Accounting Fundamentals

Accounting Fundamentals

Third Edition

FRANK HOFFMAN, B.S.C., M.A., Ed.D.

Assistant Superintendent
North Iowa Area Community College
Mason City, Iowa

ESTHER FLASHNER, A.B., M.S., C.P.A.

Associate Professor of Accounting
Hunter College of the City University of New York
New York, New York

A Gregg Text-Kit for Adult Education

GREGG DIVISION/McGRAW-HILL BOOK COMPANY

New York Atlanta Dallas St. Louis San Francisco
Auckland Bogotá Düsseldorf Johannesburg London Madrid
Mexico Montreal New Delhi Panama Paris São Paulo
Singapore Sydney Tokyo Toronto

Sponsoring Editor: Sherry Cohen
Editing Supervisors: Jane Licht, Nancy Sorensen
Production Supervisor: Laurence Charnow
Design Supervisor: Karen T. Miño
Art Supervisor: George T. Resch

Cover Designer: Richard Scott
Interior Design: Barbara Bert

Library of Congress Cataloging in Publication Data

Hoffman, Frank.
    Accounting fundamentals.

    Includes index.
    1. Accounting. I. Flashner, Esther, date
joint author. II. Title.
HF5635.H678   1980   657   79-22425
ISBN 0-07-029208-6

Accounting Fundamentals, Third Edition

Copyright © 1980, 1971, 1965 by McGraw-Hill, Inc. All Rights Reserved. Printed in the United States of America. No part of this publication may be reproduced, stored in a retrieval system, or transmitted, in any form or by any means, electronic, mechanical, photocopying, recording, or otherwise, without the prior written permission of the publisher.

1 2 3 4 5 6 7 8 9 0   WCWC   8 9 8 7 6 5 4 3 2 1 0

Contents

	Preface	vii
1	Principles of Accounting	1
2	The Effect of Revenue and Expenses	8
3	Asset, Liability, and Owner's Equity Accounts	13
4	Revenue and Expense Accounts	20
5	The Trial Balance	25
6	Financial Statements	29
	Summary Problem I	33
7	The General Journal	34
8	The General Ledger	42
9	The Worksheet and the Financial Statements	49
10	Closing the Ledger	55
11	The Accounting Cycle and Data Processing	62
	Summary Problem II	68
12	Sales and Purchases Procedures in Merchandising Businesses	69
13	Special Accounts for Merchandising Businesses	76
14	The Sales Journal	89
15	The Purchases Journal	94
16	The Cash Receipts Journal	99
17	The Cash Payments Journal	107
18	The Accounts Receivable Ledger	117
19	The Accounts Payable Ledger	126
	Summary Problem III	132
20	Worksheet Adjustments	134
21	Inventory, Cost of Goods Sold, and Statements	140
22	Adjusting and Closing the General Ledger	148
	Summary Problem IV	157
23	Banking Procedures	158
24	Petty Cash and Other Special Cash Procedures	165
25	Payroll Records	170
26	Special Procedures Related to Sales	180
27	Special Procedures Related to Purchases	191
28	The Combined Journal	198
	Comprehensive Project	204
	Index	209

Preface

A knowledge of accounting is highly useful in modern business. Many of the people connected with business—owners, managers, and office employees—work with some phase of accounting. They record financial data, read financial reports, interpret financial information, and express themselves in financial terms.

This third edition of *Accounting Fundamentals*, like the previous editions, is specially designed to meet the needs of adult students who want a brief but comprehensive introduction to accounting. The coverage of accounting principles and procedures is up to date, practical, and straightforward.

Objectives

Accounting Fundamentals, Third Edition, is one of the publications in the Gregg Continuing Education Series, a group of text-kits written for adult students who wish to increase their business skills and enhance their career opportunities. This text-kit has been carefully planned to give students who have no previous knowledge of accounting a basic understanding of accounting principles and the procedures used to record, classify, and summarize financial data. In addition, this text-kit has been designed to familiarize the students with accounting terminology and with many of the financial records, forms, and statements used in business today.

Organization

Accounting Fundamentals, Third Edition, consists of three items: a textbook, a study guide, and a workbook. These items are contained in a box for ease in carrying and storing the materials. The text-kit is a complete instructional package. No other student materials are needed for the course.

Textbook. The textbook contains 28 chapters, each covering a specific aspect of accounting. The chapters are arranged in a logical sequence so that the students can move from the simple to complex and constantly build upon prior learning. The material is concise and easy to read. Numerous illustrations graphically demonstrate the principles and procedures being taught. Each chapter is followed by business application problems and a management case. Summary problems are provided at four major points in the textbook, and a comprehensive project is given at the end of the textbook.

Study Guide. The study guide is correlated with the textbook on a chapter-by-chapter basis. It contains performance goals for each chapter, instructions for completing the chapter, and exercises that help the students to evaluate their knowledge of the text material. Self-checks for the exercises are provided at the back of the study guide.

Workbook. The workbook contains all the working papers needed to complete the business application problems, summary problems, and comprehensive project given in the textbook. Brief self-checks are provided at the back of the workbook. These self-checks consist of one or more important figures for each problem, which allow the students to verify the accuracy of their work. (Complete solutions for the problem material are only available in the instructor's manual and key.)

Application Activities

Accounting Fundamentals, Third Edition, provides a wide range of carefully planned application activities. These activities vary in type, length, and purpose.

Business Application Problems. The business application problems allow the students to put their knowledge into practice as they complete each chapter. These problems are correlated with the performance goals that appear in the study guide. The business application problems usually involve the analysis and classification of transactions and the preparation of financial records.

Managerial Analysis. The management case given at the end of each chapter is related to the material covered in the chapter. This activity provides the students with an opportunity to analyze business situations and interpret financial information.

Summary Problems. The summary problems are short projects that help the students to integrate their knowledge and skills at four important points in the course. Each summary problem covers the material taught in a group of chapters.

Comprehensive Project. The comprehensive project is a culminating activity for the course. It takes the students through an entire accounting cycle for a retail merchandising business. This project is similar to a short practice set without source documents.

Special Features

Accounting Fundamentals, Third Edition, has a number of features that make it especially well suited for adult students.

Short Chapters. Each chapter is short and to the point. Essential facts are presented in a simple, easy-to-understand manner. Numerous examples and illustrations help the students to master concepts quickly and without long, elaborate discussions.

Performance Goals. The performance goals that appear in the study guide give the students a sense of direction and purpose. They specify exactly what the students should be able to do after completing each chapter.

Chapter Summaries. At the end of each chapter, the main points that were covered are summarized for the students. This material reinforces the content of the chapter when the students complete their initial reading. Later on, the chapter summary provides a method for quickly reviewing the chapter.

Marginal Notes. The marginal notes that appear throughout the textbook pages are designed to reinforce the accounting terms, rules, and procedures introduced in each chapter. These notes consist of brief definitions of the terms and brief statements of the rules and procedures. The marginal notes also serve as a handy review device.

Self-Checks. The self-checks for the study guide exercises and the problem material give the students immediate feedback about the level of their knowledge and the quality of their work. This information shows the students whether they need to reread a chapter or redo a problem.

Teaching Aids

The *Instructor's Manual and Key for Accounting Fundamentals*, Third Edition, contains detailed information about the text-kit, teaching suggestions for the course, a set of comprehensive tests, and complete solutions for the problem material. The comprehensive tests are designed for use at four major points in the course. They can be reproduced in their entirety, or they can serve as test banks for instructor-prepared examinations. The solutions for the business application problems, summary problems, and comprehensive project are given on facsimile workbook pages for ease in checking student assignments.

Acknowledgments

Over the years, many accounting instructors have provided helpful suggestions that were used in planning this edition of *Accounting Fundamentals*. Their assistance is gratefully acknowledged. Special appreciation must go to the following people who gave valuable aid in reviewing manuscript, checking solutions, and performing other vital tasks: Vivan Pacsy of Monroe Business Institute, Jane Gammardella of Suffolk Community College, Evelyn Klapholtz of Drake Business Schools, and James Smiley of Morehead State University.

Frank Hoffman
Esther Flashner

DEDICATION

Accounting Fundamentals, Third Edition, is dedicated to the memory of a distinguished business educator and author—Noble Fritz, late Supervisor of Business Education for the Montgomery County, Maryland, Public Schools. Mr. Fritz devoted a major part of his life to training people for business careers and to creating high quality instructional materials.

Principles of Accounting

The pressure of competition in business calls for maximum efficiency. In the never-ending battle for economic survival, business owners and managers need to make wise decisions and to plan every move with the greatest care. Their decisions and plans must be based on complete and accurate financial information. Adequately kept records provide this vital information about business operations. When properly interpreted, these records also serve as an excellent guide for improving policies and procedures.

Accounting involves recording, classifying, and summarizing financial information and then interpreting the results to owners, managers, and other interested parties. For small businesses, relatively simple accounting systems provide enough information. Large businesses, however, need a much wider range of information. These businesses must have complex accounting systems and a large staff of workers.

> Accounting: Recording, classifying, and summarizing financial information; interpreting the results.

The people who have the training necessary for accounting work are known as *bookkeepers, accounting clerks,* and *accountants.* In some businesses, these people have specialized job titles such as accounts receivable clerk, accounts payable clerk, payroll clerk, office cashier, financial analyst, and controller.

The major purpose of every private business is to make a profit. The functions of accounting are to keep track of money and other property invested in a business and to determine the gains or losses that result from the business's operations.

Beginning an Accounting System

Obviously, the time to start a set of financial records is when a business opens. The *proprietor,* or owner, should make a list of the money and other property that is being used to begin the business. After operations get under way, changes will take place in the amount and nature of the business's money and other property. Information about these changes must be recorded as they occur. By keeping records on a continuous basis, the owner will be able to see how profitable the business's activities are and where the business stands financially.

> Proprietor: Owner of a business.

Let's consider how an accounting system is set up for the City Machine Repair Service. Alan West plans to open this new business on July 24, 19X1. He will be repairing typewriters, adding machines, calculators, and duplicating machines. Before starting operations, West contributes money and other property to the business.

- The first item he contributes is $1,500 in *cash.* West withdraws this money from his personal bank account and deposits it in a separate account set up for the new business.
- The second item he contributes is *equipment* that cost $700. This equipment includes repair tools, work tables, and furniture.

Assets: Property that a business owns.

Thus West invests a total of $2,200 in the business. This investment includes two kinds of property: cash and equipment. All the property the business owns is called its *assets*. Since this property belongs to West, the amount of his *investment*, or financial interest, is $2,200 (the total amount of the assets). In accounting, West's investment is called his *capital*. The financial position of the City Machine Repair Service at this time is as follows.

Assets		Financial Interest	
Cash	$1,500	Alan West, Capital	$2,200
Equipment	700		
Total Assets	$2,200	Total Financial Interest	$2,200

Before the opening day, West buys a used delivery truck for $2,000 on credit from the Ace Truck Company. As a result of this transaction, the business now owns assets totaling $4,200 ($2,200 + $2,000). Until West pays for the truck, however, a second party, Ace Truck Company, is making a contribution and therefore has a financial interest in the business's assets.

Liabilities: Debts owed by a business.

Accounts Payable: Short-term debts owed for credit purchases.

Creditors: Companies and individuals to whom money is owed.

Debts owed by a business are known as *liabilities*. All the short-term debts owed for credit purchases are called *accounts payable*. Companies and individuals to whom money is owed are *creditors*. The Ace Truck Company is a creditor of the City Machine Repair Service. Because West owes $2,000 for the delivery truck, the Ace Truck Company has an interest of $2,000 in his business.

The Ace Truck Company's interest in the repair service is shown under the heading "Liabilities" in the following illustration. West's interest appears under the heading "Owner's Equity."

Assets		Financial Interest	
Cash	$1,500	Liabilities	
Equipment	700	Accounts Payable	$2,000
Delivery Truck	2,000	(Ace Truck Company)	
		Owner's Equity	
		Alan West, Capital	2,200
Total Assets	$4,200	Total Financial Interest	$4,200

Owner's Equity: Financial interest of the owner in a business.

Owner's equity is an accounting term that indicates the financial interest of the owner in a business. *Proprietorship* and *net worth* are other terms sometimes used in place of owner's equity. The amount of the owner's equity can be found by subtracting the total of the liabilities from the total of the assets.

Note that the assets equal the financial interest of the creditors plus the financial interest of the owner; that is, assets equal liabilities plus owner's equity. This equality is shown in the *accounting equation*.

Assets	=	Liabilities	+	Owner's Equity
$4,200	=	$2,000	+	$2,200

This equation is very important. It is a device that provides checks and balances in financial recordkeeping, and it is also the basis for the formal statement of a business's financial position—the *balance sheet*.

Accounting Fundamentals

The Balance Sheet

The *balance sheet*, or *statement of financial position*, is an itemized list of the assets, liabilities, and owner's equity of a business on a certain date. The balance sheet for the City Machine Repair Service, giving the firm's financial position when operations begin, is shown below.

Balance Sheet: Itemized list of assets, liabilities, and owner's equity, showing financial position of a business on a certain date.

City Machine Repair Service
Balance Sheet
July 24, 19X1

Assets		Liabilities and Owner's Equity	
Cash	1500 00	Liabilities	
Equipment	700 00	Accounts Payable	2000 00
Delivery Truck	2000 00	Owner's Equity	
		Alan West, Capital	2200 00
		Total Liabilities	
Total Assets	4200 00	and Owner's Equity	4200 00

At the top of every balance sheet is a heading that includes the name of the business, the name of the statement, and the date. This heading answers the questions: Who? What? and When? Property and financial interests are arranged on the balance sheet in the order they appeared in the accounting equation and in previous illustrations. The assets are listed on the *left side* and totaled. Cash, equipment, and a truck are the only assets of the business when it opens on July 24, 19X1.

Note that liabilities are listed on the upper *right side* of the balance sheet. At present, West's liabilities consist only of accounts payable. Remember that accounts payable are sums of money owed to creditors for credit purchases. The Owner's Equity section follows the Liabilities section on the right side of the balance sheet.

The total liabilities and the amount of owner's equity are added. The totals of both sides of the balance sheet are recorded on the same horizontal line so that the equality can be seen clearly. When the total assets equal the total of the liabilities and the owner's equity, the balance sheet is *in balance*.

Certain practices should be followed in preparing a financial statement such as the balance sheet. The heading should be on three lines. When ruled accounting paper is used, it is customary to omit dollar signs and commas from the amounts. A single line drawn across each column means that figures above the line are either added or subtracted. Double lines show that the work is completed. All the lines should be drawn with a ruler.

The Effect of Business Activities on the Balance Sheet

Business activities such as buying, selling, receiving money, and paying bills cause continual changes in the amounts of the assets, liabilities, and owner's equity. These activities are called *business transactions*. They involve the exchange of one item of value for another.

Business Transactions: Business activities involving the exchange of one item of value for another.

The effect of each transaction on the assets, liabilities, and owner's equity of a business must be analyzed.

Principles of Accounting   **3**

Trans. A—Purchase of an asset for cash.

Transaction A. Alan West buys some tools for his business for $100 in cash.

As a result of this transaction, additional equipment in the form of tools is acquired and cash is paid out. In accounting terms, one would say:

1. The asset Equipment is *increased* by $100.
2. The asset Cash is *decreased* by $100.

	Assets					=	Liabilities	+	Owner's Equity
	Cash	+	Equipment	+	Delivery Truck	=	Accounts Payable	+	Alan West, Capital
Totals	$1,500	+	$700	+	$2,000	=	$2,000	+	$2,200
1. Tools acquired			+100						
2. Cash paid out	−100								
New totals	$1,400	+	$800	+	$2,000	=	$2,000	+	$2,200
	$4,200					=	$4,200		

This transaction, like all business transactions, affects *at least two items*. Cash is reduced by $100, but there is now additional equipment that cost $100. The form of the assets has changed, but their total is still $4,200. The liabilities and the owner's equity have not been affected. The accounting equation balances because each side still totals $4,200.

Sale of an asset for cash.

If West sold some tools for cash, the form of the assets would change in a different way.

1. The asset Cash would be *increased*.
2. The asset Equipment would be *decreased*.

Trans. B—Payment of a liability (an account payable).

Transaction B. A notice from the Ace Truck Company reminds West that a monthly payment of $200 is due on the delivery truck he bought on credit. He sends the company a check for $200.

1. The asset Cash is *decreased* by $200.
2. The liability Accounts Payable (Ace Truck Company) is *decreased* by $200.

	Assets					=	Liabilities	+	Owner's Equity
	Cash	+	Equipment	+	Delivery Truck	=	Accounts Payable	+	Alan West, Capital
Previous totals	$1,400	+	$800	+	$2,000	=	$2,000	+	$2,200
1. Cash paid out	−200								
2. Amt. owed Ace Truck Company decreased							−200		
New totals	$1,200	+	$800	+	$2,000	=	$1,800	+	$2,200
	$4,000					=	$4,000		

The assets have decreased by $200, and the liabilities have also decreased by $200. Each side of the equation now totals $4,000. Thus the equation still balances.

Trans. C—Investment of cash by the owner.

Transaction C. West takes $400 from his personal bank account and deposits it in the business's account as an additional cash investment.

1. The asset Cash is *increased* by $400.
2. Alan West, Capital is *increased* by $400.

4   Accounting Fundamentals

	Assets			=	Liabilities	+	Owner's Equity
	Cash +	Equipment +	Delivery Truck	=	Accounts Payable	+	Alan West, Capital
Previous totals	$1,200 +	$800 +	$2,000	=	$1,800	+	$2,200
1. Cash received	+400						
2. Owner's equity increased							+400
New totals	$1,600 +	$800 +	$2,000	=	$1,800	+	$2,600
	$4,400			=	$4,400		

Again, the form and amount of the assets have changed. Their total is now $4,400. The owner's equity has increased by the same amount, and the equation still balances.

Transaction D. West buys a cash register for $300 from the Acme Equipment Company, which allows him 60 days to pay.

1. The asset Equipment is *increased* by $300.
2. The liability Accounts Payable (Acme Equipment Company) is *increased* by $300.

Trans. D—Purchase of an asset on credit (incurring a liability—an account payable).

	Assets			=	Liabilities	+	Owner's Equity
	Cash +	Equipment +	Delivery Truck	=	Accounts Payable	+	Alan West, Capital
Previous totals	$1,600 +	$800 +	$2,000	=	$1,800	+	$2,600
1. New equipment acquired		+300					
2. New debt incurred					+300		
New totals	$1,600 +	$1,100 +	$2,000	=	$2,100	+	$2,600
	$4,700			=	$4,700		

Equipment and Accounts Payable have each been increased by $300. The assets total $4,700, and the liabilities and the owner's equity also total $4,700. The financial interest in the assets of the business is now shared by the Ace Truck Company and the Acme Equipment Company as creditors and by West as the owner.

Chapter Summary

☐ Assets are the property owned by a business. Liabilities are debts owed by a business. Owner's equity is the difference between the assets and the liabilities. It is the financial interest of the owner in a business.

☐ Liabilities represent the claims of creditors to the assets of a business, and owner's equity is the claim of the owner to the assets.

☐ The fundamental accounting equation is Assets = Liabilities + Owner's Equity. This equation serves as a basis for accounting procedures and for the balance sheet. The equation may also be stated as Assets − Liabilities = Owner's Equity.

☐ The balance sheet is a statement of assets, liabilities, and owner's equity. It shows the financial position of a business on a certain date.

☐ Every business transaction affects at least two items. When transactions are properly analyzed and recorded in equation form, the total assets will always equal the total of the liabilities plus the owner's equity.

Checking Your Knowledge

BUSINESS APPLICATION

Problem 1-1. From the information below, complete the accounting equation for the Rapid Printing Service. Then prepare a balance sheet dated May 31, 19X1. Use the forms on page 1 of the workbook.

Cash	$1,000
Equipment	1,500
Delivery Truck	2,000
Accounts Payable	600
David Hess, Capital	3,900

Problem 1-2. From the information below, complete the accounting equation for the Gallo Furniture Repair Shop. You will have to find the owner's equity for Ray Gallo, who operates and owns the business. Then prepare a balance sheet dated May 31, 19X1. Use the forms on pages 1 and 2 of the workbook.

Cash	$ 400
Equipment	900
Delivery Truck	1,800
Accounts Payable	100

Problem 1-3. The balance sheet for the Mode Beauty Salon, owned and operated by Ann Cox, is shown here.

MODE BEAUTY SALON
Balance Sheet
July 1, 19X1

Assets		Liabilities and Owner's Equity	
Cash	$ 600	Liabilities	
Shop Equipment	800	Accounts Payable	$ 100
Office Equipment	200	Owner's Equity	
Furniture	300	Ann Cox, Capital	1,800
Total Assets	$1,900	Total Liabilities and Owner's Equity	$1,900

Various business transactions that occurred at the Mode Beauty Salon during July are listed in the next column.

On the form provided on page 2 of the workbook, do the following: (1) enter the balance sheet items that would be affected by these transactions, (2) indicate whether each item would be increased or decreased, and (3) enter the amount of the transaction. The information for the first transaction is shown as an example. (See Transaction A in the workbook.)

A. Ann Cox made an additional cash investment of $500 in the business.
B. Paid $200 in cash for additional shop equipment.
C. Bought two chairs for the reception area from Arco Furniture for $150 and agreed to pay in 60 days.
D. Paid $90 in cash for a used typewriter.
E. Paid $80 in cash for a used hair dryer.
F. Paid $75 in cash to Arco Furniture for one-half the amount owed for the two chairs.
G. Paid $25 in cash for a magazine rack for the reception area.
H. Ann Cox made an additional cash investment of $1,500 in the business.

Problem 1-4. The following business transactions will cause changes in the balance sheet of Jimmy's Delivery Service. The information for the balance sheet is given in an equation on page 3 of the workbook. Record the business transactions on the form provided. The first transaction is given as an example. (See Transaction A in the workbook.)

A. Paid $80 in cash for a used typewriter.
B. Paid $250 in cash to a creditor.
C. James Daley made an additional cash investment of $1,000 in the business.
D. Bought a used truck from A & B Used Cars for $1,200 and agreed to pay in 60 days.
E. Paid $80 in cash for a new desk for the office.
F. Paid $600 in cash to A & B Used Cars for one-half the amount owed for the truck.
G. Bought a new file cabinet for the office from Kelly Furniture for $25 and agreed to pay in 30 days.
H. Paid $250 in cash to a creditor.
I. James Daley made an additional cash investment of $1,000 in the business.

Accounting Fundamentals

MANAGERIAL ANALYSIS

Case 1. Linda Sanchez opened a camera store. She had no knowledge of financial recordkeeping, and she did not employ an accountant to set up an accounting system. After operating for two months, however, she hired an accountant to install a suitable accounting system.

1. Why do you think Linda Sanchez decided to hire an accountant after operating the business for two months?

2. Did she hire the accountant at the correct time?

3. What are the first things the accountant would need to find out in order to set up the business's financial records properly?

The Effect of Revenue and Expenses

As shown in the previous chapter, the amount of the owner's equity in a business is increased by additional investments. However, a more important way in which the owner's equity grows is through profits from the business's operations.

Revenue, Expenses, and Net Income

Revenue: Income from business operations, usually from the sale of services or goods.

Expenses: Costs of operating a business.

Net Income: The amount remaining when revenue exceeds expenses.

Net Loss: The amount remaining when expenses exceed revenue.

The sale of repairs by the City Machine Repair Service will produce *revenue*, or *income*. In producing this revenue, the repair service will incur certain business costs, which are known as *expenses*. These include such items as salaries, rent, supplies used, electricity, telephone service, and truck maintenance.

The revenue remaining after the expenses have been deducted is *net income* (also called *net profit*). When there is net income, the owner's equity is increased. On the other hand, if expenses are greater than revenue, the result is a *net loss*, which decreases the owner's equity. Some typical revenue and expense transactions follow.

Trans. E—Sale of services for cash.

Transaction E. At the end of the first week of operations, Alan West has received $220 in cash for repair work. The revenue received causes changes in the assets and the owner's equity.

1. The asset Cash is *increased* by $220.
2. Owner's equity is *increased* by $220.

	Assets					=	Liabilities	+	Owner's Equity		
	Cash	+	Equipment	+	Delivery Truck	=	Accounts Payable	+	Alan West, Capital	+	Revenue
Previous totals	$1,600	+	$1,100	+	$2,000	=	$2,100	+	$2,600	+	$ 0
1. Cash received	+220										
2. Owner's equity increased by revenue											+220
									$2,600	+	$220
New totals	$1,820	+	$1,100	+	$2,000	=	$2,100	+	$2,820		
			$4,920			=			$4,920		

The increase in cash is recorded, as usual, under assets. Note that a separate column has been added under owner's equity for recording revenue. This column will make revenue figures easily available when financial reports are prepared. The total of

8 Accounting Fundamentals

the assets has increased to $4,920. Owner's equity has also increased because of the revenue. The new total of the liabilities and the owner's equity (including revenue) is $4,920 ($2,100 + $2,820).

In modern business, sales of services and goods are often made on credit. Customers who buy on credit do not pay cash immediately. Instead, they promise to pay later. The amounts that a business's customers have promised to pay in the future are an asset known as *accounts receivable*. (Remember that the liability incurred by a business when *it* promises to pay its creditors is called *accounts payable*.)

Accounts Receivable: Amounts customers have promised to pay in the future for services or goods bought on credit.

Transaction F. West does repair work on credit for a customer, Donna Ryan, and bills her for $150. Revenue is obtained in the form of an account receivable. This causes changes in the assets and in the owner's equity.

Trans. F—Sale of services on credit.

1. The asset Accounts Receivable is *increased* by $150.
2. Owner's equity is *increased* by $150.

	Assets	=	Liabilities	+	Owner's Equity
	Cash + Accounts Receivable + Equipment + Delivery Truck	=	Accounts Payable	+	Alan West, Capital + Revenue
Previous totals	$1,820 + $ 0 + $1,100 + $2,000	=	$2,100	+	$2,600 + $220
1. Account receivable obtained	+150				
2. Owner's equity increased by revenue					+150
					$2,600 + $370
New totals	$1,820 + $150 + $1,100 + $2,000	=	$2,100	+	$2,970
	$5,070			=	$5,070

Note that a separate column has been added under assets to record accounts receivable. The total of the assets has increased to $5,070. Owner's equity has also increased through additional revenue. The new total of the liabilities and the owner's equity (including revenue) is $5,070 ($2,100 + $2,970).

Transaction G. At the end of the first week of operations, West pays wages of $100 in cash to the person who does repair work part-time. This expense causes changes in the assets and the owner's equity.

Trans. G—Payment of an expense (wages).

1. The asset Cash is *decreased* by $100.
2. Owner's equity is *decreased* by $100.

	Assets	=	Liabilities	+	Owner's Equity
	Cash + Accounts Receivable + Equipment + Delivery Truck	=	Accounts Payable	+	Alan West, Capital + Revenue − Expenses
Previous totals	$1,820 + $150 + $1,100 + $2,000	=	$2,100	+	$2,600 + $370 − $ 0
1. Cash paid out	−100				
2. Owner's equity decreased by expense					100
					$2,600 + $370 − $100
New totals	$1,720 + $150 + $1,100 + $2,000	=	$2,100	+	$2,870
	$4,970			=	$4,970

The Effect of Revenue and Expenses 9

Note that a separate column has now been included under Owner's Equity for recording expenses. Thus the expense figures will be easily available for financial reports. The total of the assets has decreased to $4,970. Owner's equity has also decreased because of the expense for wages. The new total of the liabilities and the owner's equity (including expenses) is $4,970 ($2,100 + $2,870).

When a business sells on credit, it sends bills to its customers and then receives payments from the customers. The amounts from these customers are referred to as money *received on account*. Similarly, the amounts that the business pays to its creditors are referred to as money *paid on account*.

Received on Account: Money is received from customers who have bought on credit.

Paid on Account: Money is paid to creditors.

Trans. H—Receipt of cash on account from a customer.

Transaction H. West receives a check for $50 on account from Donna Ryan, who owes $150 for repair work. This is a partial payment of her bill.

1. The asset Cash is *increased* by $50.
2. The asset Accounts Receivable is *decreased* by $50.

	Assets				=	Liabilities	+	Owner's Equity		
	Cash +	Accounts Receivable +	Equipment +	Delivery Truck	=	Accounts Payable +		Alan West, Capital +	Revenue −	Expenses
Previous totals	$1,720 +	$150 +	$1,100 +	$2,000	=	$2,100 +		$2,600 +	$370 −	$100
1. Cash received	+50									
2. Amount owed by customer decreased		−50								
								$2,600 +	$370 −	$100
New totals	$1,770 +	$100 +	$1,100 +	$2,000	=	$2,100 +			$2,870	
		$4,970			=			$4,970		

The total of the assets remains at $4,970 because there has merely been a substitution of one asset (cash) for another asset (accounts receivable). No change has occurred in the liabilities or the owner's equity.

Trans. I—Payment of an expense (truck repairs).

Transaction I. West pays $30 in cash to a service station for repairs on the delivery truck. The following financial changes are caused by this expense transaction.

1. The asset Cash is *decreased* by $30.
2. Owner's equity is *decreased* by $30.

	Assets				=	Liabilities	+	Owner's Equity		
	Cash +	Accounts Receivable +	Equipment +	Delivery Truck	=	Accounts Payable +		Alan West, Capital +	Revenue −	Expenses
Previous totals	$1,770 +	$100 +	$1,100 +	$2,000	=	$2,100 +		$2,600 +	$370 −	$100
1. Cash paid out	−30									
2. Owner's equity decreased by expense										30
								$2,600 +	$370 −	$130
New totals	$1,740 +	$100 +	$1,100 +	$2,000	=	$2,100 +			$2,840	
		$4,940			=			$4,940		

After the transactions involving revenue and expenses have been recorded, the accounting equation is still in balance. Each side now totals $4,940. The owner's equity is $2,840, or $240 more than Alan West's personal investment in the business. The $240

10 Accounting Fundamentals

is the net income from business operations (found by subtracting the expenses of $130 from the revenue of $370).

Compare the present balance sheet with the one prepared when the business opened on July 24, 19X1. Both of these balance sheets are shown below. Note the overall effects of the nine recorded transactions.

In the Owner's Equity section of the July 31, 19X1 balance sheet, observe that West's original investment ($2,200) has been increased by the additional cash investment of $400 plus the net income of $240 for the period.

City Machine Repair Service
Balance Sheet
July 24, 19X1

Assets		Liabilities and Owner's Equity	
Cash	1,500.00	Liabilities	
Equipment	700.00	Accounts Payable	2,000.00
Delivery Truck	2,000.00	Owner's Equity	
		Alan West, Capital	2,200.00
		Total Liabilities	
Total Assets	4,200.00	and Owner's Equity	4,200.00

City Machine Repair Service
Balance Sheet
July 31, 19X1

Assets		Liabilities and Owner's Equity		
Cash	1,740.00	Liabilities		
Accounts Receivable	100.00	Accounts Payable		2,100.00
Equipment	1,100.00	Owner's Equity		
Delivery Truck	2,000.00	A. West, Cap. 7/24/X1	2,200.00	
		Additional Inv.	400.00	
		Net Income	240.00	
		A. West, Cap. 7/31/X1		2,840.00
		Total Liabilities		
Total Assets	4,940.00	and Owner's Equity		4,940.00

Chapter Summary

☐ The income received from business operations—usually from the sale of services or goods—is known as revenue. The costs of business operations are called expenses.
☐ Revenue can be obtained in the form of cash or accounts receivable.
☐ Accounts receivable are amounts that customers have promised to pay in the future for services or goods bought on credit.
☐ The difference between revenue and expenses is net income (net profit) or net loss.
☐ When revenue is greater than expenses, there is a net income. When expenses are greater than revenue, there is a net loss.
☐ Net income results in an increase in the owner's equity. Additional investments also cause an increase in the owner's equity.
☐ Net loss results in a decrease in the owner's equity.

Checking Your Knowledge

BUSINESS APPLICATION

Problem 2-1. The Plaza Employment Service, owned and operated by Carl Berg, has assets, liabilities, and owner's equity as shown in the equation given on page 5 of the workbook. On the form that follows the equation, record the transactions listed below. Enter the new totals after each transaction. Remember that the total assets must equal the total of the liabilities and the owner's equity.

A. Paid $85 in cash for the month's rent.
B. Provided services for $50 in cash.
C. Paid $10 in cash for the telephone bill.
D. Provided services for $100 in cash.
E. Provided services for $120 on credit.
F. Paid $100 in cash to creditors on account.
G. Received $180 in cash from customers on account.

Problem 2-2. The Ott Accounting Service, owned and operated by Jane Ott, has assets, liabilities, and owner's equity as shown in the equation given on page 6 of the workbook.

1. On the form that follows the equation, record the transactions listed below.

A. Provided services for $250 in cash.
B. Bought a new typewriter for $272, made a down payment of $100, and agreed to pay the balance in 60 days.
C. Paid $200 in cash for the month's rent.
D. Provided services for $80. The customer paid one-half in cash now and agreed to pay the balance in 30 days.
E. Paid $100 in cash to creditors on account.
F. Paid $20 in cash for the telephone bill.
G. Received $120 in cash from customers on account.
H. The owner made an additional cash investment of $600.

2. Find the result of operations for the period. Use the space on page 6 of the workbook to record the necessary information.

MANAGERIAL ANALYSIS

Case 2. Ralph Corso has been operating a carpet store for two months. At the end of the first month's operations, his balance sheet showed a decrease in owner's equity. At the end of the second month's operations, his balance sheet showed an increase in owner's equity.

1. How might you explain the decrease in owner's equity at the end of the first month?
2. How might you explain the increase in owner's equity at the end of the second month?
3. Which type of increase in owner's equity would probably be of special interest to Corso?

Asset, Liability, and Owner's Equity Accounts

In the first two chapters, the effects of business transactions were analyzed and recorded through the use of the basic accounting equation: Assets = Liabilities + Owner's Equity. However, keeping actual records in this way would be very difficult and would take too much time. Businesses therefore use a *separate* record for each asset, liability, and owner's equity item. This record is known as an *account*.

Account: Record showing increases and decreases in a single asset, liability, or owner's equity item.

The Form of Accounts

The simplest form of account looks like the letter "T" and is therefore called a *T account*. The name of the account is written at the top of the form. The left side of the account is known as the *debit side*. The right side is referred to as the *credit side*.

Debit Side: Left side of an account.

Credit Side: Right side of an account.

Account Name	
Debit side	Credit side

The entire group of accounts that a business uses for its assets, liabilities, and owner's equity is known as the *general ledger*. In many businesses, especially small businesses, the general ledger is kept by hand in a bound book, a looseleaf binder, or a tray of cards. Other businesses, usually larger ones, use mechanical or electronic devices to keep their general ledgers. At this time, we will be discussing financial records that are kept by hand.

General Ledger: Entire group of accounts for a business's assets, liabilities, and owner's equity.

Opening Accounts for the Balance Sheet Items

Look again at the beginning balance sheet of the City Machine Repair Service, shown on page 3. The assets are listed on the left side of the balance sheet. Similarly, the beginning amount of each asset is entered on the left side—the debit side—of its account. The assets of the City Machine Repair Service appear in the accounts as shown on page 14.

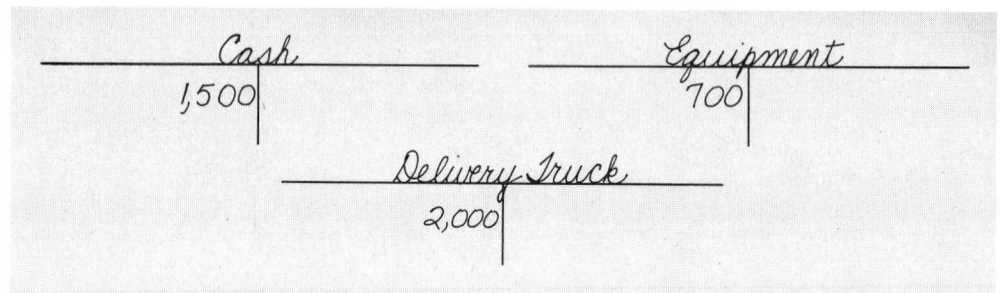

Liabilities are listed on the right side of the balance sheet. Similarly, the beginning amounts are recorded on the right side—the credit side—of each liability account. The amount of owner's equity, representing the owner's investment, is also listed on the right side of the balance sheet. It is therefore entered on the right side—the credit side—of the capital account. Thus the amounts for the liability Accounts Payable and the owner's equity of the City Machine Repair Service appear in the accounts as shown below.

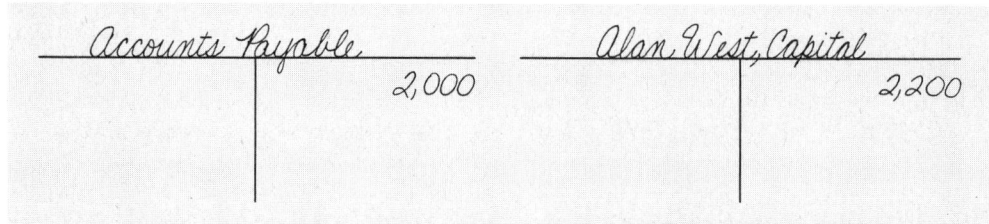

Debiting: Entering an amount on the left side of an account.

Crediting: Entering an amount on the right side of an account.

Entering an amount on the left side of an account is known as *debiting* the account. Entering an amount on the right side is known as *crediting* the account. The amount entered is called a *debit* or a *credit* according to the side on which it is recorded. The abbreviation for debit is *Dr.*, and for credit it is *Cr.*

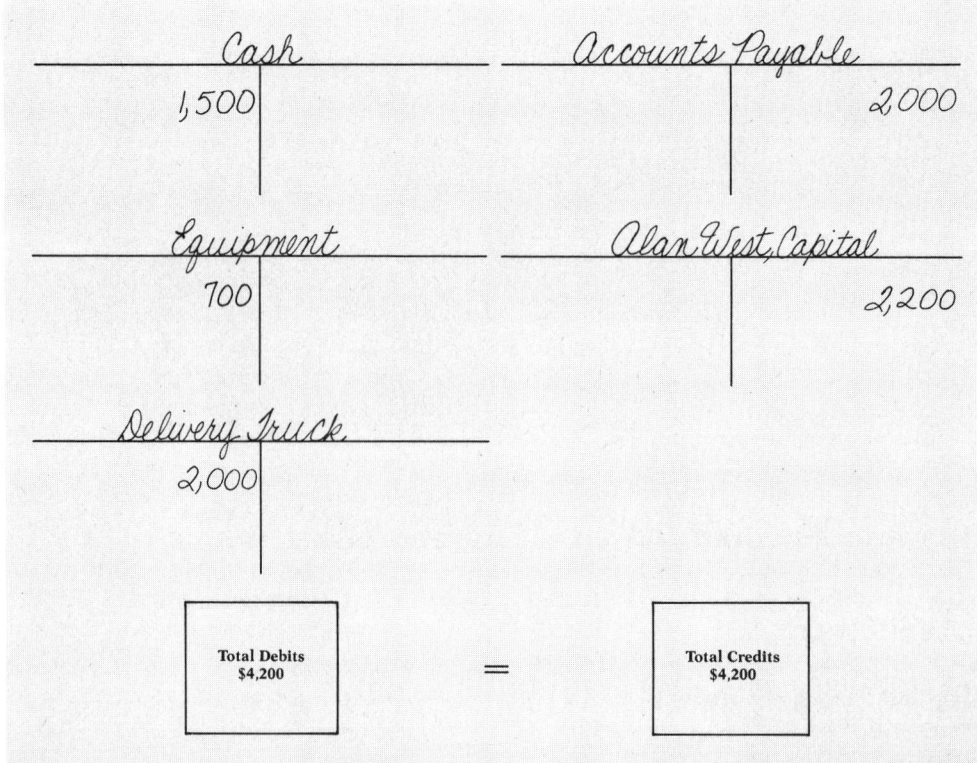

14 Accounting Fundamentals

The illustration on page 14 shows how the beginning amounts (opening balances) were recorded in the T accounts for the City Machine Repair Service. Note that the asset accounts were debited, but the liability Accounts Payable and the owner's capital account were credited. Now that all the balance sheet accounts have been opened, the amounts on the left side of the asset accounts (debits) are equal to the amounts on the right side of the liability and owner's equity accounts (credits). The total of the debits is $4,200, and the total of the credits is also $4,200. This is the same as the total on each side of the balance sheet.

In addition to a method for recording the opening balances, a business needs a way to record later increases and decreases in asset accounts. Increases in an asset account must be added to the opening balance. This can easily be done if each increase is recorded on the same side (the debit side) and listed just below the previous entry. Decreases in an asset account are of an opposite nature and must be kept separate from increases. Therefore, the right, or credit, side is used for decreases.

Since the opening balances of the liability account and the owner's equity account were entered on the right, or credit, side of the accounts, any increases in them must also be entered on that side. Decreases must be entered on the left, or debit, side.

The procedure for recording each part of a business transaction depends on two considerations: (1) the kind of account affected (asset, liability, or owner's equity) and (2) whether an increase or a decrease is involved.

Rules for Debiting and Crediting

Asset Accounts:
- Record increases as debits.
- Record decreases as credits.

Liability and Owner's Equity Accounts:
- Record increases as credits.
- Record decreases as debits.

Asset Accounts	
The original amount is entered on this (debit) side.	Decreases are entered on this (credit) side.
Increases are entered on this side.	

Liability and Owner's Equity Accounts	
Decreases are entered on this (debit) side.	The original amount is entered on this (credit) side.
	Increases are entered on this side.

Recording Changes in Accounts

To see how changes are entered in accounts, let us review the transactions of the City Machine Repair Service.

Recording Increases and Decreases in Asset Accounts. Transaction A (page 4) involved the purchase of additional equipment for $100 in cash. This transaction resulted in an increase in one asset (Equipment) and a decrease in another asset (Cash).

The increase of $100 in the asset Equipment is entered on the debit side of the Equipment account, since increases in assets are recorded as debits. The offsetting $100 decrease in the asset Cash is entered on the credit side of the Cash account, since decreases in assets are recorded as credits.

Account Balance: Difference between total debits and total credits in an account.

The $1,400 left in the Cash account (a debit of $1,500 minus a credit of $100) is known as the *balance* of the account. This is the amount by which the larger side of the account exceeds the smaller side. Because the debit side of the Cash account is larger, it is said to have a *debit balance*.

Recording Decreases in Liability Accounts. Transaction B (page 4) involved the $200 check given to the Ace Truck Company in partial payment for the delivery truck. This transaction caused a decrease of $200 in the liability Accounts Payable and a decrease of $200 in the asset Cash.

The original amount of Accounts Payable ($2,000) is on the credit side of the account. The decrease of $200 is entered on the debit side to show a reduction from the original amount. The balance of Accounts Payable is now $1,800 (a credit of $2,000 minus a debit of $200). Note that this account has a *credit balance*.

The $200 decrease in the asset Cash is entered on the credit side of the Cash account, since decreases in assets are recorded as credits. The balance of the Cash account is now $1,200 (a debit of $1,500 minus credits of $300).

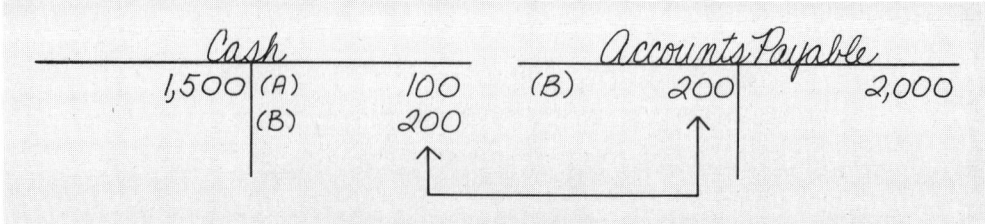

Recording Increases in the Owner's Equity Account. Transaction C (pages 4 and 5) involved Alan West's additional cash investment of $400 in the business. This transaction caused a $400 increase in the asset Cash and a $400 increase in the owner's equity Alan West, Capital.

The Cash account is, of course, debited for $400 to record an increase. The increase of $400 in Alan West, Capital is entered on the credit side, since increases in the owner's equity are recorded as credits. After this transaction is recorded, the Cash account has a balance of $1,600 (debits of $1,900 minus credits of $300) and the capital account has a balance of $2,600 (credits of $2,200 and $400).

16 Accounting Fundamentals

Recording Increases in Liability Accounts. In Transaction D (page 5), West bought a cash register for $300 and agreed to pay for it in 60 days. This transaction caused a $300 increase in the asset Equipment and a $300 increase in the liability Accounts Payable.

The Equipment account is debited for $300 to show the increase in this asset account. The increase of $300 in Accounts Payable is entered on the credit side, since increases in liabilities are recorded as credits.

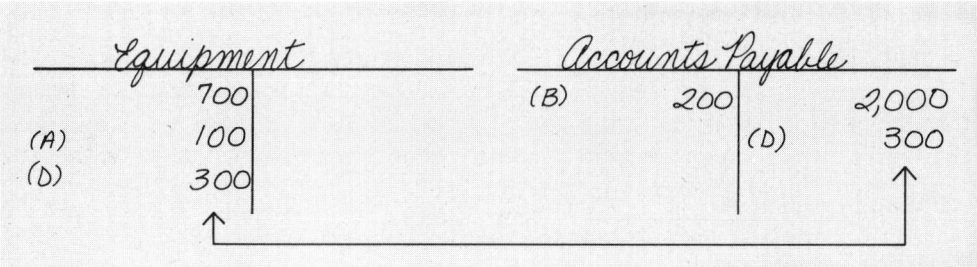

Finding the Balances of Accounts

The balance of an account can easily be found whenever the information is needed. If there are entries on only one side of the account, the procedure for finding the balance is as follows: (1) All the amounts recorded in the account are added, and (2) the total is written in small pencil figures at the foot (bottom) of the column of amounts. Look at the Equipment account shown below. Since there are no entries on the credit side, the total of the debits ($1,100) is the account balance.

A total or balance written in small pencil figures is called a *pencil footing*. Pencil is used to set these amounts apart from regular entries, which are made in ink.

If there are entries on both sides of an account, some additional steps are involved in finding the balance: (1) The debits and credits are each added. (2) The totals are pencil-footed on each side of the account. (3) The smaller total is subtracted from the larger total. (4) The difference—the balance—is pencil-footed on the side with the larger total.

The Accounts Payable account on page 18 has a credit balance of $2,100 (credits of $2,300 minus debits of $200). There is no need to pencil-foot the debit side since it contains only one amount. However, the credit side has two pencil footings—the total of the credits ($2,300) and the account balance ($2,100).

Pencil Footing: Total or balance written in small pencil figures.

Asset, Liability, and Owner's Equity Accounts 17

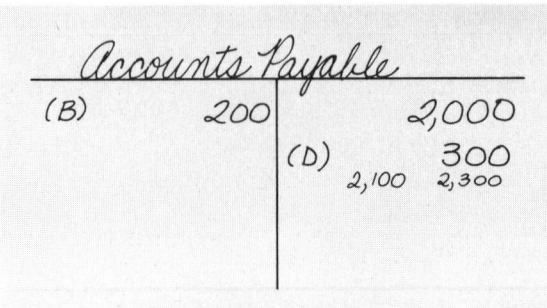

Chapter Summary

☐ A separate account is kept for every asset, liability, and owner's equity item in a business. The accounts are used to record the increases and decreases caused by daily transactions. All accounts together are known as the general ledger.

☐ Two things must be considered when analyzing and recording each part of a business transaction: (1) the kind of account affected (asset, liability, or owner's equity) and (2) whether an increase or a decrease is involved.

☐ The left side of an account is the debit side, and the right side is the credit side.

☐ The following rules apply when business transactions are analyzed and recorded.
  1. Increases in assets are recorded as debits.
  2. Decreases in assets are recorded as credits.
  3. Increases in liabilities and in owner's equity are recorded as credits.
  4. Decreases in liabilities and in owner's equity are recorded as debits.

Checking Your Knowledge

BUSINESS APPLICATION

Problem 3-1. Financial information for the Rapid Delivery Service as of June 1, 19X1, is given below. The business is owned and operated by Paul Lema.

Cash	$ 800
Accounts Receivable	600
Office Equipment	200
Delivery Equipment	2,000
Accounts Payable	500

Do the following work for the business. Use the forms on page 7 of the workbook.

1. Prepare a balance sheet dated June 1, 19X1. (You will have to find the amount of the owner's equity.)
2. Open a T account for each item on the balance sheet.
3. Record the opening balances in the accounts.

Problem 3-2. Financial information for the Metro Insurance Agency as of January 1, 19X1, is given below. The business is owned and operated by Ruth Carr.

Cash	$4,000
Accounts Payable	500
Office Equipment	700
Accounts Receivable	800
Office Furniture	600

Do the following work for the business. Use the forms on page 8 of the workbook.

1. Prepare a balance sheet dated January 1, 19X1. (You will have to find the amount of the owner's equity.)
2. Open a T account for each item on the balance sheet.
3. Record the opening balances in the accounts.

18 Accounting Fundamentals

4. Record the following transactions in the accounts.
A. Bought new office equipment for $100 in cash.
B. Paid $200 in cash to creditors on account.
C. Bought new office furniture for $150 and agreed to pay in 60 days.
D. Ruth Carr made an additional cash investment of $2,000 in the business.
E. Received $50 in cash from a customer on account.

5. Pencil-foot the accounts in order to find the balances.

MANAGERIAL ANALYSIS

Case 3. Donald Grant, who is the owner of a restaurant, has no knowledge of accounting. He cannot understand why his accountant requires that an account be used for every asset, liability, and owner's equity item.

Grant also wonders why the names of many of the accounts opened for his business differ from those used for the clothing store that his sister owns.

1. What explanation should the accountant give Grant as to why accounts are needed for every asset, liability, and owner's equity item?
2. How should the accountant explain why many of the account names differ in the two businesses?

Revenue and Expense Accounts

Accounts must also be provided for recording the receipt of revenue and the payment of expenses. In this way, a business's financial records will contain complete information. The revenue and expense transactions are important because they affect the owner's equity. As discussed in Chapter 2, if revenue is greater than expenses, there is a net income. If expenses exceed revenue, there is a net loss. The owner's equity is increased by a net income and decreased by a net loss.

The illustration below shows the relationship of revenue and expenses to the owner's equity.

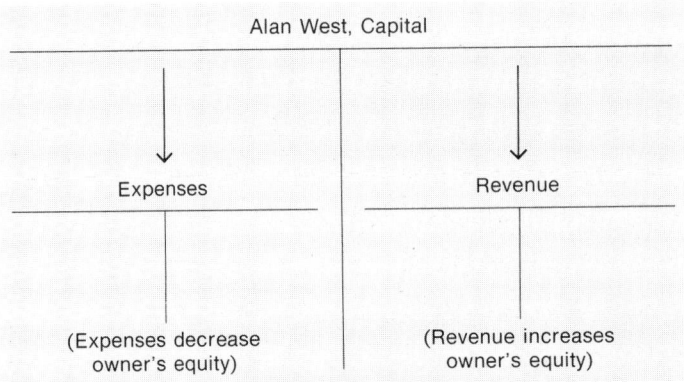

Specific accounts are used to show the kinds of revenue and expenses that are connected with the operation of a business. To see how revenue and expenses are recorded in such accounts, let us review the transactions of the City Machine Repair Service that were discussed in Chapter 2.

Recording Revenue

In Transaction E (page 8), Alan West received $220 in cash for repair work. The increase in cash is recorded as a debit to the Cash account. Because revenue has been earned, there is an increase in owner's equity. This increase must be recorded as a credit to an owner's equity account. The Alan West, Capital account is not used to record this transaction. Just as a business has separate accounts for each asset and each liability, it must keep a separate account for each item of owner's equity—capital, revenue, and expenses.

The increase in the owner's equity that results from revenue is therefore recorded in a separate revenue account. The name of the revenue account usually shows the source of the revenue. In Alan West's business, the name Repair Service Revenue is used. West credits this account for $220 to record the revenue he received during the first week of operations.

20   Accounting Fundamentals

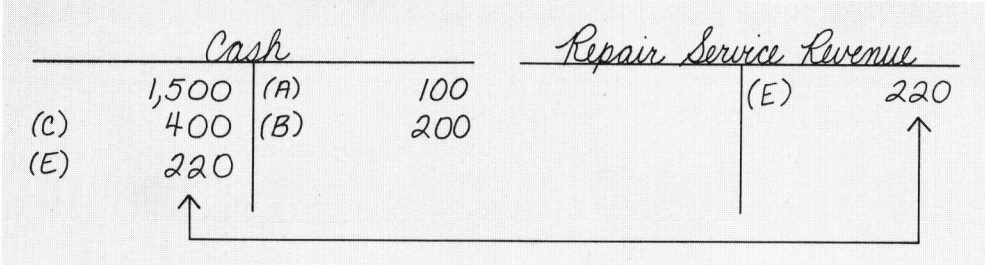

In Transaction F (page 9), West did repair work for $150 on credit for a customer, Donna Ryan. The increase in the asset Accounts Receivable is recorded as a debit to the Accounts Receivable account. Since revenue was earned, owner's equity increased. This increase is recorded by crediting the Repair Service Revenue account for $150.

Let us skip to Transaction H (page 10), in which West received $50 on account from Donna Ryan. This transaction involves only an exchange of one asset (accounts receivable) for another asset (cash). It is recorded by debiting the Cash account to show the increase in cash and by crediting the Accounts Receivable account to show the decrease in accounts receivable. Note that the owner's equity is not affected by this transaction.

Recording Expenses

In Transaction G (page 9), West paid wages of $100 in cash to the person who does repair work part time. The decrease in the asset Cash is recorded as a credit to the Cash account. An expense account is used to record the decrease in the owner's equity resulting from the expense for wages.

Just as a business needs a separate revenue account to record increases in the owner's equity from revenue, it must also have a separate expense account for each type of expense incurred. Since expenses decrease the owner's equity, the $100 that West paid in wages is debited to a Wages Expense account.

Revenue and Expense Accounts

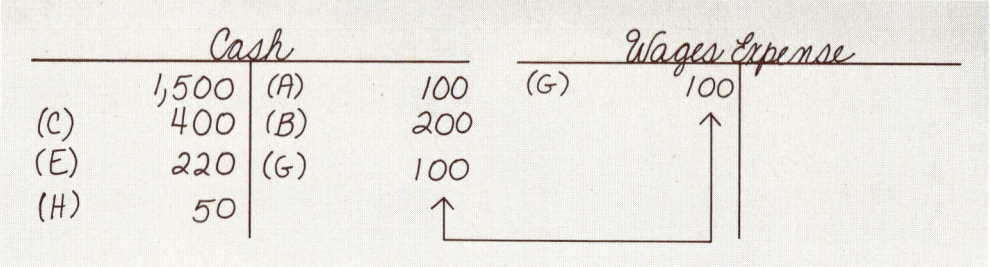

West will need more expense accounts besides Wages Expense. An account must be opened for each major expense item in a business so that the owner can easily identify the various costs of operations. In addition, when federal income tax reports are prepared, expenses must be itemized by certain categories. Therefore, West opens another expense account—Truck Expense—when he pays $30 in cash for truck repairs (Transaction I on page 10). This expense is recorded by debiting the Truck Expense account for $30 and by crediting the Cash account for $30.

Cash		Truck Expense
1,500 (A) 100		(I) 30
(C) 400 (B) 200		
(E) 220 (G) 100		
(H) 50 (I) 30		

Recording the Owner's Withdrawals

Most owners of small businesses live on money that comes from their businesses. Thus they usually withdraw cash or other assets for their personal use on a regular basis. The business is expected to make up the resulting decrease in the owner's equity through net income.

Trans. J—Withdrawal of cash by the owner.

Transaction J. West withdraws $180 in cash from his business for his personal use. This transaction has the following effects.

1. Owner's equity is *decreased* by $180.
2. The asset Cash is *decreased* by $180.

A separate account, called a *drawing account* or a *personal account*, is used to record decreases in the owner's equity due to withdrawals. This account provides a complete record of the owner's withdrawals from the business. The $180 that West withdrew is therefore debited to a new owner's equity account—Alan West, Drawing. The Cash account is credited.

Owner's Equity Accounts:
- Capital Account—use for changes in owner's investment.
- Drawing Account—use for withdrawals by owner.
- Revenue Accounts—use for revenue earned by business.
- Expense Accounts—use for expenses incurred by business.

Cash		Alan West, Drawing
1,500 (A) 100		(J) 180
(C) 400 (B) 200		
(E) 220 (G) 100		
(H) 50 (I) 30		
(J) 180		

22 Accounting Fundamentals

The Relationship of Revenue, Expenses, and Withdrawals to Owner's Equity

The City Machine Repair Service earned revenue totaling $370 during its first week of operations. It also had expenses totaling $130 in the period. The $240 difference between revenue and expenses is net income. However, West withdrew $180 for his personal use in anticipation of the net income. Thus, there is a net increase of $60 in his owner's equity for the period ($240 in net income minus $180 in withdrawals).

The following illustration shows the relationship of the various elements of owner's equity.

Owner's Equity for City Machine Repair Service
From July 24, 19X1, to July 31, 19X1

Decreased by		Increased by	
Expenses	130	Beginning investment (money and property)	2,200
Withdrawals	180	Additional money invested	400
Total Decreases	310	Revenue	370
		Total Increases	2,970

Present Owner's Equity = $2,660
(Total Increases of $2,970 − Total Decreases of $310)

If a new balance sheet were prepared for the City Machine Repair Service, the information about the owner's equity would appear as shown below.

```
Owner's Equity
    Alan West, Capital 7/24/X1                    2,200
    Additional Investment                           400
    Total Investment                              2,600
    Net Income                           240
    Less Withdrawals                     180
    Net Increase in Owner's Equity                   60
    Alan West, Capital 7/31/X1                    2,660
```

Chapter Summary

- Many business transactions involve earning revenue and incurring expenses.
- A separate account is opened for each major revenue and expense item. The account name describes the source of the revenue or the type of expense involved. The following rules are used for making entries in these accounts:
  1. Increases in owner's equity caused by revenue are recorded as credits to a revenue account.
  2. Decreases in owner's equity caused by expenses are recorded as debits to the appropriate expense accounts.
- A separate drawing account is opened to record the owner's withdrawals. Decreases in owner's equity caused by withdrawals are debited to this account.
- At the end of the period of operations, all revenue and expenses are totaled. The total expenses are subtracted from the total revenue to find the net income, which increases the owner's equity. Withdrawals are subtracted from the net income to show the net increase in the owner's equity. If expenses are greater than revenue or if withdrawals are greater than the net income, there will be a decrease in the owner's equity.

Checking Your Knowledge

BUSINESS APPLICATION

Problem 4-1. The T accounts for the Ramos Accounting Service, owned by John Ramos, are provided on page 9 of the workbook. The balances as of January 1, 19X1, are already entered.

1. Record the following transactions in the accounts. Enter the amount and identifying letter of each transaction. The first transaction has been recorded as an example.

A. Bought additional office equipment for $200 in cash.
B. Paid $250 in cash for rent for the month.
C. Provided accounting services for $400 in cash.
D. Paid $350 in cash to creditors on account.
E. Paid $300 in cash to employees for salaries.
F. Provided accounting services for $500 on credit.
G. Paid $50 in cash for gas and oil for the automobile used in the business.
H. John Ramos withdrew $175 in cash from the business.
I. Paid $25 in cash for repairs on the automobile used in the business.
J. Received $100 in cash from customers on account.
K. Bought additional file cabinets for the office for $150 and agreed to pay in 60 days.

2. Find the net income for the period and the net increase in the owner's equity. Use the form on page 9 of the workbook. Obtain the information about the revenue and expenses from the T accounts. (You will have to pencil-foot some of these accounts to determine the balances.)

Note: Save the accounts for use in Problem 5-2 of Chapter 5.

Problem 4-2. The O'Neill Advertising Agency, owned by Rita O'Neill, does most of its work for clothing stores. It performs two separate services for these clients—preparing layout designs for advertisements and organizing fashion shows.

The T accounts for the business are provided on page 10 of the workbook. The balances as of April 1, 19X1, are already entered. Note that there are two revenue accounts—one for each type of service the business performs.

1. Record the following transactions in the accounts. Enter the amount and identifying letter of each transaction.

A. Organized a fashion show for Berger Stores for $900 on credit.
B. Paid $500 in cash for rent for the month.
C. Provided layout designs for $550 in cash.
D. Paid $25 in cash for repairs to the office typewriter.
E. Received $400 in cash from customers on account.
F. Bought materials and supplies for $220 on credit.
G. Paid $600 in cash to creditors on account.
H. Because of a reduction in the time allotted to the fashion show for Berger Stores (Transaction A), Rita O'Neill reduced the bill by $100.
I. Returned some supplies (Transaction F) and received credit for $50.
J. Rita O'Neill withdrew $250 in cash for her personal use.
K. Provided layout designs for $420 on credit.
L. Paid $75 in cash for painting the office.
M. Rita O'Neill withdrew $30 in cash for her personal use.
N. Bought additional equipment for $200 on credit.
O. Paid $800 in cash to employees for salaries.

2. Find the net income for the period and the net increase in the owner's equity. Use the form on page 10 of the workbook.

Note: Save the accounts for use in Problem 5-3 of Chapter 5.

MANAGERIAL ANALYSIS

Case 4. Gary Larson is starting a trucking service. His accountant plans to open five expense accounts for the business. However, Larson feels that one account called Expenses would be enough.

1. What arguments would you use to show Larson that it is necessary to have five expense accounts instead of only one account?

2. Name five account names that Larson's accountant may possibly use when he opens accounts for the different kinds of expenses.

24 Accounting Fundamentals

The Trial Balance

5

The procedure for recording a business's transactions in its accounts has now been discussed. One of the major reasons for having accounts is to provide the information needed for financial reports. However, before the information in the accounts can be used to prepare these reports, it is necessary to check the accuracy of the entries that were recorded.

Remember that every entry consists of two parts—a debit and a credit. Therefore, the total of all the debits recorded in the accounts should equal the total of all the credits. This equality is checked by *taking a trial balance*.

Taking a Trial Balance: Checking equality of total debits and total credits in ledger accounts.

Taking the Trial Balance

The first step in taking a trial balance is finding the balance of each account. This is done by pencil-footing the accounts, as described in Chapter 3. The amounts recorded in the accounts are added, and the totals are written in small pencil figures. If an account has entries on only one side, the total of that side is the balance. If there are entries on both sides, the smaller total is subtracted from the larger total. The balance is then recorded—also in small pencil figures.

The accounts of the City Machine Repair Service are shown here and on page 26 as they would appear after the balances have been determined.

	Cash				Accounts Payable		
	1,500	(A)	100	(B)	200		2,000
(C)	400	(B)	200			(D)	300
(E)	220	(G)	100		2,100		2,300
(H)	50	(I)	30				
		(J)	180				
1,560	2,170		610				

	Alan West, Capital	
		2,200
	(C)	400
		2,600

	Accounts Receivable		
(F)	150	(H)	50
100			

	Alan West, Drawing
(J)	180

	Equipment
	700
(A)	100
(D)	300
	1,100

	Repair Service Revenue	
	(E)	220
	(F)	150
		370

The Trial Balance **25**

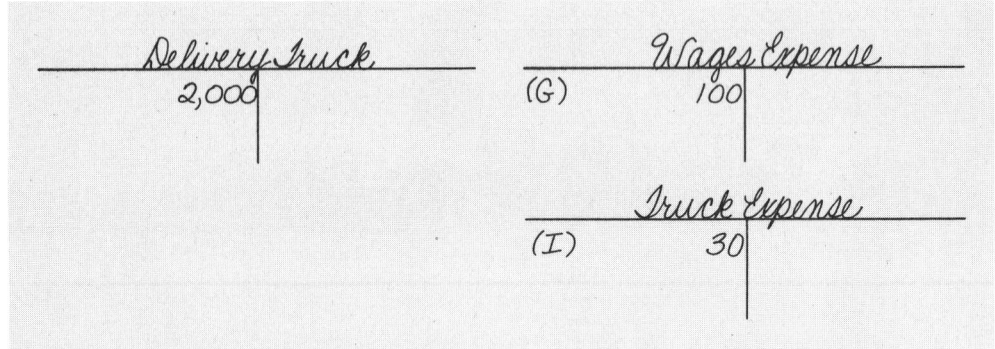

Steps in Taking a Trial Balance:
- Find balances of accounts.
- List accounts and balances.
- Add balances to see if total debits and total credits are equal.

The next step in taking the trial balance is to list the accounts and their balances. Then the debits and credits are totaled. This work is often done on a ruled form, as shown below.

Account Name	Debit	Credit
Cash	1560 00	
Accounts Receivable	100 00	
Equipment	1110 00	
Delivery Truck	2000 00	
Accounts Payable		2100 00
Alan West, Capital		2600 00
Alan West, Drawing	180 00	
Repair Service Revenue		370 00
Wages Expense	100 00	
Truck Expense	30 00	
Totals	5070 00	5070 00

City Machine Repair Service
Trial Balance
July 31, 19X1

Note that the heading consists of three lines, which answer these questions: Who? What? and When? The accounts are listed on the trial balance form in the order they appear in the ledger. The debit balances are recorded in the Debit money column, and the credit balances are recorded in the Credit money column. A single line is drawn across each money column with a ruler, and the balances are added. If the totals of the two money columns agree, the trial balance is in balance. Then, two lines are drawn under the totals. These lines show that the trial balance has been completed.

If the total debit balances do not equal the total credit balances, the trial balance is not in balance. This means that there is an error in the trial balance or in the accounts.

Finding Errors in the Trial Balance and the Accounts

Time may be saved in finding errors by working back systematically from the trial balance to the accounts. It is usually possible to locate errors by completing one or more of the following steps.

1. Total the trial balance money columns again to make sure that the addition is correct.
2. Check to see whether any account balance has not been recorded on the trial balance.
3. Compare the figures on the trial balance with the account balances to verify that the correct amounts have been listed on the trial balance and that they were placed in the proper money columns.
4. Total the debits and credits in the accounts again, and find the balances again.
5. Check the entries in the accounts to make sure that a matching debit and credit were recorded for each transaction.

Errors Not Revealed by the Trial Balance

Even if the trial balance is in balance, there is still a possibility that the accounts are not correct. Some errors that do not affect the equality of the trial balance totals are as follows.

- Omitting a transaction completely.
- Debiting and crediting the wrong accounts.
- Entering the amount of a transaction incorrectly.
- Entering the same transaction twice.

Chapter Summary

☐ The accuracy of the accounts must be checked before financial reports are prepared.
☐ The procedure for checking the equality of the debits and credits in the accounts is called taking a trial balance.
☐ The first step in taking a trial balance is to find the balances of the accounts. The next step is to list the accounts and their balances. Then, the debits and credits are totaled. The total of the debits should be equal to the total of the credits.
☐ The accounts are listed on the trial balance form in the order they appear in the ledger.
☐ If the trial balance is in balance, it is probable that the accounts in the ledger are correct. If the total debits and the total credits are not equal, the trial balance and the accounts must be checked to find the error.

Checking Your Knowledge

BUSINESS APPLICATION

Problem 5-1. The ledger accounts of the Suburban Real Estate Agency, owned by Karen Bell, are shown on page 11 of the workbook.

1. Pencil-foot the accounts and find the balances.
2. Prepare a trial balance as of March 31, 19X1, on the form at the bottom of page 11 in the workbook.

Problem 5-2. Using the ledger accounts that were completed in Problem 4-1 for the Ramos Accounting Service, do the following work.

1. Pencil-foot the accounts and find the balances.
2. Prepare a trial balance as of January 31, 19X1, on the form at the top of page 12 in the workbook.

Problem 5-3. Using the ledger accounts that were completed in Problem 4-2 for the O'Neill Advertising Agency, do the following work.

1. Pencil-foot the accounts and find the balances.

2. Prepare a trial balance as of April 30, 19X1, on the form at the bottom of page 12 in the workbook.

MANAGERIAL ANALYSIS

Case 5. The bookkeeper of the Southern Collection Agency found that the October trial balance was out of balance. The credits exceeded the debits by $400. She wonders what kind of errors she could have made.

1. What are three possible errors that could have caused the trial balance to be out of balance?

2. If the amount of the difference were only $4, why would it still be important for the bookkeeper to find and correct the error?

Financial Statements

After the trial balance is in balance, formal reports summarizing the information in the accounts can be prepared. These reports are called *financial statements*. They show the financial position of a business and the results of its operations.

The Accounting Period

The period for which results are summarized is known as the *accounting period*, or *fiscal period*. The length of the accounting period is not the same for all businesses. Each owner chooses the period that seems best for his or her type of business. It may be one month, three months (quarterly period), six months (semiannual period), or twelve months (annual period). Whatever time period is chosen, it should be used consistently.

If a year is used for the accounting period, it need not be the calendar year (January 1 to December 31). It might be any twelve-month period that covers the normal business year in that particular industry, such as July 1 to June 30. An accounting period of twelve consecutive months is called a *fiscal year*.

> **Accounting Period:** Period of time for which financial results of business operations are summarized.

> **Fiscal Year:** Any accounting period of twelve consecutive months.

Completion of the Income Statement

The method for finding the net income or net loss for a period was explained in Chapter 2. Since information about revenue, expenses, and net income or net loss is very important to business owners and managers, it is presented in a financial statement known as the *income statement*.

Look at the trial balance of the City Machine Repair Service that was prepared as of July 31, 19X1 (see page 26). This trial balance will now be used to prepare the business's financial statements. The revenue and expense figures needed for the income statement are shown on the lower part of the trial balance.

The income statement is prepared on accounting paper with two money columns. The balance of the revenue account ($370) is entered in the second money column. This is followed by the balances of each of the expense accounts, which are listed in the first money column. The expenses are added, and the total ($130) is written in the second money column below the revenue figure. The total of the expenses is then subtracted from the revenue to find the net income ($370 − $130 = $240).

Of course, if the expenses had been greater than the revenue, the result would have been a net loss. This would have been shown on the income statement by using the words Net Loss instead of Net Income.

Observe that the heading of the income statement answers the three questions: Who? What? and When? The last line of the heading usually shows both the length of the business's accounting period and the ending date of the period. For example, a business with a monthly accounting period would use Month Ended January 31, 19X1 on its income statement for January. The City Machine Repair Service will have a

> **Income Statement:** Report of revenue, expenses, and net income or net loss, showing results of business operations for a period of time.

Financial Statements   **29**

monthly accounting period. However, since the business has been open for only a week, the heading of its current income statement says Period Ended July 31, 19X1.

```
           City Machine Repair Service
                 Income Statement
              Period Ended July 31, 19X1

Revenue
    Repair Service Revenue                        370 00
Operating Expenses
    Wages Expense                   100 00
    Truck Expense                    30 00
        Total Operating Expenses                  130 00
Net Income                                        240 00
```

After the income statement is proved correct, it is often typewritten, as shown below.

```
           City Machine Repair Service
                 Income Statement
              Period Ended July 31, 19X1


Revenue
    Repair Service Revenue                    $370
Operating Expenses
    Wages Expense              $100
    Truck Expense                30
        Total Operating Expenses                130
Net Income                                    $240
```

Completion of the Statement of Owner's Equity and the Balance Sheet

Balance Sheet: Itemized list of assets, liabilities, and owner's equity, showing financial position of a business on a certain date.

Statement of Owner's Equity: Report of changes in owner's equity during a period of time.

A balance sheet is also prepared at the end of the accounting period. While the income statement reports the results of operations for the period, the balance sheet shows the financial position of the business on the last day of the period.

Before the balance sheet is prepared, many businesses prepare a *statement of owner's equity,* or *capital statement.* This statement supplements the balance sheet by showing all the details of the changes in owner's equity during the accounting period. When a statement of owner's equity is used, the Owner's Equity section of the balance sheet can be kept very simple and easy to read. The illustration on page 23 shows how long and complex this section can be if there is no separate statement of owner's equity.

Preparing the Statement of Owner's Equity. Like the income statement, the statement of owner's equity is usually first prepared on two-column accounting paper. The heading again answers the questions: Who? What? and When?

30 Accounting Fundamentals

(Handwritten statement of owner's equity)

```
              City Machine Repair Service
               Statement of Owner's Equity
                 Period Ended July 31, 19X1

Alan West, Capital, July 24, 19X1              2 200 00
Additional Investment                             400 00
   Total Investment                             2 600 00
Net Income                            240 00
Less Withdrawals                      180 00
   Net Increase in Owner's Equity                  60 00
Alan West, Capital, July 31, 19X1               2 660 00
```

The information needed to prepare the statement of owner's equity comes from several sources. The amount of the owner's capital at the beginning of the period ($2,200) and the amount of the additional investment ($400) are taken from the capital account (see page 16). Notice that these two figures are written in the second money column and added to find West's total investment ($2,200 + $400 = $2,600).

The net income for the period ($240) comes from the income statement and is listed in the first money column. The amount of the withdrawals ($180) comes from the balance of the drawing account shown on the trial balance (page 26). This figure is also listed in the first money column and is subtracted from the net income to find the net increase in owner's equity ($240 − $180 = $60).

The net increase in owner's equity ($60) is written in the second money column. It is then added to the amount of the total investment ($2,600) to find the owner's capital at the end of the period ($2,600 + $60 = $2,660).

After the statement of owner's equity is proved correct, it is also typewritten.

```
              City Machine Repair Service
               Statement of Owner's Equity
                 Period Ended July 31, 19X1


Alan West, Capital, July 24, 19X1              $2,200
Additional Investment                              400
   Total Investment                             $2,600
Net Income                             $240
Less Withdrawals                        180
   Net Increase in Owner's Equity                   60
Alan West, Capital, July 31, 19X1               $2,660
```

Preparing the Balance Sheet. If a statement of owner's equity is used, it is simple to prepare the balance sheet. The balances of the asset and liability accounts are taken from the trial balance (page 26). The Owner's Equity section of the balance sheet shows only one figure—the owner's capital at the end of the period. This figure comes from the statement of owner's equity.

Look at the balance sheet on page 32. It shows that Alan West's capital on July 31, 19X1, is $2,660. This balance sheet was first prepared on accounting paper, as discussed in Chapter 1 (see page 3). Then, after it was proved to be correct, the balance sheet was typewritten. Notice that when financial statements are typewritten, dollar signs and commas are used for the amounts.

```
              City Machine Repair Service
                     Balance Sheet
                    July 31, 19X1


         Assets                    Liabilities and Owner's Equity

Cash                    $1,560     Liabilities
Accounts Receivable        100         Accounts Payable      $2,100
Equipment                1,100
Delivery Truck           2,000     Owner's Equity
                                       Alan West, Capital     2,660

                                   Total Liabilities and
Total Assets            $4,760         Owner's Equity        $4,760
```

After the financial statements are completed, they are studied carefully by owners, managers, and accountants. These people interpret the information on the statements and use it to make decisions and plans.

Chapter Summary

- The accounting period is the period of time for which financial results are summarized. Another name for the accounting period is fiscal period.
- Most of the information used in preparing the financial statements comes from the trial balance, which is taken on the last day of the accounting period.
- The income statement summarizes the revenue and expenses for an accounting period and shows how the net income or the net loss came about.
- The statement of owner's equity shows the details of the changes in owner's equity that occurred during an accounting period. This information may be reported on the balance sheet instead of being shown on a separate statement.
- The balance sheet shows the financial position of a business on a certain date.
- The financial statements permit owners, managers, and accountants to interpret business activities.

Checking Your Knowledge

BUSINESS APPLICATION

Problem 6-1. The trial balance of the Quality Photo Studio, owned and operated by Paul Chang, is given on page 13 of the workbook. Forms for the financial statements appear on pages 13 and 14.

1. Prepare an income statement for the month ended January 31, 19X1.

2. Prepare a statement of owner's equity for the month ended January 31, 19X1. The balance of the capital account on January 1 was $3,700. Chang made an additional investment of $500 during the month.

3. Prepare a balance sheet dated January 31, 19X1.

MANAGERIAL ANALYSIS

Case 6. Robert Dunn owns and operates a dry cleaning store. When Dunn received the financial statements of the business at the end of the first quarter's operation, he was confused by two things: (1) The income statement showed a net income although the cash figure on the balance sheet was less than when he began operations. (2) The net income figure appeared on both the income statement and the statement of owner's equity.

If you were Dunn's accountant, how would you explain to Dunn the two things he doesn't understand about the financial statements of his business?

SUMMARY PROBLEM I

Chapters 1-6. The Home Decorating Service is owned and operated by Joan Novak. On December 1, 19X1, the business's accounts contained the following balances.

Cash	$ 2,600
Accounts Receivable	100
Accounts Payable	300
Building	10,000
Office Equipment	400
Automobile	2,500

1. Prepare a balance sheet dated December 1, 19X1. (You will have to find the amount of the owner's equity.) Use the form on page 15 of the workbook.

2. Enter the account balances in the accounts provided on page 15 of the workbook.

3. Record the following transactions in the accounts. Enter the amount and the identifying letter of each transaction.

A. Paid $100 in cash to the local newspaper for advertising.
B. Provided services for $200 in cash.
C. Bought an office file cabinet for $75 in cash.
D. Paid $10 in cash for gasoline for the automobile used in the business.
E. Returned $15 in cash to a client for an overcharge made on services provided in Transaction B.
F. Joan Novak made an additional cash investment of $300 in the business.
G. Provided services for $150 in cash.
H. Paid $170 in cash to a creditor on account.
I. Received $70 in cash from a client on account.
J. Paid $20 in cash for postage stamps.
K. Paid $15 in cash for the telephone bill.
L. Provided services for $260 in cash.
M. Bought a new typewriter for $250 and agreed to pay in 90 days.
N. Provided services for $80 on credit.
O. Paid $25 in cash for gasoline and oil for the automobile used in the business.
P. Paid $50 in cash for the heat and electricity bill.
Q. Received a refund of $20 in cash from the local newspaper because one of the business's ads did not appear.
R. Joan Novak withdrew $400 in cash for her personal use.
S. Paid $10 in cash for postage stamps.
T. Provided services for $250 in cash.

4. Pencil-foot the accounts to find the balances.

5. Prepare a trial balance as of December 31, 19X1. Use the form at the top of page 16 of the workbook.

6. Prepare an income statement for the month ended December 31, 19X1. Use the form at the bottom of page 16 of the workbook.

7. Prepare a statement of owner's equity for the month ended December 31, 19X1. Use the form at the top of page 17 of the workbook.

8. Prepare a balance sheet dated December 31, 19X1. Use the form at the bottom of page 17 of the workbook.

7
The General Journal

Entering transactions directly into T accounts is a good way to learn the principles of debit and credit, but this arrangement is not adequate for keeping a complete record of business operations. For one thing, errors cannot be found easily because related debits and credits are scattered throughout the accounts. Even if both sides of a transaction can be traced, the T account provides no information except the name of the account and the amount of each entry.

For example, the T accounts illustrating Transaction G in Chapter 4—the payment of the part-time employee's weekly wages of $100 in cash—give very little information.

Cash		Wages Expense
1,500	100	100
400	200	
220	100	
50		

There is no way to tell from the Cash account which of the two $100 payments was made for wages. Also, the Wages Expense account does not show to whom the wages were paid or when. Thus in addition to ledger accounts, a business needs an easy-to-follow, day-by-day record of its transactions.

The Use of the General Journal

Journal: Chronological record of business transactions.

Chronological Order: Order in which transactions happen day by day.

Journalizing: Recording transactions in the journal.

General Journal: A record in which all business transactions can be entered as they occur.

An accounting record known as a *journal* is used to list in one place all the necessary information about a transaction. The journal is the first accounting record of business transactions and is therefore referred to as a *record of original entry*. Entries are recorded in the journal in *chronological order*—in the order that the business transactions happen day by day. The process of recording these transactions in the journal is known as *journalizing*, or *making journal entries*.

There are a number of different types of journals. One common type is the *general journal*, which is illustrated on page 35. Note that the information about Transaction G is much more complete when journalized as shown here.

34 Accounting Fundamentals

```
                    GENERAL JOURNAL                       PAGE   2

  DATE  |   DESCRIPTION OF ENTRY    | POST. |   DEBIT   |   CREDIT
        |                           | REF.  |           |
--------|---------------------------|-------|-----------|----------
19X1    |                           |       |           |
July 28 | Wages Expense             |       |  100 00   |
        |   Cash                    |       |           |  100 00
        | Paid weekly wages to part-time employee.
```

Study the illustration carefully and observe the following details.

- The year is entered at the top of the Date column. The month and day are written below the year. (The year and month need not be repeated after the first entry on a page, except when the year or month changes.)
- The name of the account being debited is written in the Description of Entry column, beginning at the left margin of that column. The debit amount is entered in the Debit money column.
- The name of the account being credited is written on the next line of the Description of Entry column. It is indented about one-half inch from the left margin. The credit amount is entered in the Credit money column.
- A brief, clear explanation of the transaction follows on the next one or two lines of the Description of Entry column. This explanation gives additional information that is not shown by the account names.
- A blank line is left after the entry to separate it from the next entry. (This is one of several common methods used for separating entries.)
- The pages of the journal are numbered consecutively at the top right corner of each page.
- The narrow column to the left of the Debit money column is the Posting Reference column. Its use will be explained in the next chapter.

Journalizing a Business's Transactions

Let us consider how the transactions of the Quick Delivery Service, owned by John Costa, would be recorded in a general journal. Costa bought this established business, and he begins his own operation on November 1, 19X1. His balance sheet for that date is as follows.

```
                        Quick Delivery Service
                            Balance Sheet
                          November 1, 19X1

           Assets                    Liabilities and Owner's Equity

Cash                   $1,200      Liabilities
Accounts Receivable       800         Accounts Payable         $2,000
Office Equipment        1,000
Delivery Truck          6,000      Owner's Equity
                                      John Costa, Capital       7,000

                                   Total Liabilities and
Total Assets           $9,000         Owner's Equity           $9,000
```

The General Journal 35

Chart of Accounts: A list of all the accounts of a business arranged and numbered according to account classification.

The business's accountant has recommended that the accounts shown below be used. Note that a number is assigned to each account for identification and reference purposes. Account numbers are usually assigned in the order in which the accounts appear on the financial statements. The arranged list of a business's accounts is known as a *chart of accounts*. There are many numbering systems for accounts. The one shown here is a common type of numbering system.

```
              Quick Delivery Service
                 Chart of Accounts

Account
Number       Name of Account

100-199      ASSETS
   101         Cash
   102         Accounts Receivable
   111         Office Equipment
   112         Delivery Truck

200-299      LIABILITIES
   201         Accounts Payable

300-399      OWNER'S EQUITY
   301         John Costa, Capital
   302         John Costa, Drawing

400-499      REVENUE
   401         Delivery Service Revenue

500-599      EXPENSES
   501         Rent Expense
   502         Truck Expense
   503         Wages Expense
```

Opening Entry: Journal entry that starts a new set of financial records.

Costa asks the accountant to start a new set of financial records for the business on November 1, 19X1. The accountant therefore makes an *opening entry* in the general journal to record the items listed on the balance sheet. This entry is shown on page 38. It is the first entry in the journal. Note that the accountant debits the assets and credits the liabilities and the owner's equity.

During the month of November, Costa records the business's transactions in the general journal, as shown on pages 38 and 39. Before making an entry, he analyzes each transaction and selects the correct account names from the chart of accounts. Costa's analysis of the November transactions is given below and on page 37. Refer to this analysis as you study the journal entries for the Quick Delivery Service.

Date	Description of Transactions	Analysis
Nov. 1	Paid $300 in cash for the November rent.	Owner's equity decreases (debit Rent Expense). An asset decreases (credit Cash).
5	Bought a new typewriter for the office for $225 in cash.	An asset increases (debit Office Equipment). An asset decreases (credit Cash).

36 Accounting Fundamentals

Date	Description of Transactions	Analysis
Nov. 6	Provided delivery service for $650 in cash.	An asset increases (debit Cash). Owner's equity increases (credit Delivery Service Revenue).
10	Paid $150 in cash to the Hill Truck Company on account.	A liability decreases (debit Accounts Payable). An asset decreases (credit Cash).
13	Paid $50 in cash for gasoline and oil for the truck.	Owner's equity decreases (debit Truck Expense). An asset decreases (credit Cash).
15	Paid $250 in cash for the truck driver's semimonthly wages.	Owner's equity decreases (debit Wages Expense). An asset decreases (credit Cash).
18	Provided delivery service for $325 on credit to Santini's Furniture Store.	An asset increases (debit Accounts Receivable). Owner's equity increases (credit Delivery Service Revenue).
20	Provided delivery service for $675 in cash.	An asset increases (debit Cash). Owner's equity increases (credit Delivery Service Revenue).
23	John Costa made an additional cash investment of $600 in the business.	An asset increases (debit Cash). Owner's equity increases (credit John Costa, Capital).
25	Received $500 in cash from the Modern Appliance Center on account.	An asset increases (debit Cash). An asset decreases (credit Accounts Receivable).
27	Bought an office safe for $300 on credit from the Kelly Safe Company.	An asset increases (debit Office Equipment). A liability increases (credit Accounts Payable).
29	Paid $250 in cash for the truck driver's semimonthly wages.	Owner's equity decreases (debit Wages Expense). An asset decreases (credit Cash).
30	John Costa withdrew $700 in cash for his personal use.	Owner's equity decreases (debit John Costa, Drawing). An asset decreases (credit Cash).

GENERAL JOURNAL   PAGE 1

DATE	DESCRIPTION OF ENTRY	POST. REF.	DEBIT	CREDIT
19X1 Nov. 1	Cash		1200 00	
	Accounts Receivable		800 00	
	Office Equipment		1000 00	
	Delivery Truck		6000 00	
	Accounts Payable			200 00
	John Costa, Capital			7000 00
	Investment of John Costa in the business.			
1	Rent Expense		300 00	
	Cash			300 00
	Paid November rent.			
5	Office Equipment		225 00	
	Cash			225 00
	Bought typewriter.			
6	Cash		650 00	
	Delivery Service Revenue			650 00
10	Accounts Payable		150 00	
	Cash			150 00
	Paid Hill Truck Company on account.			
13	Truck Expense		50 00	
	Cash			50 00
	Paid for gasoline and oil.			
15	Wages Expense		250 00	
	Cash			250 00
	Paid semimonthly wages to truck driver.			
18	Accounts Receivable		325 00	
	Delivery Service Revenue			325 00
	Provided service on credit to Santini's Furniture Store.			
20	Cash		675 00	
	Delivery Service Revenue			675 00
23	Cash		600 00	
	John Costa, Capital			600 00

GENERAL JOURNAL   PAGE 2

DATE	DESCRIPTION OF ENTRY	POST. REF.	DEBIT	CREDIT
19X1 Nov. 25	Cash		500 00	
	Accounts Receivable			500 00
	Received from Modern Appliance Center on account.			

GENERAL JOURNAL				PAGE 2
DATE	DESCRIPTION OF ENTRY	POST. REF.	DEBIT	CREDIT
19X1 Nov.				
27	Office Equipment		300 00	
	Accounts Payable			300 00
	Bought office safe on credit from Kelly Safe Company.			
29	Wages Expense		250 00	
	Cash			250 00
	Paid semimonthly wages to truck driver.			
30	John Costa, Drawing		700 00	
	Cash			700 00

Note that explanations have been omitted from the entries of November 6, 20, 23, and 30. The account names in these entries tell what happened, and there is no need for additional information about the transactions.

Journal entries are recorded in ink. No erasures are made. If there is an error, it is neatly crossed out with a single line and the correct information is written above it, as shown here.

30	John Costa, Drawing		700 00	
	Cash			~~600 00~~ 700 00

An entry may contain more than one debit or credit. For example, a beauty salon may have separate accounts for its revenue from hairdressing and its revenue from manicures. If a customer pays $15, of which $12 is for hairdressing and $3 is for a manicure, the entry would be journalized as shown below. Note that the *total* debits and credits are equal ($15 = $12 + $3). No matter how many accounts are involved in an entry, the debits and credits must always add up to equal dollar amounts. An entry that has more than one debit or credit is called a *compound entry*. (The opening entry shown on page 38 is another example of a compound entry.)

Compound Entry: Journal entry with more than one debit or credit.

2	Cash		15 —	
	Hairdressing Revenue			12 —
	Manicuring Revenue			3 —

Instead of writing two zeros (00) in the cents column, many bookkeepers, accounting clerks, and accountants prefer to use a dash (—) to show that there are no cents. This is illustrated by the entry above. Either method is acceptable as long as it is used consistently in the accounting records.

Use of the journal is combined with use of the ledger. The information from the journal entries must be transferred to the proper ledger accounts. The procedure for this is explained in the next chapter.

The General Journal

Chapter Summary

- Entering transactions in T accounts is not adequate for providing complete information about business activities. In addition to accounts, there is a need for a chronological (day-by-day) record of transactions. This record is called a journal.
- The journal is used to list essential information about each transaction as it occurs. The journal is known as the record of original entry because it is the first accounting record of a transaction.
- The general journal is a common type of journal.
- A systematically arranged list of a business's accounts is known as a chart of accounts. The chart shows account classifications (assets, liabilities, owner's equity, revenue, and expenses) as well as the name and number of each account. The number is used for identification and reference purposes.
- A journal entry may contain more than one debit or credit. This type of entry is called a compound entry. No matter how many accounts are involved, the totals of the debits and credits in any one entry must be equal.

Checking Your Knowledge

BUSINESS APPLICATION

Problem 7-1. Kay Metz bought the Delta Cleaning Service on July 1, 19X1. Her balance sheet on that date is shown below.

DELTA CLEANING SERVICE
Balance Sheet
July 1, 19X1

Assets		Liabilities and Owner's Equity	
Cash	$1,700	Liabilities	
Accounts Receivable	225	Accounts Payable	$ 300
Cleaning Equipment	800	Owner's Equity	
Office Equipment	275	Kay Metz, Capital	6,450
Truck	3,750	Total Liabilities and	
Total Assets	$6,750	Owner's Equity	$6,750

1. Record the opening entry. Use the general journal given on page 20 of the workbook.

The first step in journalizing a business's daily transactions is to analyze each transaction and determine its effect on the accounts. The chart of accounts for the Delta Cleaning Service is shown in the next column.

2. Analyze the following transactions for July. Use the form given on page 19 of the workbook.

3. Journalize the entries for July. Use the general journal given on pages 20 and 21 of the workbook.

July 1 Bought supplies for $230 on credit from Rem Cleaning Supplies.
  4 Provided cleaning services for $300 in cash.
  8 Paid $15 in cash for gasoline and oil for the truck.
July 10 Provided cleaning services for $150 on credit to A-One Travel Agency.
  15 Paid $260 in cash for semimonthly wages of part-time employees.
  18 Provided cleaning services for $325 in cash.
  20 Received $75 in cash from A-One Travel Agency on account.
  25 Provided cleaning services for $500 in cash.
  26 Paid $160 in cash to Rem Cleaning Supplies on account.
  28 Bought an office desk for $180 from Elco Equipment, agreeing to pay in 30 days.
  30 Kay Metz withdrew $480 in cash for her personal use.
  31 Paid $260 in cash for semimonthly wages of part-time employees.

Note: Save the general journal for use in Problem 8-2 of Chapter 8.

Assets		Revenue	
101	Cash	401	Cleaning Service Revenue
102	Accounts Receivable		
111	Cleaning Equipment	**Expenses**	
112	Office Equipment	501	Cleaning Supplies Expense
113	Truck	502	Truck Expense
Liabilities		503	Wages Expense
201	Accounts Payable		
Owner's Equity			
301	Kay Metz, Capital		
302	Kay Metz, Drawing		

Problem 7-2. Leo Doyle bought the Pacific Delivery Company on August 1, 19X1. His balance sheet on that date is shown below.

PACIFIC DELIVERY COMPANY
Balance Sheet
August 1, 19X1

Assets		Liabilities and Owner's Equity	
Cash	$ 3,500	Liabilities	
Accounts Receivable	800	Accounts Payable	$ 600
Office Equipment	2,700	Owner's Equity	
Delivery Equipment	5,800	Leo Doyle, Capital	12,200
Total Assets	$12,800	Total Liabilities and Owner's Equity	$12,800

1. Record the opening entry. Use the general journal given on page 23 of the workbook.

The Pacific Delivery Company offers two types of service—delivery by messenger and delivery by truck. Because Doyle wants to know his revenue from each type of service, he will use two revenue accounts. His chart of accounts is shown below.

Assets		Revenue	
101	Cash	401	Truck Delivery Revenue
102	Accounts Receivable	402	Messenger Service Revenue
111	Office Equipment		
112	Delivery Equipment		
Liabilities		**Expenses**	
201	Accounts Payable	501	Rent Expense
Owner's Equity		502	Delivery Expense
301	Leo Doyle, Capital	503	Wages Expense
302	Leo Doyle, Drawing	504	Office Expense

2. Analyze the following transactions for August. Use the form given on page 22 of the workbook. Some of the transactions involve more than two accounts. Remember that the total debits must equal the total credits in all transactions.

3. Journalize the entries for August. Use the general journal given on pages 23 and 24 of the workbook.

Aug. 1 Paid $360 in cash for August rent.
   2 Provided truck deliveries for $380 in cash.
   3 Bought a new bicycle for the messenger for $120 from Tom's Cycle Center and agreed to pay in 60 days.
   4 Provided messenger service for $260 on credit to Martin Stockbrokers.
   7 Bought a new typewriter for $325 in cash and paid $25 in cash to the same business for repairing an old calculator. The total cash payment was $350.
   10 Provided truck deliveries for $450 on credit and messenger service for $230 on credit to Brown's Department Store. The total amount billed to this business was $680.
   12 Bought a new tire for the delivery truck for $75 at Calli's Garage, agreeing to pay in 30 days.
   14 Received $700 in cash from Klein Stores on account.
   15 Paid $550 in cash for semimonthly wages of truck driver and messenger.
   18 Paid $570 in cash to Ross Trucks on account.
   20 Leo Doyle made an additional cash investment of $1,000 in the business.
   22 Paid $15 in cash for gasoline for the delivery truck.
   24 Provided truck deliveries for $420 in cash and messenger service for $320 in cash. The total cash received was $740.
   29 Leo Doyle withdrew $600 in cash for his personal use.
   30 Paid $30 in cash to have repairs made on an office chair.
   31 Paid $550 in cash for semimonthly wages of truck driver and messenger.

Note: Save the general journal for use in Problem 8-3 of Chapter 8.

MANAGERIAL ANALYSIS

Case 7. Janet Miller is opening a furniture store. Her accountant has told her to use a general journal as part of her financial recordkeeping system. She argues that there is no need for a general journal. She believes that the accounts will supply her with all the financial information that she needs.

How would you convince Janet Miller that the general journal is a necessary part of her financial recordkeeping system and that the accounts will not supply enough information?

The General Ledger

8

Ledger: Record that contains accounts.

Posting: Transferring information from the journal to the ledger.

The journal gives a complete chronological record of a business's transactions. However, it is also necessary to sort this information so that related facts can be grouped and summarized. For example, all facts about cash transactions must be grouped together, and all facts about accounts payable transactions must also be grouped together. This is done in the *ledger*.

Since the journal is the first accounting record of transactions, sorting information about transactions involves transferring it from the journal to the ledger. Thus, the ledger becomes the second record of transactions and is often called a *record of final entry*. The process of transferring information about transactions from the journal to the ledger is known as *posting*.

Lined ledger account forms with columns are used in business instead of T accounts. These printed forms allow for the recording of more details about transactions than T accounts. An example of a standard ledger account form is shown here.

Note that the ledger account form is an elaboration of the T account shown above it. Both have a debit side and a credit side. However, each side of the ledger account form provides columns so that the date, explanation, posting reference, and amount for each debit and credit item can be recorded. At the top of the ledger account form, there is space for entering both the account name and the account number.

Posting to the Ledger

The illustrations on page 43 show how the information from the general journal entry for the payment of rent on November 1 is posted (transferred) to the two ledger accounts involved.

42 Accounting Fundamentals

GENERAL JOURNAL				PAGE 1
DATE	DESCRIPTION OF ENTRY	POST. REF.	DEBIT	CREDIT
19X1 Nov. 1	Rent Expense	501	30000	
	Cash	101		30000
	Paid November rent.	⑤		

Rent Expense   NO. 501

DATE	EXPLANATION	POST. REF.	DEBIT	DATE	EXPLANATION	POST. REF.	CREDIT
19X1 Nov. 1		J1	30000				
②	③	④	①				

Cash   NO. 101

DATE	EXPLANATION	POST. REF.	DEBIT	DATE	EXPLANATION	POST. REF.	CREDIT
				19X1 Nov. 1		J1	30000

Note the following steps in posting the debit item from the general journal.

1. The amount is entered in the Debit column of the ledger account being debited.
2. The year, month, and day are entered in the Date column. (After the first entry, the year and the month are not recorded except when continuing onto another page or when the year or the month changes.)
3. The Explanation column of the account is not used for most transactions. However, it is available for any special notations that might be helpful.
4. A *J* (for journal) and the number of the journal page from which the entry came are written in the Posting Reference column of the account. Thus page 1 of the general journal would be recorded as *J1*. This makes it easy to trace the information in the ledger account back to the original journal entry.
5. The number of the ledger account is recorded in the Posting Reference column of the journal to show that the debit item was posted.

The credit item is then posted to the ledger account being credited by following similar steps. However, the entry is made on the right (credit) side of the ledger account form. Study the Cash account shown above.

Remember that an account must be provided for each financial item involved in the business—assets, liabilities, and owner's equity (including revenue and expenses). To make posting as simple as possible, a separate ledger sheet is used for each account. All the accounts together make up the *general ledger*.

Posting Procedure:
- Enter amount in account.
- Enter date in account.
- Enter explanation in account if one is needed.
- Enter posting reference (journal page number) in account.
- Enter posting reference (account number) in journal.

General Ledger: Entire group of accounts for a business's assets, liabilities, and owner's equity.

Setting Up and Using Accounts in the General Ledger

As discussed in Chapter 7, the accountant for the Quick Delivery Service prepared a chart of accounts (page 36) and made the opening entry in the general journal. Another important task that the accountant had to perform was setting up a general ledger account for each item shown on the chart of accounts. The accountant did this by writing the account names and numbers at the top of the ledger sheets. Then the accountant posted the opening entry from the general journal to the general ledger.

The General Ledger

When the general ledger accounts are set up, they are arranged in the order that they appear on the chart of accounts. This order will make it easy to prepare the financial statements. Note that the balance sheet accounts are placed first—asset accounts, liability accounts, owner's capital account, and owner's drawing account. Next come the income statement accounts—revenue accounts and expense accounts.

After the transactions of the Quick Delivery Service have been entered in the general journal, they are posted to the general ledger. This is done on a daily basis in order to have up-to-date information in the accounts at all times.

Study the illustrations of the journal and the accounts below and on pages 45 through 47. Note the following about the illustrations.

- The account numbers in the journal are recorded as each item is posted. They show that the items were transferred from the journal to the ledger.
- In the ledger, the year and the month are written once on each side of the accounts. Only the day is used for later entries. (As already discussed, the month and year are not recorded again on the ledger sheet until there is a change.)
- The entries in the ledger accounts are recorded in ink. No erasures are made. If there is an error, it is neatly crossed out with a single line and the correct information is written above it.
- The posting reference in the ledger accounts changes from J1 to J2 when entries are posted from a new page of the journal.
- At the end of the month, the money columns of the ledger accounts are pencil-footed. Each account balance is then determined. When there are entries on both sides of an account, the balance is recorded in the Explanation column of the side with the larger total. When there is only one entry in a money column, no pencil footing is necessary.

GENERAL JOURNAL				PAGE 1
DATE	DESCRIPTION OF ENTRY	POST. REF.	DEBIT	CREDIT
9X1 Nov. 1	Cash	101	1200 00	
	Accounts Receivable	102	800 00	
	Office Equipment	111	100 00	
	Delivery Truck	112	600 00	
	Accounts Payable	201		200 00
	John Costa, Capital	301		700 00
	Investment of John Costa in the business.			
1	Rent Expense	501	30 00	
	Cash	101		30 00
	Paid November rent.			
5	Office Equipment	111	225 00	
	Cash	101		225 00
	Bought typewriter.			
6	Cash	101	65 00	
	Delivery Service Revenue	401		65 00
10	Accounts Payable	201	150 00	
	Cash	101		150 00
	Paid Hill Truck Company on account.			

44 Accounting Fundamentals

GENERAL JOURNAL   PAGE 1

DATE	DESCRIPTION OF ENTRY	POST. REF.	DEBIT	CREDIT
19X1 Nov. 13	Truck Expense	502	50 00	
	Cash	101		50 00
	Paid for gasoline and oil.			
15	Wages Expense	503	250 00	
	Cash	101		250 00
	Paid semimonthly wages to truck driver.			
18	Accounts Receivable	102	325 00	
	Delivery Service Revenue	401		325 00
	Provided service on credit to Santini's Furniture Store.			
20	Cash	101	675 00	
	Delivery Service Revenue	401		675 00
23	Cash	101	600 00	
	John Costa, Capital	301		600 00

GENERAL JOURNAL   PAGE 2

DATE	DESCRIPTION OF ENTRY	POST. REF.	DEBIT	CREDIT
19X1 Nov. 25	Cash	101	500 00	
	Accounts Receivable	102		500 00
	Received from Modern Appliance Center on account.			
27	Office Equipment	111	300 00	
	Accounts Payable	201		300 00
	Bought office safe on credit from Kelly Safe Company.			
29	Wages Expense	503	250 00	
	Cash	101		250 00
	Paid semimonthly wages to truck driver.			
30	John Costa, Drawing	302	700 00	
	Cash	101		700 00

Cash   NO. 101

DATE	EXPLANATION	POST. REF.	DEBIT	DATE	EXPLANATION	POST. REF.	CREDIT
19X1 Nov. 1		J1	1200 00	19X1 Nov. 1		J1	300 00
6		J1	650 00	5		J1	225 00
20		J1	675 00	10		J1	150 00
23		J1	600 00	13		J1	50 00
25		J2	500 00	15		J1	250 00
	1,700.00		3625 00	29		J2	250 00
				30		J2	700 00
							1925 00

The General Ledger 45

Accounts Receivable — NO. 102

DATE	EXPLANATION	POST. REF.	DEBIT	DATE	EXPLANATION	POST. REF.	CREDIT
19X1 Nov. 1		J1	800 00	19X1 Nov. 25		J2	500 00
18		J1	325 00				
	625.00		1125 00				

Office Equipment — NO. 111

DATE	EXPLANATION	POST. REF.	DEBIT	DATE	EXPLANATION	POST. REF.	CREDIT
19X1 Nov. 1		J1	1000 00				
5		J1	225 00				
27		J2	300 00				
			1525 00				

Delivery Truck — NO. 112

DATE	EXPLANATION	POST. REF.	DEBIT	DATE	EXPLANATION	POST. REF.	CREDIT
19X1 Nov. 1		J1	6000 00				

Accounts Payable — NO. 201

DATE	EXPLANATION	POST. REF.	DEBIT	DATE	EXPLANATION	POST. REF.	CREDIT
19X1 Nov. 10		J1	150 00	19X1 Nov. 1		J1	2000 00
				27	2,150.00	J2	300 00
							2300 00

John Costa, Capital — NO. 301

DATE	EXPLANATION	POST. REF.	DEBIT	DATE	EXPLANATION	POST. REF.	CREDIT
				19X1 Nov. 1		J1	7000 00
				23		J1	600 00
							7600 00

John Costa, Drawing — NO. 302

DATE	EXPLANATION	POST. REF.	DEBIT	DATE	EXPLANATION	POST. REF.	CREDIT
19X1 Nov. 30		J2	700 00				

Delivery Service Revenue — NO. 401

DATE	EXPLANATION	POST. REF.	DEBIT	DATE	EXPLANATION	POST. REF.	CREDIT
				19X1 Nov. 6		J1	650 00
				18		J1	325 00
				20		J1	675 00
							1650 00

Accounting Fundamentals

Rent Expense — NO. 501

DATE	EXPLANATION	POST. REF.	DEBIT	DATE	EXPLANATION	POST. REF.	CREDIT
19X1 Nov. 1		J1	300 00				

Truck Expense — NO. 502

DATE	EXPLANATION	POST. REF.	DEBIT	DATE	EXPLANATION	POST. REF.	CREDIT
19X1 Nov. 13		J1	50 00				

Wages Expense — NO. 503

DATE	EXPLANATION	POST. REF.	DEBIT	DATE	EXPLANATION	POST. REF.	CREDIT
19X1 Nov. 15		J1	250 00				
29		J2	250 00				
			500 00				

At the end of November, the account balances in the ledger of the Quick Delivery Service are used to prepare the trial balance shown below. The trial balance tests the accuracy of the entries in the ledger. Note that the account numbers are recorded in the first column of the trial balance for identification and reference purposes.

Quick Delivery Service
Trial Balance
November 30, 19X1

Acct. No.	Account Name	Debit	Credit
101	Cash	1700 00	
102	Accounts Receivable	625 00	
111	Office Equipment	1525 00	
112	Delivery Truck	6000 00	
201	Accounts Payable		2150 00
301	John Costa, Capital		7600 00
302	John Costa, Drawing	700 00	
401	Delivery Service Revenue		1650 00
501	Rent Expense	300 00	
502	Truck Expense	50 00	
503	Wages Expense	500 00	
	Totals	11400 00	11400 00

Although the journal, the ledger, and the trial balance are shown together here, keep in mind that each is a separate record and serves a different purpose. The journal provides a day-by-day listing of transactions. The ledger sorts this information and groups it by accounts. The trial balance proves the equality of the debits and credits in the ledger.

The General Ledger 47

Chapter Summary

☐ The facts about a business's transactions are sorted and grouped by transferring the information in the journal to the ledger.
☐ An account must be provided in the ledger for each financial item in the business.
☐ The process of transferring information from the journal to the ledger is known as posting. Lined ledger account forms with columns are used to record detailed information about each entry.
☐ In the posting process, posting references are recorded to permit easy tracing of an entry from the journal to the ledger or from the ledger to the journal.
☐ Ledger accounts are arranged in an easy-to-follow order for preparing financial statements. Balance sheet accounts are first and income statement accounts follow.
☐ After all postings for a month have been completed, a trial balance is taken to prove the accuracy of the ledger.

Checking Your Knowledge

BUSINESS APPLICATION

Problem 8-1. The accounts listed in alphabetic order below are from the ledger of Dave's Garage, owned and operated by David Orr.

Use the form on page 25 of the workbook to prepare a chart of accounts for Dave's Garage. Arrange the accounts in the correct order and then assign a number to each account.

- Accounts Payable
- Accounts Receivable
- Advertising Expense
- Cash
- David Orr, Capital
- David Orr, Drawing
- Office Equipment
- Rent Expense
- Repair Equipment
- Repair Revenue
- Telephone Expense
- Tools
- Tow Truck
- Towing Revenue
- Utilities Expense
- Wages Expense

Problem 8-2. The chart of accounts for the Delta Cleaning Service is given on page 40.

1. Using the chart of accounts, open the necessary ledger accounts on the forms provided on pages 25-28 of the workbook.
2. Post to the accounts the journal entries that were made in Problem 7-1.
3. Pencil-foot the accounts to find the balances.
4. Prepare a trial balance of the general ledger as of July 31, 19X1. Use the form on page 28 of the workbook.

Problem 8-3. The chart of accounts for the Pacific Delivery Company is given on page 41.

1. Using the chart of accounts, open the necessary ledger accounts on the forms provided on pages 29-31 of the workbook.
2. Post to the accounts the journal entries that were made in Problem 7-2.
3. Pencil-foot the accounts to find the balances.
4. Prepare a trial balance of the general ledger as of August 31, 19X1. Use the form on page 32 of the workbook.

MANAGERIAL ANALYSIS

Case 8. Maria Valdez, who owns and operates a small motel, does not have enough work for a full-time accounting clerk. Therefore, her accounting clerk also acts as desk clerk and cashier for part of each day.

The accounting clerk makes daily entries of all financial information in the general journal. However, several days usually pass before he posts the entries from the general journal to the accounts in the general ledger.

1. What difficulties could this procedure create for Maria Valdez?
2. What difficulties could this procedure create for the accounting clerk?

48 Accounting Fundamentals

The Worksheet and the Financial Statements

Journalizing transactions and posting them to the ledger are important activities. They provide the figures needed to determine the result of operations and the financial position of the business at the end of the accounting period. After these figures are checked by taking a trial balance, the information is reported on the financial statements.

Up to now, the financial statements have been prepared directly from the trial balance. However, a special form called a *worksheet* is often used to compute the net income or net loss and to plan the financial statements before they are prepared. This form serves the same purpose as a blueprint made by an architect in planning a house before it is built.

Remember that each item listed on the trial balance appears on only one of the financial statements. The revenue and expense items are shown on the income statement. The asset, liability, and owner's equity items are shown on the balance sheet. Look at the worksheet illustrated on page 50. Note that it has a series of columns that allow the trial balance items to be separated according to their use on the income statement or the balance sheet.

Worksheet: Form used to compute the net income or net loss and to plan the preparation of financial statements.

Preparing the Worksheet

Since the worksheet is only a plan, it is usually prepared in pencil. The partially completed worksheet of the Quick Delivery Service for the month ended November 30, 19X1, is shown on page 50.

Note that the trial balance is recorded in the first two money columns of the worksheet form. This is the same trial balance that was shown on page 47. Proceeding item by item, the accountant now transfers the trial balance amounts to the additional pairs of money columns. Each amount is recorded in the one money column where it belongs.

1. The debits for balance sheet items are listed in the Debit column of the Balance Sheet section. These amounts are the balances of the asset accounts and the owner's drawing account.
2. The credits for balance sheet items are listed in the Credit column of the Balance Sheet section. These amounts are the balances of the liability account and the owner's capital account.
3. The credits for income statement items are listed in the Credit column of the Income Statement section. On the worksheet shown here, there is only one income statement item with a credit amount. This is the balance of the revenue account.
4. The debits for income statement items are listed in the Debit column of the Income Statement section. These amounts are the balances of the expense accounts.

Quick Delivery Service
Worksheet
Month Ended November 30, 19X1

ACCT. NO.	ACCOUNT NAME	TRIAL BALANCE DR.	TRIAL BALANCE CR.	INCOME STATEMENT DR.	INCOME STATEMENT CR.	BALANCE SHEET DR.	BALANCE SHEET CR.
101	Cash	1,700 00				1,700 00	
102	Accounts Receivable	625 00				625 00	
111	Office Equipment	1,525 00				1,525 00	
112	Delivery Truck	6,000 00				6,000 00	
201	Accounts Payable		2,150 00				2,150 00
301	John Costa, Capital		7,600 00				7,600 00
302	John Costa, Drawing	700 00				700 00	
401	Delivery Service Revenue		1,650 00		1,650 00		
501	Rent Expense	300 00		300 00			
502	Truck Expense	50 00		50 00			
503	Wages Expense	500 00		500 00			
	Totals	11,400 00	11,400 00	850 00	1,650 00	10,550 00	9,750 00

Note that a debit on the trial balance remains a debit when it is transferred; a credit on the trial balance remains a credit when it is transferred.

The columns of the Income Statement section and the Balance Sheet section are totaled after all the amounts have been transferred. Note that double lines are not drawn under these columns yet. The result of operations must be determined before the worksheet can be completed.

Determining the Result of Operations

After the trial balance amounts have been classified on the worksheet, the result of operations can be determined quickly.

- The total of the Debit column in the Income Statement section shows the total expenses for the period.
- The total of the Credit column in the Income Statement section shows the total revenue for the period.
- The difference between the Debit and Credit columns in the Income Statement section is the net income (or net loss) from operations. (When revenue is greater than expenses, the result is a net income. When expenses are greater than revenue, the result is a net loss.)

Since the worksheet of the Quick Delivery Service lists total expenses of $850 and total revenue of $1,650, the net income for November is $800 ($1,650 − $850). The net income figure is now used in completing the worksheet. This two-step process is illustrated at the top of page 51 and is explained below.

1. The net income figure ($800) is entered in the Debit column of the Income Statement section under the expense total and added to that total. The two columns of the Income Statement section will then balance (unless an arithmetic error or some other type of error has been made).
2. The net income figure is also entered in the Credit column of the Balance Sheet section. After this amount is added to the previous total of the Credit column, the two columns of the Balance Sheet section will balance (unless an error has been made).

Accounting Fundamentals

ACCT. NO.	ACCOUNT NAME	INCOME STATEMENT DR.	CR.
401	Delivery Service Revenue		1650 00
501	Rent Expense	300 00	
502	Truck Expense	50 00	
503	Wages Expense	500 00	
	Totals	850 00	1650 00
	Net Income	800 00	
		1650 00	1650 00

ACCT. NO.	ACCOUNT NAME	BALANCE SHEET DR.	CR.
101	Cash	1700 00	
102	Accounts Receivable	625 00	
111	Office Equipment	1525 00	
112	Delivery Truck	6000 00	
201	Accounts Payable		2150 00
301	John Costa, Capital		7600 00
302	John Costa, Drawing	700 00	
	Totals	10550 00	9750 00
	Net Income		800 00
		10550 00	10550 00

If the business had a net loss, the amount would be entered in the Credit column of the Income Statement section and the Debit column of the Balance Sheet section.

The following illustration shows how the worksheet of the Quick Delivery Service appears after the net income is recorded and the final totals are computed. Note that double lines are now drawn under the Income Statement and Balance Sheet columns to show that the worksheet is completed.

Quick Delivery Service
Worksheet
Month Ended November 30, 19X1

ACCT. NO.	ACCOUNT NAME	TRIAL BALANCE DR.	CR.	INCOME STATEMENT DR.	CR.	BALANCE SHEET DR.	CR.
101	Cash	1700 00				1700 00	
102	Accounts Receivable	625 00				625 00	
111	Office Equipment	1525 00				1525 00	
112	Delivery Truck	6000 00				6000 00	
201	Accounts Payable		2150 00				2150 00
301	John Costa, Capital		7600 00				7600 00
302	John Costa, Drawing	700 00				700 00	
401	Delivery Service Revenue		1650 00		1650 00		
501	Rent Expense	300 00		300 00			
502	Truck Expense	50 00		50 00			
503	Wages Expense	500 00		500 00			
	Totals	11400 00	11400 00	850 00	1650 00	10550 00	9750 00
	Net Income			800 00			800 00
				1650 00	1650 00	10550 00	10550 00

Preparing the Financial Statements

After the worksheet has been completed, the financial statements can be prepared easily because the planning has been done and the net income (or net loss) is known. (The value of the worksheet will become even more evident later when more complex financial statements are used.)

The Worksheet and the Financial Statements

The Income Statement. The income statement of the Quick Delivery Service is illustrated below. It shows the result of operations (the net income) for November and how this result came about. The figures for the preparation of the income statement are taken from the Income Statement columns of the worksheet.

```
                   Quick Delivery Service
                      Income Statement
                Month Ended November 30, 19X1


Revenue
   Delivery Service Revenue                      $1,650
Operating Expenses
   Rent Expense                   $300
   Truck Expense                    50
   Wages Expense                   500
      Total Operating Expenses                      850
Net Income                                       $  800
```

The Statement of Owner's Equity. In addition to the balance sheet, the Quick Delivery Service uses a statement of owner's equity, which explains the details of the changes in owner's equity during the accounting period (see Chapter 6). When this statement is used, the Owner's Equity section of the balance sheet can be kept very simple.

Look at the statement of owner's equity below. The figures for the capital on November 1 and the additional investment are taken from the John Costa, Capital account in the general ledger (see page 46). The figures for the net income and the withdrawals come from the Balance Sheet section of the worksheet. (The balance of the John Costa, Drawing account shows the withdrawals.) The total investment, the net increase in the owner's equity, and the capital on November 30 are computed on the statement of owner's equity.

```
                   Quick Delivery Service
                 Statement of Owner's Equity
                Month Ended November 30, 19X1



John Costa, Capital, November 1, 19X1             $7,000
Additional Investment                                600
   Total Investment                               $7,600
Net Income                           $800
Less Withdrawals                      700
   Net Increase in Owner's Equity                    100
John Costa, Capital, November 30, 19X1            $7,700
```

The Balance Sheet. After the statement of owner's equity is completed, the balance sheet is prepared to show the financial position of the Quick Delivery Service on November 30. The figures for the Assets section and the Liabilities section are taken from the Balance Sheet columns of the worksheet. Only one amount is listed in the Owner's Equity section of the balance sheet—the amount of capital on November 30. This comes from the statement of owner's equity.

```
            Quick Delivery Service
               Balance Sheet
              November 30, 19X1

                    Assets

Assets
  Cash                          $1,700
  Accounts Receivable              625
  Office Equipment               1,525
  Delivery Truck                 6,000
Total Assets                              $9,850


         Liabilities and Owner's Equity

Liabilities
  Accounts Payable                        $2,150
Owner's Equity
  John Costa, Capital                      7,700
Total Liabilities and Owner's Equity      $9,850
```

Note that the form of the balance sheet illustrated above is different from that shown previously. The liabilities and the owner's equity are listed below the assets instead of to the right of them. This is known as the *report form of balance sheet*. The change in arrangement does not affect the content or the equality of the statement. The totals show that the assets equal the liabilities plus the owner's equity, as they did in the *account form of balance sheet* used in earlier chapters.

Report Form of Balance Sheet: A balance sheet in which liabilities and owner's equity are placed under assets.

Account Form of Balance Sheet: A balance sheet in which assets are on the left side and liabilities and owner's equity are on the right side.

Chapter Summary

- A special form known as a worksheet is often used to compute the net income or net loss and to plan the financial statements before they are prepared.
- The trial balance is completed in the first two money columns of the worksheet. Then, the items on the trial balance are classified according to the financial statements on which they will appear. This is done by recording each amount in the proper statement section and column of the worksheet.
- The net income or net loss is the difference between the totals of the Debit and Credit columns in the Income Statement section of the worksheet.
- The net income is entered in two columns of the worksheet—the Debit column of the Income Statement section and the Credit column of the Balance Sheet section. A net loss would be recorded in the Credit column of the Income Statement section and the Debit column of the Balance Sheet section.
- The income statement is prepared from the figures in the Income Statement columns of the worksheet.
- The statement of owner's equity is prepared from figures in the owner's capital account in the general ledger and from figures in the Balance Sheet columns of the worksheet.
- The balance sheet is prepared from figures in the Balance Sheet columns of the worksheet and from the ending capital figure shown on the statement of owner's equity.
- In the report form of balance sheet, the liabilities and owner's equity are placed under the assets. The account form of balance sheet shows the assets on the left side and the liabilities and owner's equity on the right side.

Checking Your Knowledge

BUSINESS APPLICATION

Problem 9-1. The trial balance for Elegant Hair Stylists, owned by Roy Reed, is entered in the first two columns of the worksheet provided on page 33 of the workbook. Using this form and the financial statement forms on pages 34 and 35 of the workbook, do the following.

1. Complete the worksheet.
2. Prepare an income statement for the month ended December 31, 19X1.
3. Prepare a statement of owner's equity for the month ended December 31, 19X1. The capital account in the general ledger had a balance of $783 on December 1. Roy Reed made an additional investment of $200 during the month.
4. Prepare a balance sheet, in report form, dated December 31, 19X1.

Problem 9-2. The accounts shown at the right are from the general ledger of Apex Dry Cleaners, owned by Ida Paulos. The balances are for April 30, 19X1. The account names are listed in alphabetic order.

Using the worksheet and financial statement forms on pages 36 and 37 of the workbook, do the following.

1. Record the account names on the worksheet in the proper order and enter a suitable number for each account. Then prepare the trial balance.
2. Complete the worksheet.
3. Prepare an income statement for the month ended April 30, 19X1.
4. Prepare a statement of owner's equity for the month ended April 30, 19X1. The capital account in the general ledger had a balance of $4,310 on April 1. Ida Paulos made an additional investment of $700 during the month.
5. Prepare a balance sheet, in report form, dated April 30, 19X1.

Accounts Payable	$ 520
Accounts Receivable	130
Cash	2,100
Cleaning Equipment	3,400
Cleaning Revenue	1,420
Ida Paulos, Capital	5,010
Ida Paulos, Drawing	450
Maintenance Expense	320
Salaries Expense	500
Utilities Expense	50

MANAGERIAL ANALYSIS

Case 9. George Lenski owns a store that sells stereo equipment, records, and tapes. After he received the financial statements of his business last month, he was concerned because his net income was lower than it had been during the previous month.

1. Which financial statement would most likely be used to compare the result of last month's operations with that of the previous month's operations? Why?
2. What proposals would you make to Lenski to help him increase his net income in the future?

Closing the Ledger

After the financial statements have been completed, the ledger must be made ready for the transactions of the next accounting period. This procedure often involves two activities: (1) recording closing entries and (2) ruling and balancing the ledger accounts.

Let us consider the general ledger of the Quick Delivery Service (pages 45 through 47) from which the worksheet and the financial statements for November were just prepared. There are several reasons why this ledger must be made ready for December.

- One of the most important pieces of information about November operations is the fact that the business had a net income of $800. Although this fact is shown on the income statement (page 52), it does not yet appear in the business's permanent records—the journal and the ledger.
- The owner's capital account needs updating. The balance in the general ledger is now $7,600, but the statement of owner's equity (page 52) shows that it should be $7,700. This is the result of the net increase of $100 in owner's equity from November operations.
- The balances of the revenue and expense accounts represent transactions that took place during November. Remember that these accounts are used to determine the result of operations for each accounting period. Thus, their balances must now be reduced to zero so that the revenue and expense transactions for the next period (December) can be recorded. The drawing account is another account that is used to gather information for each accounting period, and its balance must also be reduced to zero.

Recording the Closing Entries

The procedure used at the end of each accounting period to make the ledger ready for the next period's transactions is known as *closing the ledger*. This procedure begins with a series of *closing entries*, which are journalized and posted. The closing entries serve several purposes.

Closing the Ledger: Preparing the ledger at the end of a period so that it is ready to receive the next period's transactions.

- They summarize the balances of the revenue and expense accounts so that the net income or net loss can be recorded.
- They transfer to the capital account the net increase or net decrease in owner's equity resulting from the current period's operations.
- They reduce the balances of the revenue, expense, and drawing accounts to zero so that these accounts can be used to record information for the next period.

The closing entries for the Quick Delivery Service are shown in the general journal on page 56. Most of the information for these entries was taken from the Income Statement columns of the worksheet (page 51). The steps that are needed to make the closing entries are explained on pages 56 and 57. (Note that the journal illustrated here contains the complete closing entries, including the posting references. However, keep in mind that these numbers are not filled in when the closing entries are journalized. They are recorded as part of the posting process.)

		GENERAL JOURNAL			PAGE 2
DATE		DESCRIPTION OF ENTRY	POST. REF.	DEBIT	CREDIT
19X1 Nov.	30	Delivery Service Revenue	401	1650 00	
		Revenue and Expense Summary	399		1650 00
		To close revenue account and transfer total revenue to summary account.			
	30	Revenue and Expense Summary	399	850 00	
		Rent Expense	501		300 00
		Truck Expense	502		50 00
		Wages Expense	503		500 00
		To close expense accounts and transfer total expenses to summary account.			
	30	Revenue and Expense Summary	399	800 00	
		John Costa, Drawing	302		800 00
		To close summary account and transfer net income to drawing account.			
	30	John Costa, Drawing	302	100 00	
		John Costa, Capital	301		100 00
		To close drawing account and transfer net increase in owner's equity to capital account.			

Closing an Account: Reducing the balance of an account to zero by transferring the balance to another account.

1. The first step is to close the revenue account. Since the Delivery Service Revenue account has a credit balance of $1,650, it is closed by debiting it for this amount. Thus the balance is reduced to zero. Note that a new account called the Revenue and Expense Summary account is credited. This owner's equity account is used only at the end of the period for the closing entries.
2. The second step is to close the expense accounts. Since these accounts (Rent Expense, Truck Expense, and Wages Expense) have debit balances, they are closed by crediting each one for the amount of its balance. This reduces each balance to zero. The total of the balances of all the expense accounts ($850) is debited to the Revenue and Expense Summary account.
3. The third step is to close the Revenue and Expense Summary account. This account now shows the same basic information as the income statement. The total of the revenue ($1,650) is recorded on the credit side, and the total of the expenses ($850) is recorded on the debit side. The balance of $800 ($1,650 − $850) represents the net income. The Revenue and Expense Summary account is closed by debiting it for $800 and crediting the amount to the owner's drawing account.
4. The fourth step is to close the drawing account. This account now has the net income of $800 on the credit side. The withdrawal of $700 already made against the net income is shown on the debit side. The balance of $100 ($800 − $700) represents the net increase in owner's equity. The drawing

56 Accounting Fundamentals

account is closed by debiting it for $100 and crediting the amount to the owner's capital account. This updates the capital account so that it shows the present capital of $7,700.

The following T accounts provide a summary of the closing entries. The balances are the same as those shown on pages 46 and 47.

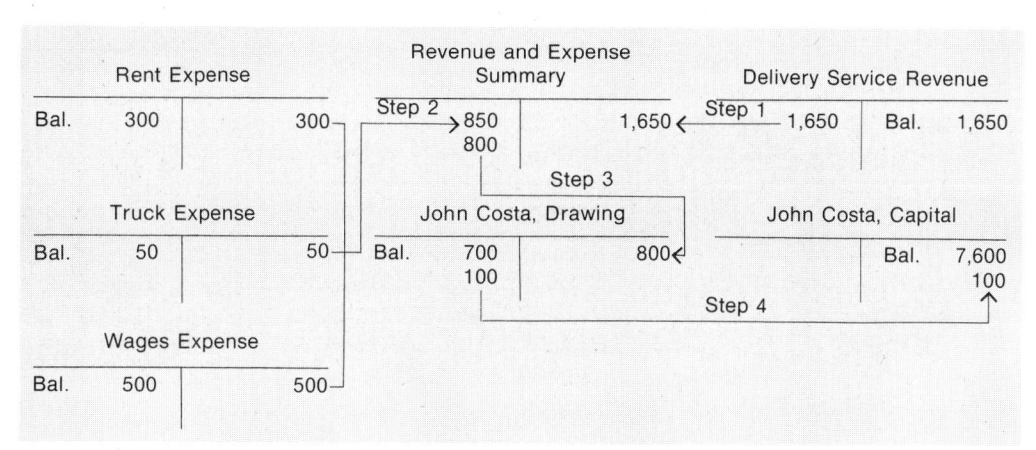

Closing Entries:
- Close revenue account to summary account.
- Close expense accounts to summary account.
- Close summary account to drawing account.
- Close drawing account to capital account.

Rent Expense		Revenue and Expense Summary		Delivery Service Revenue	
Bal. 300	300	Step 2 → 850 / 800	1,650 ← Step 1	1,650	Bal. 1,650

Truck Expense		John Costa, Drawing		John Costa, Capital	
Bal. 50	50	Bal. 700 / 100	800		Bal. 7,600 / 100

Step 3, Step 4

Wages Expense	
Bal. 500	500

The posting of the closing entries to the actual ledger accounts is illustrated on pages 58 and 59. Note that explanations are used for these entries in the accounts.

Completing the Closing Procedure

After the closing entries are posted, some businesses open new ledger accounts for recording the transactions of the new period. Other businesses continue to use the old accounts. If new accounts are opened, the only balances to be recorded are the balances of the asset, liability, and owner's capital accounts. The first day of the new period is used as the date for these entries. The revenue, expense, drawing, and summary accounts have no balances.

If the old ledger accounts are used, the entries for the period just ended must be separated from the entries of the new period. This is done by *ruling* the accounts. At the same time, the balances of the asset, liability, and owner's capital accounts are carried forward for the new period. The following illustrations show how ledger accounts appear after they are correctly ruled and balanced.

Cash NO. 101

DATE	EXPLANATION	POST. REF.	DEBIT	DATE	EXPLANATION	POST. REF.	CREDIT
19X1 Nov. 1		J1	1200 00	19X1 Nov. 1		J1	300 00
6		J1	650 00	5		J1	225 00
20		J1	675 00	10		J1	150 00
23		J1	600 00	13		J1	50 00
25	1,700.00	J2	500 00	15		J1	250 00
			3625 00	29		J2	250 00
				30		J2	700 00
				30	Carried Forward	✓	1925 00 / 1700 00
							3625 00
19X1 Dec. 1	Brought Forward	✓	1700 00				

Closing the Ledger

Accounts Receivable   NO. 102

DATE	EXPLANATION	POST. REF.	DEBIT	DATE	EXPLANATION	POST. REF.	CREDIT
19X1 Nov. 1		J1	800 00	19X1 Nov. 25		J2	500 00
18	625.00	J1	325 00	30	Carried Forward	✓	625 00
			1125 00				1125 00
19X1 Dec. 1	Brought Forward	✓	625 00				

Office Equipment   NO. 111

DATE	EXPLANATION	POST. REF.	DEBIT	DATE	EXPLANATION	POST. REF.	CREDIT
19X1 Nov. 1		J1	1000 00	19X1 Nov. 30	Carried Forward	✓	1525 00
5		J1	225 00				
27		J2	300 00				
			1525 00				1525 00
19X1 Dec. 1	Brought Forward	✓	1525 00				

Delivery Truck   NO. 112

DATE	EXPLANATION	POST. REF.	DEBIT	DATE	EXPLANATION	POST. REF.	CREDIT
19X1 Nov. 1		J1	6000 00				

Accounts Payable   NO. 201

DATE	EXPLANATION	POST. REF.	DEBIT	DATE	EXPLANATION	POST. REF.	CREDIT
19X1 Nov. 10		J1	150 00	19X1 Nov. 1		J1	2000 00
30	Carried Forward	✓	2150 00	27	2,150.00	J2	300 00
			2300 00				2300 00
				19X1 Dec. 1	Brought Forward	✓	2150 00

John Costa, Capital   NO. 301

DATE	EXPLANATION	POST. REF.	DEBIT	DATE	EXPLANATION	POST. REF.	CREDIT
19X1 Nov. 30	Carried Forward	✓	7700 00	19X1 Nov. 1		J1	7000 00
				23		J1	600 00
				30	From Drawing	J2	100 00
			7700 00				7700 00
				19X1 Dec. 1	Brought Forward	✓	7700 00

John Costa, Drawing   NO. 302

DATE	EXPLANATION	POST. REF.	DEBIT	DATE	EXPLANATION	POST. REF.	CREDIT
19X1 Nov. 30		J2	700 00	19X1 Nov. 30	Net Income	J2	800 00
30	To Capital	J2	100 00				
			800 00				800 00

58   Accounting Fundamentals

Revenue and Expense Summary — No. 399

DATE	EXPLANATION	POST. REF.	DEBIT	DATE	EXPLANATION	POST. REF.	CREDIT
19X1 Nov. 30	Expenses	J2	850 00	19X1 Nov. 30	Revenue	J2	1650 00
30	Net Income	J2	800 00				
			1650 00				1650 00

Delivery Service Revenue — No. 401

DATE	EXPLANATION	POST. REF.	DEBIT	DATE	EXPLANATION	POST. REF.	CREDIT
19X1 Nov. 30	Closing	J2	1650 00	19X1 Nov. 6		J1	650 00
				18		J1	325 00
				20		J1	675 00
			1650 00				1650 00

Rent Expense — No. 501

DATE	EXPLANATION	POST. REF.	DEBIT	DATE	EXPLANATION	POST. REF.	CREDIT
19X1 Nov. 1		J1	300 00	19X1 Nov. 30	Closing	J2	300 00

Truck Expense — No. 502

DATE	EXPLANATION	POST. REF.	DEBIT	DATE	EXPLANATION	POST. REF.	CREDIT
19X1 Nov. 13		J1	50 00	19X1 Nov. 30	Closing	J2	50 00

Wages Expense — No. 503

DATE	EXPLANATION	POST. REF.	DEBIT	DATE	EXPLANATION	POST. REF.	CREDIT
19X1 Nov. 15		J1	250 00	19X1 Nov. 30	Closing	J2	500 00
29		J2	250 00				
			500 00				500 00

Ruling Closed Accounts. A closed account (one that has no balance) is ruled in one of the following ways.

- If only one amount appears on each side of the account, a double line is drawn below the entries, across the Date, Posting Reference, Debit, and Credit columns. (Note the Rent Expense and Truck Expense accounts.)
- If two or more entries appear on either side of the account, a single line is drawn below the last amount. This line goes across the money columns on both sides of the account. A total is written below this line on both sides, and a double line is drawn across all columns except the Explanation columns. (Note the Drawing, Revenue and Expense Summary, Delivery Service Revenue, and Wages Expense accounts.)

Closing the Ledger

Ruling Accounts With Balances. The accounts for the assets, liabilities, and owner's capital have balances that must be carried forward to the new accounting period. An account with a balance is ruled as follows.

1. The account is pencil-footed to find the balance. (This was done at the time the trial balance was prepared.)
2. The account balance is entered, along with the date, on the side with the smaller footing. The notation *Carried Forward* and a check mark in the Posting Reference column show that the balance has not been posted from a journal entry.
3. The account is totaled and ruled in the same manner as a closed account.
4. The balance is entered below the double line on the side of the account with the larger footing. The beginning date of the new accounting period, the explanation *Brought Forward*, and a check mark are also recorded.

If an account contains only one entry, it remains as it is. No ruling or balancing is required. (Note the Delivery Truck account.)

Preparing the Postclosing Trial Balance

Postclosing Trial Balance: Trial balance taken after closing entries are posted.

Before recording any transactions for the new period, another trial balance, called a *postclosing trial balance*, is prepared to check the equality of the debits and credits in the ledger. This is done whether new accounts have been started or the old accounts have been ruled and balanced. The postclosing trial balance for the Quick Delivery Service on November 30 is shown below.

Quick Delivery Service
Postclosing Trial Balance
November 30, 19X1

Acct. No.	Account Name	Debit	Credit
101	Cash	1700.00	
102	Accounts Receivable	625.00	
111	Office Equipment	1525.00	
112	Delivery Truck	6000.00	
201	Accounts Payable		2150.00
301	John Costa, Capital		7700.00
	Totals	9850.00	9850.00

Permanent Accounts: Accounts that remain open from period to period.

Temporary Accounts: Accounts that are closed at the end of each period.

Note that the only accounts listed on the postclosing trial balance are the ones that are still open (have balances)—the asset, liability, and owner's capital accounts. These accounts are often called *permanent accounts*. The revenue, expense, drawing, and summary accounts do not appear on the postclosing trial balance because they are closed. These accounts are often referred to as *temporary accounts*.

Chapter Summary

- The procedure used at the end of each accounting period to make the general ledger accounts ready for recording the next period's transactions is known as closing the ledger.
- An account called Revenue and Expense Summary is used in the closing entries. The balances of the revenue and expense accounts are transferred to this account. Then the balance of Revenue and Expense Summary, which represents the net income (or net loss), is transferred to the owner's drawing account.
- After the net income (or net loss) has been transferred, the balance of the owner's drawing account shows the net increase (or net decrease) in owner's equity. This balance is transferred to the owner's capital account, which then shows the current capital.
- After the closing entries have been posted, new accounts are started for the next accounting period or the old accounts are ruled and balanced so that they can be used in the next period.
- Before any transactions are recorded for the next accounting period, a postclosing trial balance is prepared to prove the equality of the debit and credit balances in the open accounts.
- The accounts that remain open from period to period are the permanent accounts—asset, liability, and owner's capital accounts. The accounts that are closed at the end of each period are the temporary accounts—revenue, expense, drawing, and summary accounts.

Checking Your Knowledge

BUSINESS APPLICATION

Problem 10-1. The capital, drawing, summary, revenue, and expense accounts for the Deluxe Travel Service, owned by Ellen Shuster, are given on pages 39–41 of the workbook. These accounts show information for the month of January.

1. Pencil-foot the drawing, revenue, and expense accounts to find the balances.

2. Journalize the closing entries for January 31, 19X1. Use the general journal forms on pages 41 and 42 of the workbook.

3. Post the closing entries to the ledger accounts.

4. Rule the closed accounts. Rule and balance the capital account.

MANAGERIAL ANALYSIS

Case 10. Peter Morgan is a former professional tennis player, who recently opened a tennis equipment store. After his first month of operations, he cannot understand why his capital account shows a balance of $9,370 on the worksheet and $9,900 on the postclosing trial balance.

Morgan also wonders if it is really necessary to close the ledger at the end of each accounting period.

1. How would you explain the difference between the capital account balances on the worksheet and the postclosing trial balance?

2. How would you explain why it is necessary to close the ledger?

The Accounting Cycle and Data Processing

Accounting Cycle: Series of procedures repeated in each accounting period.

Accounting work follows a pattern. The same procedures are repeated in each accounting period. These procedures are referred to as the *accounting cycle*.

The methods used to perform accounting procedures vary from business to business. In some businesses, all accounting work is done by hand. In other businesses, computers play a major role in accounting work. However, no matter what method is used, the purpose of the accounting system remains the same—to provide information about the results of operations and the financial position of the business. Management needs this information to control operations and make decisions.

The Accounting Cycle

The procedures that make up the accounting cycle are listed below. You are already familiar with most of these procedures.

1. Record the business's transactions on source documents. (Source documents are explained in the next section of this chapter.)
2. Journalize the transactions.
3. Post the journal entries to the ledger accounts.
4. Prepare a trial balance to prove the ledger accounts.
5. Complete a worksheet to plan the financial statements.
6. Prepare the financial statements.
7. Journalize and post adjusting entries and closing entries. (Adjusting entries are discussed in Chapter 22.)
8. Balance and rule the ledger accounts.
9. Prepare a postclosing trial balance to prove the ledger accounts that remain open at the end of the period.

Source Documents

Source Documents: Business papers that contain important facts about transactions.

When transactions take place, *source documents* are prepared. These business papers contain the important facts about each transaction. For example, in many retail stores, a sales slip is used to record the details of each sale to a charge account customer.

Source documents provide the accounting system with information about transactions. This information is needed to make journal entries.

A wide variety of source documents are used in business. Sales slips, invoices, cash register tapes, check stubs, and credit memorandums are a few examples. These source documents and others are illustrated in later chapters.

Manual Data Processing

Business data processing involves recording, classifying, and summarizing facts about business operations. These facts are used to produce information for management and for others, such as customers, creditors, and the government. Accounting is concerned with one major area of business data processing—recording, classifying, and summarizing financial facts.

There are a number of different data processing methods. One of the most common is *manual data processing*. With this method, records are prepared by hand. Manual data processing is widely used in small businesses and small professional practices, such as the practices of doctors, dentists, and lawyers.

Journals and Ledgers. In manual accounting systems, journals are kept in bound books or binders. Ledgers are kept in the same way, or the accounts are placed on cards.

Wilson Jones Company	McBee Systems
LOOSE-LEAF BINDER FOR JOURNAL OR LEDGER	**TRAY OF LEDGER CARDS**

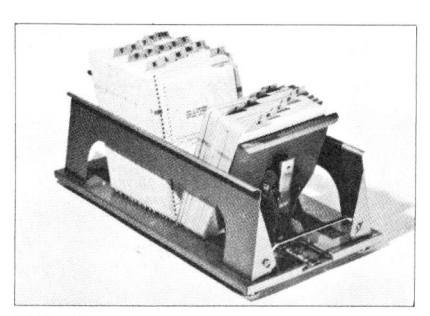

Up to this point, you have learned about the general journal and the general ledger. However, there are also other types of journals and ledgers. Some of these journals and ledgers are presented in later chapters. Keep in mind that accounting records differ from business to business because of the special needs of each firm.

Even the form for the general ledger accounts can vary. The businesses discussed in this book use the standard ledger form for their general ledger accounts. However, other businesses use the *balance ledger form* for these accounts. An example of a balance ledger form is shown below. With this form, the account balance is always known. It is recorded whenever a journal entry is posted. Thus there is no need to balance and rule the accounts at the end of each period. (Compare the following account with the one shown on page 58.)

Accounts Receivable NO. 102

DATE	EXPLANATION	POST. REF.	DEBIT	CREDIT	BALANCE DEBIT	BALANCE CREDIT
19X1 Nov. 1		J1	800 00		800 00	
18		J1	325 00		1125 00	
25		J2		500 00	625 00	

Office supply stores and mail-order companies have a variety of forms for journals, ledger accounts, and worksheets.

Adding Machines and Calculators. When accounting records are prepared by hand, certain devices are used to help with the work. For example, adding machines and calculators are often used to make computations. These devices speed up manual

---

Business Data Processing: Recording, classifying, and summarizing facts about business operations.

Manual Data Processing: Records are prepared by hand.

Balance Ledger Form: Form of ledger account that always shows the account balance.

accounting work and increase its accuracy. Models that produce a printed paper tape are preferred for accounting because the tape provides a record of the computations.

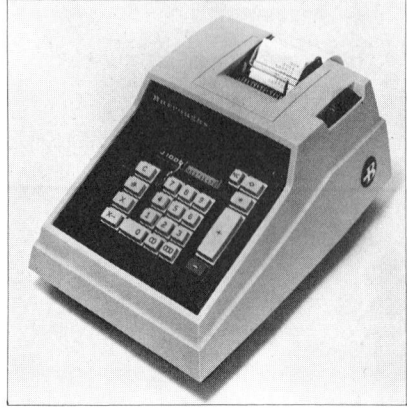

Burroughs Corporation
TEN-KEY ADDING MACHINE

Hewlett-Packard
ELECTRONIC DESK CALCULATOR

Pegboard: Device used to make an entry on several forms at one time.

The Pegboard. Another device often used to increase the efficiency of manual accounting work is the *pegboard*. This device is a flat board with metal pegs along one side. Special forms with punched holes fit over the pegs. Several different types of forms that require the same information are placed on the board at one time. The forms have carbon spots on their backs, or they are made of carbonless reproducing paper. An entry recorded on the top form is therefore transferred to the forms below it. In this way, several forms can be prepared without rewriting the same entries.

The pegboard is especially helpful for payroll, accounts receivable, and accounts payable procedures because they require repetitive entries. The same information must appear in several records. (Payroll, accounts receivable, and accounts payable procedures are discussed in later chapters.)

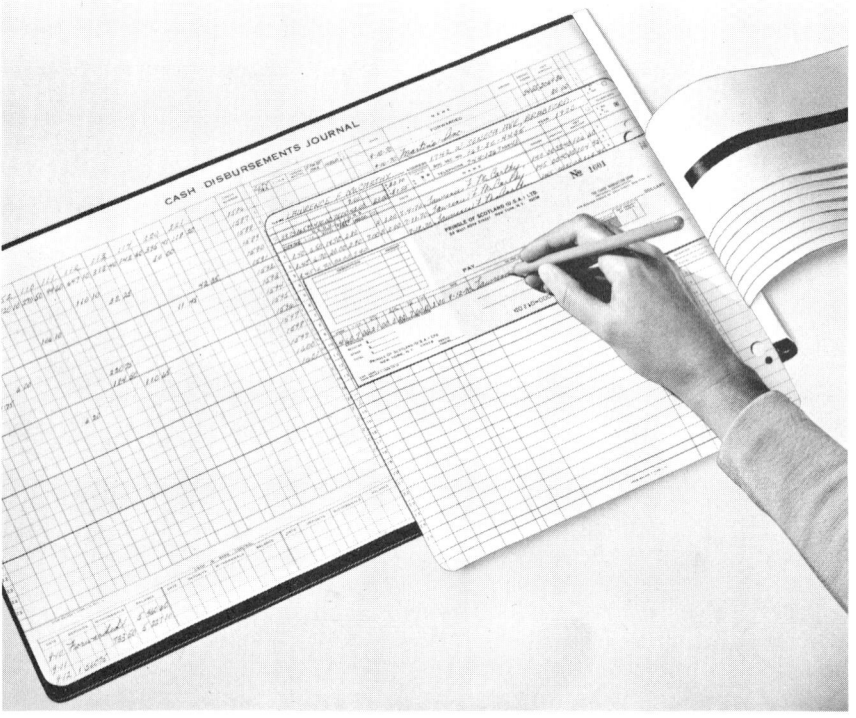

The Shaw-Walker Co.
PEGBOARD SYSTEM

64   Accounting Fundamentals

Electronic Data Processing

Manual data processing serves the needs of many businesses. However, when a business has a large number of transactions, it is not practical to keep accounting records by hand. In the past, mechanical accounting machines and punched-card machines were used to prepare records with greater speed. Now, the most common method for handling large amounts of accounting work is *electronic data processing*. With this method, computers perform accounting procedures and produce the necessary records.

A *computer* is a group of electronic devices that operate together to process data. These devices can function automatically because they follow a series of instructions called a *program*. There is a separate program for each procedure. Before the computer begins a procedure, the appropriate program is placed in its memory unit.

Some computers are small and can be run by one person. Other computers involve many pieces of equipment and require a data processing staff.

Electronic Data Processing: Records are prepared by computer.

Computer: Group of electronic devices that operate together to process data.

Program: Series of instructions that a computer follows.

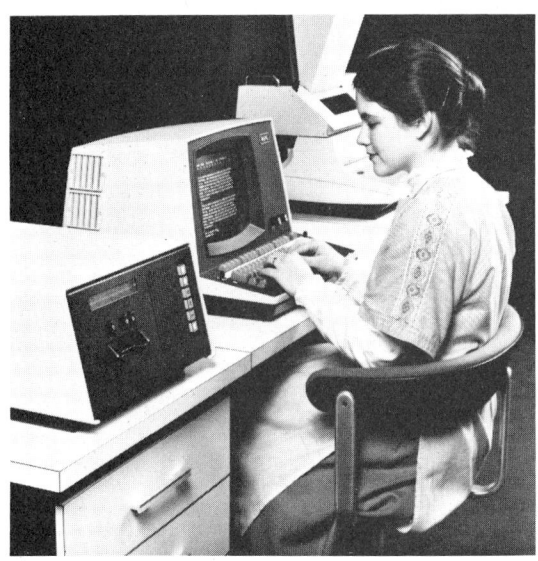

Wang Laboratories, Inc.

A SMALL COMPUTER

IBM

A LARGE COMPUTER

The Accounting Cycle and Data Processing

IBM
MAGNETIC TAPE

When transactions are recorded by a computer, the ledger accounts are usually kept on magnetic tape or magnetic disks. The accounts are updated at regular intervals, such as every day or every week. As this is done, the computer produces a printed journal. At the end of the accounting period, the computer is used to prepare a trial balance and financial statements. An example of a computer-prepared income statement is shown below.

```
                    WAYNE COMMERCIAL CLEANING COMPANY
                              INCOME STATEMENT
                            MONTH ENDED 06/30/X1

OPERATING REVENUES
    DRY CLEANING REVENUE                              10,400
    LAUNDRY REVENUE                                    5,800
    RUG CLEANING REVENUE                               2,100
        TOTAL OPERATING REVENUES                                18,300

OPERATING EXPENSES
    CLEANING AND LAUNDRY SUPPLIES EXPENSE                490
    DEPRECIATION EXPENSE - CLEANING EQUIPMENT            220
    DEPRECIATION EXPENSE - DELIVERY TRUCKS               205
    DEPRECIATION EXPENSE - OFFICE EQUIPMENT              160
    MISCELLANEOUS EXPENSE                                135
    OFFICE SUPPLIES EXPENSE                              150
    RENT EXPENSE                                       1,300
    SALARIES AND WAGES EXPENSE                        11,900
    TRUCK MAINTENANCE AND GASOLINE EXPENSE               525
    UTILITIES EXPENSE                                  1,100
        TOTAL OPERATING EXPENSES                                16,185

NET INCOME                                                       2,115
```

Computers can perform many other procedures besides the ones discussed above. For example, they can issue checks to pay creditors and prepare monthly bills for charge account customers. Computers can also use the information from transactions to produce many types of reports, such as sales reports and expense reports. These reports provide management with details that are not shown on the financial statements.

Although computers carry out a great deal of accounting work automatically, they do not remove the need for an accounting staff. Certain activities must still be performed by accounting clerks and accountants. For example, accounting clerks must check the accuracy of all source documents before transactions are fed into the computer. Accountants must help management to interpret the information on computer-prepared financial statements and reports. These are just a few of the activities performed by the accounting staff in businesses that use computers.

NCR Corporation
MAGNETIC DISKS

Chapter Summary

☐ The accounting cycle is a series of procedures that are repeated in each accounting period.

☐ When transactions take place, source documents are prepared. They provide the information needed to journalize transactions.

☐ In manual data processing, records are kept by hand. This data processing method is widely used in small businesses and small professional practices.

☐ Certain devices such as adding machines, calculators, and the pegboard are often used to increase the efficiency of a manual accounting system.

☐ In electronic data processing, records are kept by a computer. This data processing method is most often used by businesses that have a large number of transactions.

☐ A computer is a group of electronic devices that operate together to process data. These devices function automatically by following the instructions in a program.

☐ Electronic data processing offers a number of advantages. Computers can record transactions at a high speed, perform a wide variety of accounting procedures automatically, and produce many types of financial statements and reports.

Checking Your Knowledge

BUSINESS APPLICATION

Problem 11-1. Some of the procedures that make up the accounting cycle are listed on page 43 of the workbook. Fill in the missing procedures.

Problem 11-2. In businesses that use electronic data processing, the accounting staff must often work with computer-prepared financial statements and reports. Study the income statement shown on page 66. Then answer the following questions. Record your answers on page 43 of the workbook.

1. What were the sources of revenue?
2. Which source provided the most revenue?
3. How much was the total of the operating revenues?
4. What were the two largest expenses?
5. What were the two smallest expenses?
6. How much was the total of the operating expenses?
7. Did the business have a net income or a net loss for the month? What was the amount?

MANAGERIAL ANALYSIS

Case 11. The Dalton Car Rental Service has four branches and will soon add another branch at the local airport. The business's accounting records are kept by hand in a central office. An accounting supervisor and three accounting clerks do the work. However, they are having difficulty processing all the transactions on time because the amount is constantly growing. For this reason, the owner is now trying to decide whether to hire another accounting clerk or buy a small computer.

1. What advantages might a computer have for this business?
2. What factors should the owner consider before deciding whether to hire another clerk or buy a computer?

SUMMARY PROBLEM II

Chapters 7–11. Lee Olson bought the Atlas Floor Service on March 1, 19X1. His balance sheet for that date is shown below.

ATLAS FLOOR SERVICE
Balance Sheet
March 1, 19X1

Assets		Liabilities and Owner's Equity	
Cash	$3,500	Liabilities	
Accounts Receivable	300	Accounts Payable	$ 400
Office Equipment	1,250	Owner's Equity	
Service Equipment	1,800	Lee Olson, Capital	8,450
Truck	2,000	Total Liabilities and	
Total Assets	$8,850	Owner's Equity	$8,850

1. Make the opening entry in the general journal provided on page 45 of the workbook.

2. Open the following general ledger accounts. Use the forms on pages 50–54 of the workbook.

101	Cash	401	Floor Service Revenue
102	Accounts Receivable	501	Rent Expense
111	Office Equipment	502	Truck Expense
112	Service Equipment	503	Wages Expense
113	Truck	504	Supplies Expense
201	Accounts Payable	505	Advertising Expense
301	Lee Olson, Capital	506	Miscellaneous Expense
302	Lee Olson, Drawing		
399	Revenue and Expense Summary		

3. Post the opening entry to the accounts.

4. Journalize the following transactions for March.

Mar. 1 Paid $175 in cash for the March rent.
 3 Received $100 in cash from Ann Rice (a customer) on account. (This money is for work done in February when the previous owner was operating the business.)
 6 Bought a sander for $150 on credit from the Wade Equipment Company.
 7 Installed linoleum for $90 in cash.
 8 Received $200 in cash from John Casey (a customer) on account. (This money is for work done in February when the previous owner was operating the business.)
 8 Paid $25 in cash for a newspaper ad.
 10 Paid $150 in cash for wages of the part-time employee.
 10 Paid $12 in cash for gasoline for the truck.
 12 Paid $30 in cash for supplies.
 13 Installed floor tiles for $145 in cash.
 15 Paid $100 in cash to the Crown Supply Company (a creditor) on account. (This payment is for a purchase made by the previous owner in February.)
 15 Lee Olson made an additional cash investment of $300 in the business.
 17 Paid $50 in cash for an office file.
 17 Refinished floors at Dale's Restaurant for $350 on credit.
 19 Repaired a floor for $85 in cash.
 20 Paid $13 in cash for postage stamps. (Debit Miscellaneous Expense.)
 22 Paid $25 in cash for a newspaper ad.
 23 Installed floor tiles for $140 in cash.
 23 Paid $17 in cash for the telephone bill. (Debit Miscellaneous Expense.)
 24 Paid $200 in cash to the United Manufacturing Company (a creditor) on account. (This payment is for a purchase made by the previous owner in February.)
 24 Paid $90 in cash for wages of the part-time employee.
 26 Refinished floors for $220 in cash.
 28 Paid $25 in cash for supplies.
 30 Installed floor tiles at the Fashion Boutique for $350 on credit.
 31 Paid $20 in cash for gasoline for the truck.
 31 Lee Olson withdrew $600 in cash for his personal use.

5. Post the journal entries to the ledger accounts.

6. Prepare the worksheet. Use the form on page 54 of the workbook.

7. Prepare an income statement for the month ended March 31, 19X1. Use the form at the top of page 55 of the workbook.

8. Prepare a statement of owner's equity for the month ended March 31, 19X1. Use the form at the bottom of page 55 of the workbook.

9. Prepare a balance sheet in report form, dated March 31, 19X1. Use the form at the top of page 56 of the workbook.

10. Record the closing entries in the general journal. (These entries should be placed immediately after the last transaction journalized on March 31.)

11. Post the closing entries.

12. Rule and balance the accounts.

13. Prepare a postclosing trial balance. Use the form at the bottom of page 56 of the workbook.

Sales and Purchases Procedures in Merchandising Businesses

Up to this point, we have been concerned with the financial procedures and records of service businesses. Remember that a service business earns its revenue by providing some kind of service, such as repairing machines or delivering packages. We will now turn our attention to another common type of business—the *merchandising* or *trading business*. This type of business earns its revenue by selling *merchandise*, or goods, that it has purchased.

Merchandising businesses vary greatly in size and in the kind of merchandise they offer. For example, a small local grocery store and a large nationwide distributor of television sets are both merchandising businesses. Their main activities are the purchase and sale of merchandise.

Merchandising businesses are usually either wholesalers or retailers. *Wholesalers* normally buy merchandise from the manufacturers or producers and sell it at a higher price to retailers. Some wholesalers also sell to large consumers, such as hotels and hospitals. Wholesalers are often called *distributors*.

Retailers normally buy merchandise from wholesalers and sell it at a higher price to individual consumers. However, some manufacturers and producers allow retailers (especially large retailers) to buy directly. Department stores, supermarkets, and drugstores are all examples of retailers.

Merchandising Business: Business that earns its revenue by selling merchandise that it has purchased.

Merchandise: Goods purchased for resale.

Wholesalers: Merchandising businesses that sell to retailers and large consumers.

Retailers: Merchandising businesses that sell to individual consumers.

Selling at Retail

Some retailers sell only for cash. Other retailers sell both for cash and on credit. By providing credit, they allow people to obtain merchandise immediately and pay for it at a later time. *Charge accounts* are one common type of credit offered by retailers.

Cash Sales. When merchandise is sold for cash, retailers often use a cash register to record the money received from their customers. By depressing the keys of the cash register, the cashier enters the amount of each sale and any other necessary information on a tape inside the machine. This tape gives the business a complete record of its cash sales. The machine also prints another tape, which is used to provide receipts for the customers.

Charge Accounts: A type of credit offered by retailers to their customers.

RECORDING CASH SALES IN RETAIL BUSINESSES

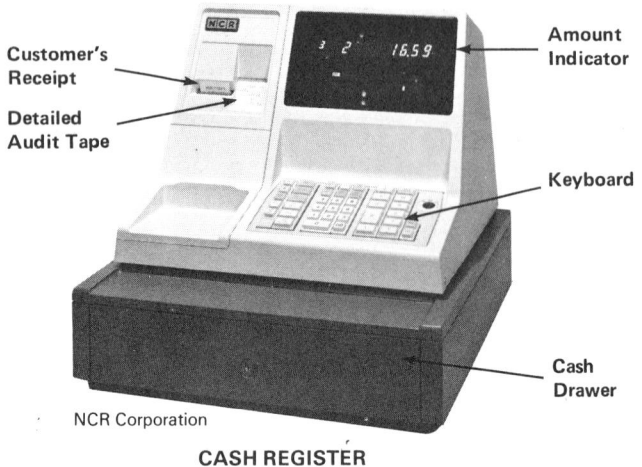

CASH REGISTER (NCR Corporation)

Labels: Customer's Receipt, Detailed Audit Tape, Amount Indicator, Keyboard, Cash Drawer

The cash register is widely used in retail businesses to record cash sales. This machine has several advantages for retailers:

- It prints a tape listing the details of all cash transactions and the totals.
- It prints a receipt for each customer.
- It provides a cash drawer for sorting the currency and coins received from customers and for storing this money until a bank deposit can be made.

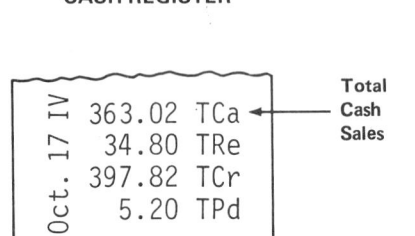

DAILY TOTALS ON DETAILED AUDIT TAPE

```
Oct. 17 IV   363.02  TCa   ← Total Cash Sales
              34.80  TRe
             397.82  TCr
               5.20  TPd
```

At the end of each business day, the tape locked inside the cash register is removed so that the retailer can see the total of the cash sales and other information. This tape is usually called the *detailed audit tape.*

Sales Slip: Form listing information about a retail sale, usually a credit sale.

Statement of Account: Form that is sent to customer who buys on credit to show transactions for a specified period and the total owed.

Credit Cards: A type of credit provided by credit services for use in retail businesses.

Charge Account Sales. When merchandise is sold on credit, most retailers use a form called a *sales slip* to record the transaction. This form usually consists of several copies. One copy is given to the customer, and the other copies are kept by the business. Some retailers use sales slips for both cash sales and credit sales. A typical sales slip is shown on page 71. Note the information listed on it.

In addition to preparing sales slips, retailers usually send a monthly *statement of account* to each charge account customer who owes money. This form summarizes all transactions involving the customer's account during the month, and it lists the total amount that is owed.

The statement of account serves two purposes: (1) It is a reminder to the customer that payment is due and (2) it gives the customer a means of checking the figures against his or her own records. A typical statement of account is shown on page 71.

Many retailers add a finance charge if the customer does not pay by a specified time. Payment may be required as soon as the statement of account is received, or the customer may be allowed an additional payment period, such as 30 days.

Credit Card Sales. Some retailers do not provide charge accounts, but they allow customers to use *credit cards* to buy on credit. The customers obtain the credit cards from credit services, such as Master Charge, Visa, and American Express. These credit cards can be used in a large number of retail businesses throughout the United States.

There are several major differences between charge accounts and credit cards. Retailers who accept credit cards collect their money from the credit service rather than from the customers. The credit service sends bills to the customers and receives payment from them.

70 Accounting Fundamentals

This arrangement is helpful to the retailers because it simplifies their accounting work. They do not have to prepare monthly bills and keep charge account records. However, the retailers must pay a fee to the credit service. This fee is a small percentage of each credit card sale.

When retailers make credit card sales, they enter the necessary information on special sales slips provided by the credit service. One copy of this form is given to the customer, a second copy goes to the credit service, and a third copy is kept by the retailer. A typical sales slip for a credit card sale is shown at the top of page 72.

Selling at Wholesale

Most selling at the wholesale level is done on credit. When merchandise is shipped, the wholesaler sends a form called an *invoice* to the customer. The invoice is a bill for the merchandise sold.

Invoice: Form used to record details of a sale and to bill the customer.

A typical invoice is shown at the bottom of page 72. It was prepared in duplicate so that the wholesaler could keep a copy. Note that the invoice lists the same kind of information as the sales slips used by retailers to record their credit sales.

Some wholesalers send a monthly statement of account to their customers in addition to the invoices for the individual sales.

RECORDING CHARGE ACCOUNT SALES IN RETAIL BUSINESSES

Two business forms that many retailers use for charge account sales are the sales slip and the statement of account. The sales slip shows details about a single sale and is prepared at the time the sale is made. The statement of account is prepared monthly. It provides the customer with a summary of all transactions during the period and a bill for the amount owed. Note how the sales slip illustrated here (Sales Slip 115) is listed on the statement of account.

SALES SLIP

PACIFIC CLOTHING CENTER
1644 Mission Drive
Los Angeles, California 90004

Date Jan. 3 19 X1

Mr. Steven Gallo
Address 38 Kent Road, Los Angeles, CA

Clerk	Cash	C.O.D.	Charge	On Acct.	Ship	Paid Out
			✓			

QUAN.	DESCRIPTION	PRICE	AMOUNT
2	Shirts #578	9.00	18 00
1	Sweater #832		16 00
		Subtotal	34 00
	6%	Tax	2 04
		Total	36 04

All claims and returned goods must be accompanied by this bill.

No. 115   Rec'd by _____

STATEMENT OF ACCOUNT

PACIFIC CLOTHING CENTER
1644 Mission Drive
Los Angeles, California 90004

STATEMENT OF ACCOUNT

Steven Gallo
38 Kent Road
Los Angeles, CA 90017

Date January 31, 19X1

Please return this stub with your check   Amount Enclosed $_____

Date	Reference	Charges	Credits	Balance
Balance Forwarded				74.85
Jan. 3	Sales Slip 115	36.04		110.89
10	Payment		74.85	36.04
17	Sales Slip 186	18.42		54.46
25	Sales Slip 223	11.20		65.66

Pay last amount in Balance column

Sales and Purchases Procedures in Merchandising Businesses

RECORDING CREDIT CARD SALES

Credit card sales are recorded on special sales slips that the credit service gives to the retailer. After listing information on one of these sales slips, the retailer places the form and the customer's credit card in an imprinting device. This device prints the customer's name and credit card number on the sales slip.

Some large retailers, such as department stores, provide their charge account customers with charge cards that look like credit cards. These businesses also use imprinting devices when preparing sales slips for charge account sales.

CREDIT CARD

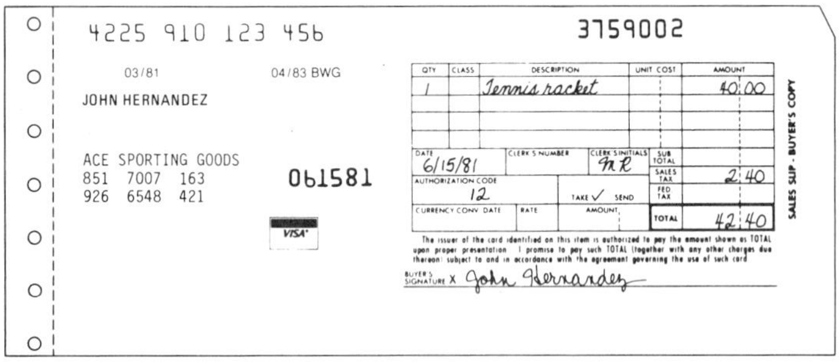

SALES SLIP

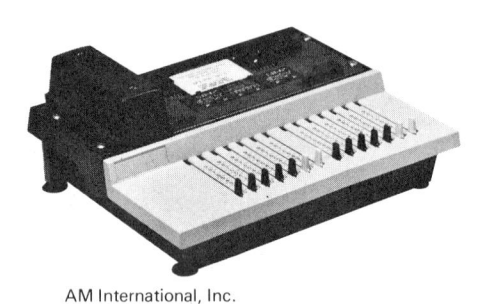

AM International, Inc.
IMPRINTING DEVICE

RECORDING SALES IN WHOLESALE BUSINESSES

The invoice is the business form that wholesalers use to record detailed information about a sale and to bill the customer. This form usually includes the following items:

1. The seller's name and address, which are preprinted.
2. The invoice number, which is often preprinted also. (This practice makes it easier for the seller to keep track of all invoices.)
3. The customer's name and address.
4. The invoice date.
5. The credit terms, which show when the customer must pay for the merchandise.
6. The number and date of the customer's order.
7. The transportation company used to ship the merchandise.
8. The quantity, stock number, description, and unit price of each type of merchandise shipped.
9. The extension, which is the total amount owed for each type of merchandise. This amount is found by multiplying the unit price by the quantity.
10. The invoice total. This amount is found by adding all the extensions.

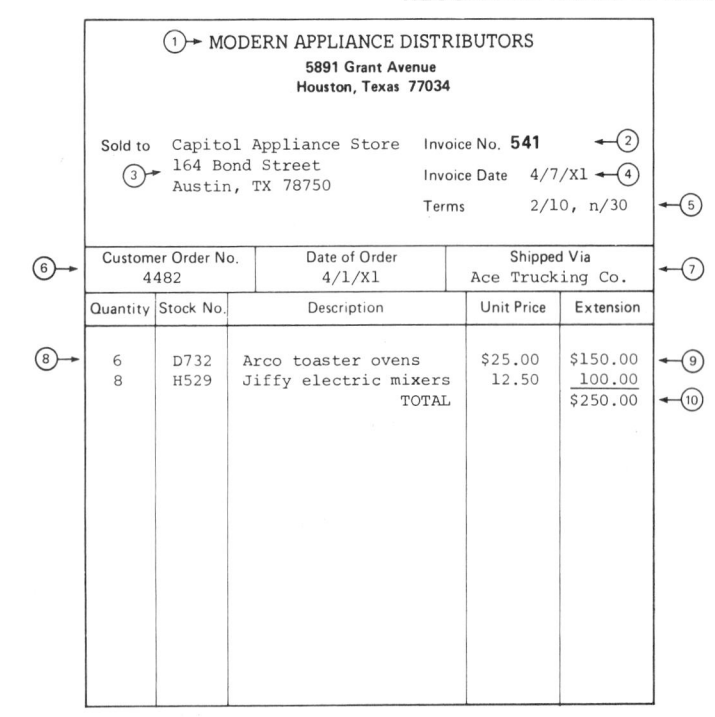

INVOICE

72 Accounting Fundamentals

Credit Terms. The credit terms on an invoice show when the customer must pay for the merchandise. To encourage early payment, wholesalers often include a *cash discount* in their credit terms. The cash discount is a deduction from the invoice total. The customer can obtain this deduction by paying within a short discount period.

Cash Discount: Deduction from invoice total given for early payment.

Some common credit terms are explained below.

- n/30—The letter *n* stands for "net" and the figure *30* stands for "30 days." Thus the net (full) amount of the invoice must be paid within 30 days of the invoice date. To find the end of the credit period, the exact number of days must be counted, starting with the day after the invoice date. For example, an invoice dated July 19 with terms of n/30 would be due on August 18.

July 20–31	12 days
August 1–18	18 days
	30 days

    Note that the credit terms *n/30* do not include a cash discount.

- 2/10, n/30—The first part of these terms (*2/10*) means that a cash discount of 2 percent will be allowed if the invoice is paid within 10 days of its date. Otherwise, the customer must pay the full amount of the invoice within 30 days. This is shown in the second part of the terms (*n/30*). Consider an invoice for $500, dated July 19, with terms of 2/10, n/30. If the invoice is paid by July 29 (10 days after July 19), the customer can take a discount of $10 ($500 × .02 = $10). Thus the amount due is $490.

Amount of invoice	$500
Less 2-percent discount	10
Amount due	$490

    If payment is not made by July 29, no discount is permitted. In this case, the customer must pay $500 by August 18 (the end of the 30-day credit period).

- 3/10, n/30 EOM—The letters *EOM* are an abbreviation for "end of month." When credit terms include EOM, the days of the discount period are counted after the last day of the month in which the invoice is dated. For example, suppose that an invoice is dated July 19 and has terms of 3/10, n/30 EOM. To obtain the 3-percent cash discount, the customer must pay by August 10 (10 days after July 31). Otherwise, the customer must pay the full amount of the invoice by August 30 (30 days after July 31).

There are many variations on the basic credit terms described here.

Making Purchases

Businesses that purchase merchandise must have orderly procedures for checking the accuracy of invoices and for making prompt payments. As we have discussed, the buyer receives an invoice from the seller for each purchase. To the seller, this form is a *sales invoice*. To the buyer, it is a *purchase invoice*.

Sometimes the invoice is included in the shipment, and sometimes it is sent separately. When the invoice arrives, the buyer must check to see that the merchandise has actually been received and that the quantities, quality, unit prices, extensions, total amount, and credit terms are correct. If there are any errors, the buyer reports them to the seller. If the invoice is accurate, it is accepted for payment.

As soon as the invoice is checked and accepted, the due date for payment must be computed. This should be done quickly because the credit terms usually begin with the date of the invoice.

It is also important to have an efficient method for keeping track of the due dates of all invoices so that payments can be made on time. There are several reasons why every effort should be made to pay promptly.

- It is usually to the advantage of the buyer to pay within the discount period and obtain the cash discount. During a year, this practice will save a lot of money.
- If it is not possible to pay within the discount period, the buyer should be sure to pay by the end of the credit period. Otherwise, the seller may charge a late payment penalty. Also, constant late payments will give a business a poor credit rating. Some sellers may refuse to provide any more credit.

Unpaid Invoices File: File in which unpaid invoices are arranged by due dates.

One simple way of keeping track of due dates is to use an *unpaid invoices file*. All approved invoices are placed in this file according to the dates on which they are to be paid. Each morning, the accounting clerk looks at the file and takes out any invoices that are due for payment. The accounting clerk makes certain that these invoices are paid in time to receive the discount, if one is offered.

Usually, the date used for filing an invoice is a few days before the end of the discount period or the credit period. For example, if the due date is July 29, the invoice might be filed under July 26. This practice allows time for preparing a check before the due date. An unpaid invoices file is shown below.

CONTROLLING PURCHASE INVOICES

Many businesses use a processing stamp to help control purchase invoices. When each invoice arrives, it is stamped with a rubber stamp. As the invoice is checked, recorded, and paid, the necessary information is written in the stamped area. Note that the due date is also entered.

An unpaid invoices file is another aid in handling purchase invoices efficiently. All the invoices are arranged in chronological (day-by-day) order according to the due dates on which they are to be paid. This type of file is often called a *tickler file*.

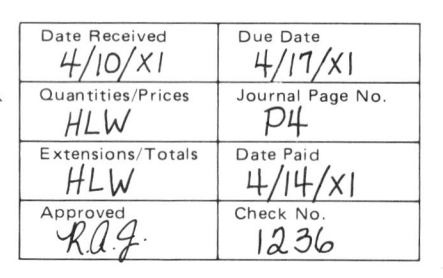

INVOICE WITH PROCESSING STAMP

UNPAID INVOICES FILE

Chapter Summary

- A merchandising business earns its revenue by selling merchandise (goods) that it has purchased.
- Merchandising businesses are usually either wholesalers or retailers.
- Some retailers sell only for cash, and others sell both for cash and on credit. Charge accounts and credit cards are two common types of credit used in retail stores. Wholesalers make most of their sales on credit.

- When sales are made, merchandising businesses must record information about them on source documents. Retailers prepare cash register tapes and sales slips. Wholesalers prepare invoices.
- The invoice is a bill for the merchandise. The seller considers it a sales invoice, and the buyer considers it a purchase invoice.
- Many merchandising businesses send a monthly statement of account to customers who have bought on credit. This form shows the transactions that took place during the month and the total amount that is owed.
- Wholesalers often include a cash discount in their credit terms to encourage early payment. This discount is deducted from the invoice total if payment is made within a specified number of days.
- It is important for a merchandising business to have orderly procedures for checking invoices and making prompt payments.

Checking Your Knowledge

BUSINESS APPLICATION

Problem 12-1. During the first week of June, the Top Value Furniture Store received the three invoices shown on pages 57 and 58 of the workbook. Check the accuracy of the extensions and totals on these invoices.

If there is an error, cross out the incorrect amount and write the correct one above it. When you complete work on an invoice, enter your initials in the Extensions/Total section of the processing stamp.

Remember that an extension is found by multiplying the unit price of an item by its quantity.

Problem 12-2. Information about seven invoices received by the Alpine Sporting Goods Shop is given in the tables on page 58 of the workbook.

1. For each invoice listed in the first table, enter the last day of the discount period (if any) and the last day of the credit period.

2. The dates when the invoices were actually paid are shown in the second table. For each invoice, enter the amount of the discount (if any) and the amount of the payment. Then indicate whether the payment was late—made after the end of the credit period. (Look at the due dates in the first table as you work on the second table. Remember that a cash discount should only be taken if payment is made on or before the last day of the discount period.)

MANAGERIAL ANALYSIS

Case 12. Gary Hoffman owns a wholesale business that sells dental equipment and supplies. One of his customers makes a practice of paying each invoice a few days after the end of the discount period but deducting the cash discount anyway.

1. What possible actions can Hoffman take to discourage this practice?
2. How do you suggest that Hoffman handle the problem? Give reasons for your choice.

Sales and Purchases Procedures in Merchandising Businesses

Special Accounts for Merchandising Businesses

In the previous chapter, we discussed the procedures for handling purchases and sales. After these transactions are listed on source documents such as invoices and sales slips, they must be journalized and posted. The information needed for the journal entries comes from the source documents.

We will now discuss the accounts that merchandising businesses use to record their purchases and sales.

Recording Purchases of Merchandise

Remember that expense accounts are used to record the costs of operating a business, such as salaries, rent, and electricity. Merchandising businesses also have another type of cost—the amounts that must be paid to obtain merchandise for resale.

The purchase of merchandise for resale is recorded in an account called Merchandise Purchases. This account is usually referred to as a *cost account*. Like the expense accounts, it decreases owner's equity.

Because cost and expense accounts are so similar, they are often grouped together on the chart of accounts. For example, see the Costs and Expenses section of the chart of accounts on page 82.

The Merchandise Purchases account is debited for the amount of each purchase. The account to be credited depends on the terms of the purchase. The Cash account is used for a cash purchase, and the Accounts Payable account is used for a credit purchase. These two kinds of merchandise purchases are journalized and posted in the following illustrations.

GENERAL JOURNAL PAGE 3

DATE	DESCRIPTION OF ENTRY	POST. REF.	DEBIT	CREDIT
19X1 Mar. 2	Merchandise Purchases	501	680 00	
	Cash	101		680 00
4	Merchandise Purchases	501	950 00	
	Accounts Payable	202		950 00
	Purchased merchandise on credit from National Electric Products; Invoice J7632, dated 3/2/X1, terms 2/10, n/30.			

Accounting Fundamentals

			Merchandise Purchases				NO. 501	
DATE	EXPLANATION	POST. REF.	DEBIT	DATE	EXPLANATION	POST. REF.	CREDIT	
19X1 Mar. 2		J3	680 00					
4		J3	950 00					

			Cash				NO. 101	
DATE	EXPLANATION	POST. REF.	DEBIT	DATE	EXPLANATION	POST. REF.	CREDIT	
				19X1 Mar. 2		J3	680 00	

			Accounts Payable				NO. 202	
DATE	EXPLANATION	POST. REF.	DEBIT	DATE	EXPLANATION	POST. REF.	CREDIT	
				19X1 Mar. 4		J3	950 00	

Recording Other Purchases

Be careful to record only *purchases of merchandise for resale* in the Merchandise Purchases account. Purchases of permanent assets, such as office furniture and delivery equipment, should be debited to an appropriate asset account and credited to Cash or Accounts Payable. The procedure for recording these purchases is the same in both service and merchandising businesses.

Purchases of supplies may be treated in several ways. If a business buys large amounts of supplies for use over a period of several months, the purchase is usually debited to an asset account called Supplies. For example, a wholesaler might make large purchases of cartons, sealing tape, and shipping labels, which it needs to send merchandise to customers.

The same wholesaler might make small purchases of office supplies such as file folders, typing paper, and rubber bands. Purchases of small amounts of supplies, which will probably be used up quickly, are usually debited to an appropriate expense account such as Miscellaneous Expense or Office Expense. Study the following illustrations, which show the two types of entries for purchases of supplies.

	GENERAL JOURNAL			PAGE 3
DATE	DESCRIPTION OF ENTRY	POST. REF.	DEBIT	CREDIT
19X1 Mar. 5	Supplies	115	390 00	
	Cash	101		390 00
	Purchased shipping cartons and sealing tape.			
6	Miscellaneous Expense	511	15 00	
	Cash	101		15 00
	Purchased file folders and typing paper.			

Special Accounts for Merchandising Businesses

Ledger Accounts

Supplies — NO. 115

DATE	EXPLANATION	POST. REF.	DEBIT	DATE	EXPLANATION	POST. REF.	CREDIT
19X1 Mar. 5		J3	390 00				

Miscellaneous Expense — NO. 511

DATE	EXPLANATION	POST. REF.	DEBIT	DATE	EXPLANATION	POST. REF.	CREDIT
19X1 Mar. 6		J3	15 00				

Cash — NO. 101

DATE	EXPLANATION	POST. REF.	DEBIT	DATE	EXPLANATION	POST. REF.	CREDIT
				19X1 Mar. 5		J3	390 00
				6		J3	15 00

Recording Amounts Paid for Purchases of Merchandise on Credit

SUMMARY OF ENTRIES FOR PURCHASES

Purchases of Merchandise for Resale
Debit to the cost account Merchandise Purchases.

Purchases of Permanent Assets
Debit to an appropriate asset account, such as Office Equipment.

Purchases of Supplies
Debit to the asset account Supplies if a large amount is bought for use over several months.
Debit to an appropriate expense account, such as Miscellaneous Expense, if a small amount is bought and it will probably be used up quickly.

Cash Discount for a Purchase of Merchandise
Credit to the cost account Purchases Discount when the invoice is paid.

The amount to be paid for merchandise bought on credit depends on whether a cash discount is involved. If there is no cash discount, the buyer must pay the total amount of the invoice. This transaction is recorded in the same way as the payments on account discussed in earlier chapters. Accounts Payable is debited, and Cash is credited.

If the credit terms of the purchase include a cash discount and the buyer pays within the discount period, the amount of the payment is less than the total of the invoice. For example, consider an invoice for $950 on which a discount of 2 percent is taken. The amount to be paid is $931.

Total of invoice	$950
Less 2-percent discount	19
Amount of payment	$931

Three accounts are used to record this transaction. The total of the invoice is debited to Accounts Payable. The amount of cash actually paid is credited to Cash. The amount of the discount is credited to a cost account called Purchases Discount. The following illustrations show how this payment is journalized and posted.

GENERAL JOURNAL — PAGE 3

DATE	DESCRIPTION OF ENTRY	POST. REF.	DEBIT	CREDIT
19X1 Mar. 10	Accounts Payable	202	950 00	
	Cash	101		931 00
	Purchases Discount	504		19 00
	Paid to National Electric Products			
	for Invoice J7632 less discount.			

78 Accounting Fundamentals

Accounts Payable — No. 202

DATE	EXPLANATION	POST. REF.	DEBIT	DATE	EXPLANATION	POST. REF.	CREDIT
19X1 Mar. 10		J3	950 00	19X1 Mar. 4		J3	950 00

Cash — No. 101

DATE	EXPLANATION	POST. REF.	DEBIT	DATE	EXPLANATION	POST. REF.	CREDIT
				19X1 Mar. 10		J3	931 00

Purchases Discount — No. 504

DATE	EXPLANATION	POST. REF.	DEBIT	DATE	EXPLANATION	POST. REF.	CREDIT
				19X1 Mar. 10		J3	19 00

Notice that the Purchases Discount account has a credit balance unlike the other cost and expense accounts, which have debit balances. This is because purchase discounts reduce the cost of the purchases recorded in the Merchandise Purchases account. Thus the balance of the Purchases Discount account represents an increase in owner's equity.

Recording Sales of Merchandise

Sales of merchandise are recorded in an account called Sales Revenue. This revenue account is similar to Repair Service Revenue and Delivery Service Revenue, which were used in earlier chapters for recording sales of services. Look at the entries shown below. The amount of each sale of merchandise is credited to Sales Revenue. The offsetting debits are to Cash or Accounts Receivable, depending on the terms of the sale.

GENERAL JOURNAL — PAGE 3

DATE	DESCRIPTION OF ENTRY	POST. REF.	DEBIT	CREDIT
19X1 Mar. 7	Cash	101	760 00	
	Sales Revenue	401		760 00
	Cash sales for first week of March.			
8	Accounts Receivable	112	300 00	
	Sales Revenue	401		300 00
	Sold merchandise on credit to Sterling Appliance Store; Invoice 536, terms 3/15, n/60.			

Special Accounts for Merchandising Businesses

				Cash				NO. 101
DATE	EXPLANATION	POST. REF.	DEBIT	DATE	EXPLANATION	POST. REF.	CREDIT
19X1 Mar. 7		J3	760 00				

				Accounts Receivable				NO. 112
DATE	EXPLANATION	POST. REF.	DEBIT	DATE	EXPLANATION	POST. REF.	CREDIT
19X1 Mar. 8		J3	300 00				

				Sales Revenue				NO. 401
DATE	EXPLANATION	POST. REF.	DEBIT	DATE	EXPLANATION	POST. REF.	CREDIT
				19X1 Mar. 7		J3	760 00
				8		J3	300 00

Recording Amounts Received for Sales of Merchandise on Credit

If a credit sale does not involve a cash discount, the amount received from the customer is recorded by debiting Cash and crediting Accounts Receivable. However, if the seller offers a cash discount and the customer pays in time to obtain it, three accounts must be used in recording the amount received. For example, suppose that a seller allows a 3-percent discount on an invoice of $300. The customer deducts $9 for the discount, and the seller receives $291.

Total of invoice	$300
Less 3-percent discount	9
Amount received	$291

The amount of cash actually received from the customer is debited to Cash. The amount of the discount is debited to a revenue account called Sales Discount. The total of the invoice is credited to Accounts Receivable. Study the entries shown below and on page 81.

GENERAL JOURNAL				PAGE 4
DATE	DESCRIPTION OF ENTRY	POST. REF.	DEBIT	CREDIT
19X1 Mar. 23	Cash	101	291 00	
	Sales Discount	403	9 00	
	Accounts Receivable	112		300 00
	Received from Sterling Appliance Store for Invoice 536 less discount.			

80 Accounting Fundamentals

Cash NO. 101

DATE	EXPLANATION	POST. REF.	DEBIT	DATE	EXPLANATION	POST. REF.	CREDIT
19X1 Mar. 23		J4	291 00				

Sales Discount NO. 403

DATE	EXPLANATION	POST. REF.	DEBIT	DATE	EXPLANATION	POST. REF.	CREDIT
19X1 Mar. 23		J4	9 00				

Accounts Receivable NO. 112

DATE	EXPLANATION	POST. REF.	DEBIT	DATE	EXPLANATION	POST. REF.	CREDIT
19X1 Mar. 8		J3	300 00	19X1 Mar. 23		J4	300 00

To the buyer, a cash discount is a *purchase discount*. To the seller, it is a *sales discount*. Notice that the Sales Discount account has a debit balance, whereas the Sales Revenue account has a credit balance. This is because sales discounts reduce the amount of revenue from sales and, therefore, represent a decrease in owner's equity.

Recording Typical Transactions for a Merchandising Business

Ann Lang was employed as the manager of Modern Appliance Distributors for a number of years. When the owner retired, she bought this wholesale merchandising business. The chart of accounts for the business is shown on page 82.

Notice that certain account numbers have been skipped so that new accounts can be set up later in the correct order. (This is a common accounting practice that allows new accounts to be added in their correct numeric order.) Also notice that the assets include an account called Merchandise Inventory. The stock of merchandise that a business has on hand for resale is referred to as *merchandise inventory*. This is one of the assets that Ann Lang obtained when she bought the business.

On April 1, 19X1, the new owner begins operations. During the month of April, the transactions described on pages 82 and 83 are completed. The general journal entries to record the beginning investment and the transactions for April are shown on pages 84–87. After you read the description of each transaction, study the related journal entry.

Notice that unlike most wholesalers, Modern Appliance Distributors has many cash sales. This is because it does much of its business with small local retailers who prefer to buy small quantities and receive quick deliveries. The retailers find such an arrangement convenient and are willing, therefore, to pay cash for the merchandise.

SUMMARY OF ENTRIES FOR SALES

Sales of Merchandise
Credit to the revenue account Sales Revenue.

Cash Discount for a Sale of Merchandise
Debit to the revenue account Sales Discount when the money is received for the invoice.

Merchandise Inventory: Stock of merchandise that a business has on hand for resale to its customers.

```
                Modern Appliance Distributors
                      Chart of Accounts


    Account
    Number          Name of Account


    100-199         ASSETS
      101           Cash
      112           Accounts Receivable
      114           Merchandise Inventory
      115           Supplies
      116           Delivery Equipment
      118           Warehouse Equipment
      120           Office Equipment
      122           Building


    200-299         LIABILITIES
      202           Accounts Payable


    300-399         OWNER'S EQUITY
      301           Ann Lang, Capital
      302           Ann Lang, Drawing
      399           Revenue and Expense Summary


    400-499         REVENUE
      401           Sales Revenue
      403           Sales Discount


    500-599         COSTS AND EXPENSES
      501           Merchandise Purchases
      504           Purchases Discount
      511           Miscellaneous Expense
      512           Truck Expense
      513           Wages Expense
```

Date	Description of Transactions
April 1	Ann Lang began her operations with the following assets and liabilities: Cash, $6,000; Accounts Receivable, $1,000; Merchandise Inventory, $5,000; Delivery Equipment, $4,000; Warehouse Equipment, $1,000; Office Equipment, $200; Building, $20,000; and Accounts Payable, $2,200. Her owner's equity is therefore $35,000 (assets of $37,200 minus liabilities of $2,200).
2	Purchased new bins, shelves, and conveyors for the warehouse for $3,000 in cash.
3	Purchased merchandise for $1,500 on credit from Allied Manufacturing Company; Invoice 1167, dated 4/1/X1, terms 3/10, n/60.
3	Purchased a new typewriter, electronic calculator, and postage meter for the office for $600 in cash.
4	Paid $1,400 in cash to Reliable Products (a creditor) for Invoice B2895. (This money is for a purchase made by the previous owner in March.)

April 5 Purchased shipping cartons for $320 in cash.
     7 Sold merchandise for $1,800 in cash during the first week of April.
     7 Sold merchandise for $250 on credit to the Capitol Appliance Store; Invoice 541, terms 2/10, n/30.
     8 Received $550 in cash from the Town Appliance Center (a customer) for Invoice 540. (This money is for merchandise sold by the previous owner in March.)
     9 Paid $1,455 in cash to the Allied Manufacturing Company for Invoice 1167 ($1,500), less discount ($45).
    11 Purchased merchandise for $450 in cash.
    12 Paid $90 in cash for gasoline, oil, and repairs for the delivery truck.
    14 Paid $50 in cash for the electric bill.
    14 Paid $35 in cash for the telephone bill.
    14 Sold merchandise for $2,200 in cash during the second week of April.
    16 Ann Lang made an additional cash investment of $2,000 in the business.
    16 Sold merchandise for $350 on credit to Bristol Appliances; Invoice 542, terms 2/10, n/30.
    17 Received $245 in cash from the Capitol Appliance Store for Invoice 541 ($250), less discount ($5).
    17 Purchased merchandise for $1,960 in cash.
    18 Purchased merchandise for $600 on credit from Arco Electric Products; Invoice 6281, dated 4/16/X1, terms 1/10, n/30.
    19 Paid $20 in cash for pencils, pens, and typing paper.
    21 Sold merchandise for $1,350 in cash during the third week of April.
    24 Received $343 in cash from Bristol Appliances for Invoice 542 ($350), less discount ($7).
    24 Sold merchandise for $1,280 on credit to the Economy Appliance Center; Invoice 543, terms 1/10, n/60.
    24 Purchased merchandise for $1,750 on credit from Dow Industries; Invoice 327, dated 4/21/X1, terms 3/10 EOM.
    24 Paid $594 in cash to Arco Electric Products for Invoice 6281 ($600), less discount ($6).
    25 Purchased a file cabinet for the office for $70 in cash.
    28 Sold merchandise for $1,670 in cash during the fourth week of April.
    29 Sold merchandise for $880 on credit to the Capitol Appliance Store; Invoice 544, terms 2/10, n/30.
    30 Paid $1,620 in cash for the monthly wages of the truck driver and the shipping clerk.
    30 Purchased merchandise for $3,000 on credit from the Allied Manufacturing Company; Invoice 1191, dated 4/28/X1, terms 3/10, n/60.
    30 Ann Lang withdrew $900 in cash for her personal use.

Chapter Summary

☐ Purchases of merchandise for resale are debited to a cost account called Merchandise Purchases.

☐ Purchases of permanent assets, such as equipment, are debited to an appropriate asset account. Supplies purchased in large amounts for use during several months are considered assets and are debited to the asset account Supplies. When supplies are purchased in small amounts and will probably be used up quickly, they are debited to an appropriate expense account.

☐ Sales of merchandise are credited to a revenue account called Sales Revenue.

☐ When a cash discount is offered and payment is made in time to take advantage of it, the buyer credits the amount of the discount to a cost account called Purchases Discount. The seller debits the amount of the discount to a revenue account called Sales Discount.

GENERAL JOURNAL
PAGE 1

DATE	DESCRIPTION OF ENTRY	POST. REF.	DEBIT	CREDIT
19X1 Apr. 1	Cash		6000 00	
	Accounts Receivable		1000 00	
	Merchandise Inventory		5000 00	
	Delivery Equipment		4000 00	
	Warehouse Equipment		1000 00	
	Office Equipment		200 00	
	Building		20000 00	
	Accounts Payable			2200 00
	Ann Lang, Capital			35000 00
	Investment of Ann Lang in the business.			
2	Warehouse Equipment		3000 00	
	Cash			3000 00
	Purchased bins, shelves, and conveyors.			
3	Merchandise Purchases		1500 00	
	Accounts Payable			1500 00
	Purchased merchandise on credit from Allied Manufacturing Co.; Invoice 1167, dated 4/1/X1, terms 3/10, n/60.			
3	Office Equipment		600 00	
	Cash			600 00
	Purchased typewriter, electronic calculator, and postage meter.			
4	Accounts Payable		1400 00	
	Cash			1400 00
	Paid to Reliable Products for Invoice B2895.			
5	Supplies		320 00	
	Cash			320 00
	Purchased shipping cartons.			
7	Cash		1800 00	
	Sales Revenue			1800 00
	Cash sales for first week of April.			
7	Accounts Receivable		250 00	
	Sales Revenue			250 00
	Sold merchandise on credit to Capital Appliance Store; Invoice 541, terms 2/10, n/30.			

84   Accounting Fundamentals

GENERAL JOURNAL
PAGE 2

DATE	DESCRIPTION OF ENTRY	POST. REF.	DEBIT	CREDIT
19X1 Apr. 8	Cash		550 00	
	Accounts Receivable			550 00
	Received from Town Appliance Center for Invoice 540.			
9	Accounts Payable		1500 00	
	Cash			1455 00
	Purchases Discount			45 00
	Paid to Allied Manufacturing Co. for Invoice 1167 less discount.			
11	Merchandise Purchases		450 00	
	Cash			450 00
12	Truck Expense		90 00	
	Cash			90 00
	Paid for gasoline, oil, and repairs for the delivery truck.			
14	Miscellaneous Expense		50 00	
	Cash			50 00
	Paid electric bill.			
14	Miscellaneous Expense		35 00	
	Cash			35 00
	Paid telephone bill.			
14	Cash		2200 00	
	Sales Revenue			2200 00
	Cash sales for second week of April.			
16	Cash		2000 00	
	Ann Lang, Capital			2000 00
16	Accounts Receivable		350 00	
	Sales Revenue			350 00
	Sold merchandise on credit to Bristol Appliances; Invoice 542, terms 2/10, n/30.			

Special Accounts for Merchandising Businesses 85

GENERAL JOURNAL

PAGE 3

DATE	DESCRIPTION OF ENTRY	POST. REF.	DEBIT	CREDIT
19X1 Apr. 17	Cash		245 00	
	Sales Discount		5 00	
	Accounts Receivable			250 00
	Received from Capitol Appliance			
	Store for Invoice 541 less discount.			
17	Merchandise Purchases		1960 00	
	Cash			1960 00
18	Merchandise Purchases		600 00	
	Accounts Payable			600 00
	Purchased merchandise on credit			
	from Arco Electric Products; Invoice			
	6281, dated 4/16/X1, terms 1/10, n/30.			
19	Miscellaneous Expense		20 00	
	Cash			20 00
	Purchased pencils, pens, and typing paper.			
21	Cash		1350 00	
	Sales Revenue			1350 00
	Cash sales for third week of April.			
24	Cash		343 00	
	Sales Discount		7 00	
	Accounts Receivable			350 00
	Received from Bristol Appliances			
	for Invoice 542 less discount.			
24	Accounts Receivable		1280 00	
	Sales Revenue			1280 00
	Sold merchandise on credit to Economy			
	Appliance Center; Invoice 543, terms 1/10, n/60.			
24	Merchandise Purchases		1750 00	
	Accounts Payable			1750 00
	Purchased merchandise on credit from			
	Dow Industries; Invoice 327, dated 4/21/X1,			
	terms 3/10 EOM.			

GENERAL JOURNAL

PAGE 4

DATE	DESCRIPTION OF ENTRY	POST. REF.	DEBIT	CREDIT
19X1 Apr. 24	Accounts Payable		600 00	
	Cash			594 00
	Purchases Discount			6 00
	Paid to Arco Electric Products for Invoice 6281 less discount.			
25	Office Equipment		70 00	
	Cash			70 00
	Purchased a file cabinet.			
28	Cash		1670 00	
	Sales Revenue			1670 00
	Cash sales for fourth week of April.			
29	Accounts Receivable		880 00	
	Sales Revenue			880 00
	Sold merchandise on credit to Capitol Appliance Store; Invoice 544, terms 2/10, n/30.			
30	Wages Expense		1620 00	
	Cash			1620 00
	Paid monthly wages to truck driver and shipping clerk.			
30	Merchandise Purchases		3000 00	
	Accounts Payable			3000 00
	Purchased merchandise on credit from Allied Manufacturing Co.; Invoice 1191, dated 4/28/X1, terms 3/10, n/60.			
30	Ann Long, Drawing		900 00	
	Cash			900 00

Special Accounts for Merchandising Businesses

Checking Your Knowledge

BUSINESS APPLICATION

Problem 13-1. General Hardware Distributors, owned and operated by Ralph Gomez, had the following transactions during the month of May, 19X1. Record these transactions in the journal given on pages 59 and 60 of the workbook. Use the same accounts as are shown on page 82 of the textbook.

May 1 Purchased new desks, chairs, and file cabinets for the office for $1,500 in cash.
 3 Purchased merchandise for $3,000 on credit from Western Manufacturing Company; Invoice 1861, dated 5/1/X1, terms 3/10, n/60.
 4 Purchased shipping cartons for $400 in cash.
 5 Purchased merchandise for $500 in cash.
 8 Paid $388 in cash to Glen Industries for Invoice J765 ($400), less discount ($12). (This invoice was dated April 16 and had terms of 3/10 EOM.)
 9 Paid $2,910 in cash to Western Manufacturing Company for Invoice 1861 ($3,000), less discount ($90).
 12 Sold merchandise for $450 on credit to Bailey's Hardware Store; Invoice 220, terms 2/10, n/30.
 14 Paid $17 in cash for stationery and envelopes.
 15 Sold merchandise for $500 in cash during the first half of May.
 22 Received $441 in cash from Bailey's Hardware Store for Invoice 220 ($450), less discount ($9).
 24 Purchased merchandise for $575 on credit from Glen Industries; Invoice J788, dated 5/22/X1, terms 3/10 EOM.
 26 Sold merchandise for $1,200 on credit to the House of Hardware; Invoice 221, terms 2/10, n/30.
 31 Sold merchandise for $640 in cash during the second half of May.

MANAGERIAL ANALYSIS

Case 13. Mary Hurlbut owns a retail store that sells musical instruments. She recently bought a new cash register for use in the store. While looking at her general journal, she found that the bookkeeper had recorded this purchase in the Merchandise Purchases account.

She also found that the bookkeeper correctly deducts the cash discount when he pays for merchandise during the discount period, but he does not record the amount of the discount in the journal. He simply debits Accounts Payable and credits Cash for the total of the invoice.

1. Explain why the entry for the purchase of the cash register was incorrect.

2. How should the bookkeeper record payments that involve a cash discount? Why will his current entries for these transactions cause serious errors in the business's financial records?

88 Accounting Fundamentals

The Sales Journal

Every business has certain types of transactions that take place often and require similar journal entries. For example, the general journal prepared by Modern Appliance Distributors during April shows four entries for sales of merchandise on credit. Notice that each of the journal entries consists of a debit to Accounts Receivable and a credit to Sales Revenue. From these entries, eight separate postings had to be made to the general ledger. There were four postings to the Accounts Receivable account and four postings to the Sales Revenue account.

As Modern Appliance Distributors expands its business activities, it will have many more credit sales each month. This will lead to even greater repetition in its journal entries and postings.

GENERAL JOURNAL PAGE 1

DATE	DESCRIPTION OF ENTRY	POST. REF.	DEBIT	CREDIT
19X1 Apr. 7	Accounts Receivable	112	250 00	
	Sales Revenue	401		250 00
	Sold merchandise on credit to Capitol Appliance Store; Invoice 541, terms 2/10, n/30.			
16	Accounts Receivable	112	350 00	
	Sales Revenue	401		350 00
	Sold merchandise on credit to Bristol Appliances; Invoice 542, terms 2/10, n/30.			
24	Accounts Receivable	112	1280 00	
	Sales Revenue	401		1280 00
	Sold merchandise on credit to Economy Appliance Center; Invoice 543, terms 1/10, n/60.			
29	Accounts Receivable	112	880 00	
	Sales Revenue	401		880 00
	Sold merchandise on credit to Capitol Appliance Store; Invoice 544, terms 2/10, n/30.			

Accounts Receivable — No. 112

Date	Explanation	Post. Ref.	Debit	Date	Explanation	Post. Ref.	Credit
19X1 Apr. 7		J1	250 00				
16		J2	350 00				
24		J3	1 280 00				
29		J4	880 00				

Sales Revenue — No. 401

Date	Explanation	Post. Ref.	Debit	Date	Explanation	Post. Ref.	Credit
				19X1 Apr. 7		J1	250 00
				16		J2	350 00
				24		J3	1 280 00
				29		J4	880 00

Recording Transactions in the Sales Journal

Special Journal: Journal in which only one kind of transaction is entered.

Sales Journal: Chronological record of credit sales of merchandise.

One way to reduce the repetition in journalizing and posting is to have a *special journal* for all sales of merchandise on credit. Since this special journal is used to record *only sales of merchandise on credit*, it is called a *sales journal*.

Modern Appliance Distributors will be using a sales journal from now on. The business's credit sales for April are shown below as they would be recorded in the sales journal.

SALES JOURNAL for Month of April 19X1 — Page 1

Date	Invoice No.	Sold To	Terms	✓	Amount
19X1 Apr. 7	541	Capitol Appliance Store	2/10, n/30		250 00
16	542	Bristol Appliances	2/10, n/30		350 00
24	543	Economy Appliance Center	1/10, n/60		1 280 00
29	544	Capitol Appliance Store	2/10, n/30		880 00

Notice the advantages of the sales journal.

- All entries for sales of merchandise on credit are grouped together in one place rather than being scattered throughout the general journal. Thus information about credit sales can be located quickly and easily.
- The important facts about each transaction are written on a single line. These facts include the date, the invoice number, the name of the customer, the credit terms, and the amount of the sale.
- The information is neatly organized in separate columns.
- There is no need to enter account titles, record the amount twice, or write a long explanation for each transaction.

The source of information for each entry in the sales journal is the sales invoice or sales slip. A wholesaler like Modern Appliance Distributors uses a duplicate copy of the sales invoice that is sent to each customer who buys on credit. A retailer uses a duplicate copy of the sales slip that is given to each charge account customer. Notice how the information on the following invoice is entered on the first line of the sales journal shown on page 90.

```
              MODERN APPLIANCE DISTRIBUTORS
                     5891 Grant Avenue
                     Houston, Texas  77034

Sold to   Capitol Appliance Store    Invoice No. 541
          164 Bond Street
          Austin, TX 78750           Invoice Date  4/7/X1

                                     Terms         2/10, n/30

Customer Order No.   Date of Order         Shipped Via
     4482               4/1/X1             Ace Trucking Co.

Quantity  Stock No.   Description         Unit Price   Extension

   6       D732    Arco toaster ovens       $25.00      $150.00
   8       H529    Jiffy electric mixers     12.50       100.00
                                  TOTAL                 $250.00
```

Since the source documents are numbered in order and the numbers are recorded in the sales journal, it is easy to check that all credit sales have been entered. It is also easy to find the correct source document later if there is a need to refer to the form. The copies of the sales invoices or sales slips are filed for this purpose after the journalizing is completed.

Not every sales journal is exactly the same as the one shown on page 90. Some businesses add more columns in order to enter additional information. For example, large businesses often assign an identification number to each customer, and these numbers are recorded in the sales journal.

Posting From the Sales Journal

Another major advantage of the special sales journal is that it simplifies the posting of credit sales to the general ledger. At the end of each month, the figures in the Amount column of this journal are added. The total represents all the credit sales made during the month. This amount is posted as a single debit to the Accounts Receivable account and as a single credit to the Sales Revenue account.

The single posting to each account saves time and reduces the possibility of error. Remember that when the general journal was used, eight separate postings were needed to transfer the same information to the general ledger.

Posting of Monthly Total From Sales Journal With One Money Column

Debit
Accounts Receivable

Credit
Sales Revenue

The Sales Journal 91

SALES JOURNAL for Month of April 19X1   PAGE 1

DATE	INVOICE NO.	SOLD TO	TERMS	✓	AMOUNT
19X1 Apr. 7	541	Capitol Appliance Store	2/10, n/30		250 00
16	542	Bristol Appliances	2/10, n/30		350 00
24	543	Economy Appliance Center	1/10, n/60		1 280 00
29	544	Capitol Appliance Store	2/10, n/30		880 00
30		Total	Debit 112 Credit 401	✓✓	2 760 00

Accounts Receivable   NO. 112

DATE	EXPLANATION	POST. REF.	DEBIT	DATE	EXPLANATION	POST. REF.	CREDIT
19X1 Apr. 30		S1	2 760 00				

Sales Revenue   NO. 401

DATE	EXPLANATION	POST. REF.	DEBIT	DATE	EXPLANATION	POST. REF.	CREDIT
				19X1 Apr. 30		S1	2 760 00

Posting Reference for Sales Journal: The letter S and the journal page number.

Observe how the sales journal is totaled and how the postings are recorded. In the journal, both account numbers are placed on the same line as the total amount. They are checked off when they are posted. The abbreviation *S* and the journal page number are written in the Posting Reference columns of the ledger accounts to identify the postings from the sales journal.

Chapter Summary

- ☐ The sales journal is a special journal that is used for recording sales of merchandise on credit. It allows a business to save time and avoid repetition in the journalizing and posting of its credit sales.
- ☐ The sales journal groups together in one place all information about credit sales. It also organizes the information in columns and permits all the information for one transaction to be entered on a single line.
- ☐ The information needed for entries in the sales journal is taken from copies of the sales invoices in a wholesale business and from copies of the sales slips in a retail business.
- ☐ At the end of each month, the figures in the sales journal are added. The total is posted to the general ledger as a debit to the Accounts Receivable account and a credit to the Sales Revenue account. There is no need to post individual credit sales to these accounts during the month.

Accounting Fundamentals

Checking Your Knowledge

BUSINESS APPLICATION

Problem 14-1. The Champion Sporting Goods Company is a wholesaler of golf, tennis, and skiing equipment. During the month of January, 19X1, this business made the sales of merchandise on credit that are shown below.

1. Record each sale in the sales journal provided on page 61 of the workbook.
2. Total and rule the sales journal.
3. Open general ledger accounts for Accounts Receivable 112 and Sales Revenue 401.
4. Post the total of the sales journal to the general ledger accounts.

Date	Invoice Number	Sold To	Credit Terms	Amount of Sale
Jan. 2	121	Tennis World	2/10, n/30	$ 724.50
4	122	Fairview Pro Shop	2/10, n/30	415.80
7	123	Active Sports Mart	2/10, n/30	110.00
8	124	Ray's Ski Shop	2/10, n/30	617.50
12	125	Tennis World	2/10, n/30	115.00
15	126	Star Golf and Tennis Center	n/15	319.10
18	127	Active Sports Mart	2/10, n/30	236.50
21	128	Fairview Pro Shop	2/10, n/30	859.30
22	129	Mason's Sporting Gear	n/15	170.00
25	130	Ray's Ski Shop	2/10, n/30	755.00
28	131	Tennis World	2/10, n/30	115.00
30	132	Olympic Ski Shop	3/10, n/60	1,350.00

MANAGERIAL ANALYSIS

Case 14. George O'Brien owns a retail clothing business. He has just started using a sales journal to speed up his journalizing and posting work. He is wondering whether he can record the amount of his weekly cash sales in this journal. He is also wondering whether he can record the sale of some used store equipment there.

1. Should O'Brien enter his weekly cash sales in the sales journal? Why or why not?
2. Should O'Brien enter the sale of his used store equipment in the sales journal? Why or why not?
3. What three requirements must a transaction meet in order to be entered in a sales journal?

15

The Purchases Journal

The use of a sales journal simplifies accounting work and saves time. To achieve even more efficiency, many businesses also have a special journal for purchases of merchandise on credit.

The recording of credit purchases in the general journal involves the same kind of repetition as the recording of credit sales in the general journal. Look at the following general journal entries. They show four purchases of merchandise on credit made by Modern Appliance Distributors during April. In each entry, Merchandise Purchases was debited and Accounts Payable was credited. Then, eight separate postings were needed to transfer the information to the general ledger. There were four postings to the Merchandise Purchases account and four postings to the Accounts Payable account.

GENERAL JOURNAL PAGE 1

DATE	DESCRIPTION OF ENTRY	POST. REF.	DEBIT	CREDIT
19X1 Apr. 3	Merchandise Purchases	501	1500 00	
	Accounts Payable	202		1500 00
	Purchased merchandise on credit from Allied Manufacturing Co.; Invoice 1167, dated 4/1/X1, terms 3/10, n/60.			
18	Merchandise Purchases	501	600 00	
	Accounts Payable	202		600 00
	Purchased merchandise on credit from Arco Electric Products; Invoice 6281, dated 4/16/X1, terms 1/10, n/30.			
24	Merchandise Purchases	501	1750 00	
	Accounts Payable	202		1750 00
	Purchased merchandise on credit from Dow Industries; Invoice 327, dated 4/21/X1, terms 3/10 EOM.			
30	Merchandise Purchases	501	3000 00	
	Accounts Payable	202		3000 00
	Purchased merchandise on credit from Allied Manufacturing Co.; Invoice 1191, dated 4/28/X1, terms 3/10, n/60.			

Accounting Fundamentals

Merchandise Purchases   NO. 501

DATE	EXPLANATION	POST. REF.	DEBIT	DATE	EXPLANATION	POST. REF.	CREDIT
19X1 Apr. 3		J1	1500 00				
18		J3	600 00				
24		J3	1750 00				
30		J4	3000 00				

Accounts Payable   NO. 202

DATE	EXPLANATION	POST. REF.	DEBIT	DATE	EXPLANATION	POST. REF.	CREDIT
				19X1 Apr. 3		J1	1500 00
				18		J3	600 00
				24		J3	1750 00
				30		J4	3000 00

By using a *purchases journal* as well as a sales journal, Modern Appliance Distributors will further reduce repetition in the journalizing and posting of its transactions. Purchases of merchandise on credit can be recorded easily and quickly in the special purchases journal.

Note that purchases of merchandise for cash, purchases of supplies, and purchases of permanent assets cannot be entered in the purchases journal. This special journal is used to record *only purchases of merchandise on credit.*

Purchases Journal: Chronological record of credit purchases of merchandise.

Recording Transactions in the Purchases Journal

The purchases journal offers the same type of advantages as the sales journal. All journal entries for purchases of merchandise on credit are grouped together in one place. The column headings permit the important facts about each transaction to be recorded in a minimum amount of space and with a minimum amount of work. Only a single line is needed to enter a purchase. No account titles are used, and the amount of the purchase is written only once.

The purchases of merchandise on credit made by Modern Appliance Distributors during April are shown below as they would be recorded in a purchases journal.

The source documents for entries in the purchases journal are the purchase invoices received from suppliers. These invoices must be checked carefully before journalizing the transactions. (The procedures for handling purchase invoices were discussed on pages 73 and 74 of Chapter 12.)

PURCHASES JOURNAL FOR MONTH OF April 19X1   PAGE 1

DATE	PURCHASED FROM	INVOICE NO.	INVOICE DATE	TERMS	✓	AMOUNT
19X1 Apr. 3	Allied Manufacturing Co.	1167	4/1/X1	3/10,n/60		1500 00
18	Arco Electric Products	6281	4/16/X1	1/10,n/30		600 00
24	Dow Industries	327	4/21/X1	3/10EOM		1750 00
30	Allied Manufacturing Co.	1191	4/28/X1	3/10,n/60		3000 00

The Purchases Journal

The following invoice is recorded on the first line of the purchases journal shown on page 95. Notice that the date used for the journal entry (April 3) is the date on which the invoice was received. (This date appears in the processing stamp.) The date that the supplier prepared the invoice (April 1) is recorded in the Invoice Date column of the journal. The other important facts taken from the invoice are the name of the supplier, the invoice number, the credit terms, and the total of the purchase.

```
Allied Manufacturing Company
1268 Water Street   Chicago, Illinois 60628

SOLD TO  Modern Appliance Distributors        INVOICE NO. 1167
         5891 Grant Avenue
         Houston, TX 77034             INVOICE DATE    TERMS
                                         4/1/X1      3/10,n/60

DATE OF ORDER  CUSTOMER ORDER NO.  SHIPPED VIA         SALES REPRESENTATIVE
  3/22/X1           081            Ward Motor Freight    Sadowski

QUAN.  STOCK NO.   DESCRIPTION                   UNIT PRICE   EXTENSION
  25   A113X20     Electric rotisserie broilers   $32.00     $  800.00
  50   A164X68     Electric coffee makers          14.00        700.00
                                       TOTAL                 $1,500.00
```

Processing stamp:
- Date Received: 4/3/X1
- Quantities & Prices: GYB
- Extensions & Total: amL
- Due Date: 4/11/X1
- Journal Page No.: P1
- Payment Date:
- Check No.:

Observe that Modern Appliance Distributors uses a processing stamp on its purchase invoices. After an invoice is entered in the purchases journal, the number of the journal page is written in the stamped area. Then the invoice is placed in an unpaid invoices file until the due date for payment. When payment is made, information about the payment is recorded in the stamped area of the invoice. Finally, the invoice is placed in a paid invoices file in case it is needed for future reference.

The form used for the purchases journal may vary. Some businesses arrange the columns of this journal in a different order. Other businesses add more columns so that they can record additional information.

Posting From the Purchases Journal

Posting of Monthly Total From Purchases Journal With One Money Column

Debit
Merchandise Purchases

Credit
Accounts Payable

At the end of each month, the figures in the Amount column of the purchases journal are added. The total represents the cost of all the purchases of merchandise on credit made during the month. This amount is posted as a single debit to the Merchandise Purchases account and as a single credit to the Accounts Payable account.

PURCHASES JOURNAL FOR MONTH OF April 19X1   PAGE 1

DATE	PURCHASED FROM	INVOICE NO.	INVOICE DATE	TERMS	✓	AMOUNT
19X1 Apr. 3	Allied Manufacturing Co.	1167	4/1/X1	3/10,n/60		1 500 00
18	Arco Electric Products	6281	4/16/X1	1/10,n/30		600 00
24	Dow Industries	327	4/21/X1	3/10 EOM		1 750 00
30	Allied Manufacturing Co.	1191	4/28/X1	3/10,n/60		3 000 00
30	Total Debit 501 Credit 202				✓	6 850 00

Merchandise Purchases — NO. 501

DATE	EXPLANATION	POST. REF.	DEBIT	DATE	EXPLANATION	POST. REF.	CREDIT
19X1 Apr. 30		P1	6850 00				

Accounts Payable — NO. 202

DATE	EXPLANATION	POST. REF.	DEBIT	DATE	EXPLANATION	POST. REF.	CREDIT
				19X1 Apr. 30		P1	6850 00

Notice that both account numbers are placed on the same line of the journal as the total amount. These numbers are checked off as they are posted. The abbreviation *P* and the journal page number are used in the Posting Reference columns of the general ledger accounts to identify postings from the purchases journal.

Posting Reference for Purchases Journal: The letter *P* and the journal page number.

Chapter Summary

- The purchases journal is a special journal for recording purchases of merchandise on credit.
- The information about each transaction is taken from a purchase invoice and is entered on a single line of the purchases journal.
- The journal entry for each purchase shows the date the invoice was received, the supplier's name, the invoice number, the invoice date, the credit terms, and the amount of the purchase.
- At the end of each month, the total of the purchases journal is posted as a single debit to the Merchandise Purchases account and as a single credit to the Accounts Payable account.

Checking Your Knowledge

BUSINESS APPLICATION

Problem 15-1. Alice's Corner Shop is a retail business that sells books, records, adult games, and posters. During July, 19X1, the shop made the purchases of merchandise on credit that are shown on page 98.

1. Record each purchase in the purchases journal provided on page 63 of the workbook.
2. Total and rule the purchases journal.
3. Open general ledger accounts for Accounts Payable 202 and Merchandise Purchases 501.
4. Post the total of the purchases journal to the general ledger accounts.

The Purchases Journal   **97**

Date	Purchased From	Invoice Number	Date of Invoice	Terms	Amount of Invoice
July 3	Hamilton Wholesalers	824-J	7/1	2/10, n/30	$385.60
7	Alden Supply Company	1132	7/5	1/15, n/60	450.00
11	Lane Brothers	4736	7/10	n/30	452.80
20	Marcus Company	555	7/18	n/30 EOM	260.40
22	Alden Supply Company	1158	7/20	1/15, n/60	755.50
25	Hamilton Wholesalers	908-J	7/23	2/10, n/30	220.75
28	Allen-Kirby, Inc.	1361	7/26	n/30	640.00
31	Marcus Company	648	7/29	n/30 EOM	935.30

MANAGERIAL ANALYSIS

Case 15. Martin Beck has just opened a camera store. He will buy all of his merchandise on credit. He wants to be sure that the purchase invoices are checked for accuracy, that they are journalized and posted efficiently, and that they are paid in time to obtain the cash discounts.

What procedures should Beck follow to achieve these goals?

16

The Cash Receipts Journal

Cash transactions are very common in most businesses. Cash is constantly received and constantly paid out. For example, during April, Modern Appliance Distributors had eight transactions involving the receipt of cash.

GENERAL JOURNAL   PAGE 1

DATE	DESCRIPTION OF ENTRY	POST. REF.	DEBIT	CREDIT
19X1 Apr. 7	Cash	101	1800 00	
	Sales Revenue	401		1800 00
	Cash sales for first week of April.			
8	Cash	101	550 00	
	Accounts Receivable	112		550 00
	Received from Town Appliance Center for Invoice 540.			
14	Cash	101	2200 00	
	Sales Revenue	401		2200 00
	Cash sales for second week of April.			
16	Cash	101	2000 00	
	Ann Lang, Capital	301		2000 00
17	Cash	101	245 00	
	Sales Discount	403	5 00	
	Accounts Receivable	112		250 00
	Received from Capitol Appliance Store for Invoice 541 less discount.			

The Cash Receipts Journal   **99**

GENERAL JOURNAL PAGE 1

DATE	DESCRIPTION OF ENTRY	POST. REF.	DEBIT	CREDIT
19X1 Apr. 21	Cash	101	1350.00	
	Sales Revenue	401		1350.00
	Cash sales for third week of April.			
24	Cash	101	343.00	
	Sales Discount	403	7.00	
	Accounts Receivable	112		350.00
	Received from Bristol Appliances for Invoice 542 less discount.			
28	Cash	101	1670.00	
	Sales Revenue	401		1670.00
	Cash sales for fourth week of April.			

Notice that the Cash account was debited eight times during the month (not including the opening entry). The journal entries for cash receipts required eight separate postings to the Cash account in the general ledger. There were also two debits to the Sales Discount account, which required two separate postings.

In addition, the Accounts Receivable account was credited three times, the owner's capital account was credited once, and the Sales Revenue account was credited four times. All of these credits had to be posted separately to the general ledger.

Thus, 18 postings were needed for the business's cash receipts transactions.

Cash NO. 101

DATE	EXPLANATION	POST. REF.	DEBIT	DATE	EXPLANATION	POST. REF.	CREDIT
19X1 Apr. 1		J1	6000.00				
7		J1	1800.00				
8		J2	550.00				
14		J2	2200.00				
16		J2	2000.00				
17		J3	245.00				
21		J3	1350.00				
24		J3	343.00				
28		J4	1670.00				

Accounts Receivable NO. 112

DATE	EXPLANATION	POST. REF.	DEBIT	DATE	EXPLANATION	POST. REF.	CREDIT
				19X1 Apr. 8		J2	550.00
				17		J3	250.00
				24		J3	350.00

100 Accounting Fundamentals

Ann Lang, Capital No. 301

DATE	EXPLANATION	POST. REF.	DEBIT	DATE	EXPLANATION	POST. REF.	CREDIT
				19X1 Apr. 16		J2	2000 00

Sales Revenue No. 401

DATE	EXPLANATION	POST. REF.	DEBIT	DATE	EXPLANATION	POST. REF.	CREDIT
				19X1 Apr. 7		J1	1800 00
				14		J2	2200 00
				21		J3	1350 00
				28		J4	1670 00

Sales Discount No. 403

DATE	EXPLANATION	POST. REF.	DEBIT	DATE	EXPLANATION	POST. REF.	CREDIT
19X1 Apr. 17		J3	5 00				
24		J3	7 00				

Obviously, the use of a special *cash receipts journal* will make the accounting system of Modern Appliance Distributors more efficient. Like the sales journal and the purchases journal, the cash receipts journal offers important advantages. All the cash receipts transactions will be grouped in one place. The journalizing of these transactions will be easier and quicker, and their posting will be greatly simplified.

Cash Receipts Journal: Chronological record of cash receipts.

Setting Up a Cash Receipts Journal

The cash receipts journal that Modern Appliance Distributors will use is shown below. The transactions for April would appear as follows in this journal.

CASH RECEIPTS JOURNAL FOR MONTH OF April 19 X1 PAGE 1

		DEBITS			CREDITS				
DATE	EXPLANATION	CASH	SALES DISCOUNT	✓	ACCOUNTS RECEIVABLE	SALES REVENUE	OTHER ACCOUNTS		
							ACCOUNT TITLE	POST. REF.	AMOUNT
19X1 Apr. 1	Balance on hand, $6,000								
7	Cash sales for first week	1800 00				1800 00			
8	Town Appliance Center — Inv. 540	550 00			550 00				
14	Cash sales for second week	2200 00				2200 00			
16	Additional investment by owner	2000 00					Ann Lang, Capital		2000 00
17	Capitol Appliance Store — Inv. 541	245 00	5 00		250 00				
21	Cash sales for third week	1350 00				1350 00			
24	Bristol Appliances — Inv. 542	343 00	7 00		350 00				
28	Cash sales for fourth week	1670 00				1670 00			

The Cash Receipts Journal 101

Notice that this journal has five money columns. The accounts most often used in recording cash receipts transactions at Modern Appliance Distributors are Cash, Sales Discount, Accounts Receivable, and Sales Revenue. A special column is set up for each of these four accounts. Since other accounts are sometimes involved in cash receipts transactions, a fifth money column—Other Accounts—must also be set up. (It is not worthwhile to have special columns for accounts that are used only occasionally.)

The Debits section of the cash receipts journal contains two money columns. The Cash column is used to record the amount of cash received in each transaction. The Sales Discount column is used to record any sales discounts taken by credit customers who are paying invoices within the discount period. The debits to the Cash account and the Sales Discount account are entered in these two columns during the month.

The Credits section of the cash receipts journal contains three money columns. The Accounts Receivable column is used to record the amounts of the invoices that credit customers are paying. The Sales Revenue column is used to record the amounts received from cash sales. The credits to the Accounts Receivable account and the Sales Revenue account are entered in these two columns during the month.

The Accounts Receivable and Sales Revenue columns take care of the two regular sources of cash receipts for the business: (1) amounts received on account from credit customers and (2) amounts received from cash sales. Occasionally, however, cash comes from other sources, such as an additional investment by the owner. The last money column in the Credits section—Other Accounts—is used to record the credit entries for these transactions.

Recording Transactions in the Cash Receipts Journal

Since the cash receipts journal has special money columns for all the accounts commonly used by the business in recording cash receipts transactions, it is easy to make entries in this journal. Observe the following about the entries for April.

- The notation *Balance on hand, $6,000* is written on the first line of the journal. This figure comes from the Cash account. It is customary to record the amount of cash on hand at the beginning of each month in the cash receipts journal. Because this notation simply provides information and is not a regular entry to be posted, the amount is listed in the Explanation column. A line is drawn through the Cash Debit column. The notation of the cash balance is called a *memorandum entry*.

Memorandum Entry: Journal entry that is not to be posted.

- The entries for April 7, 14, 21, and 28 involve cash received from weekly cash sales. In each entry, the amount is recorded in the Cash Debit column and the Sales Revenue Credit column.
- The entry for April 8 involves cash received from a credit customer who is paying an invoice after the discount period. Thus there is no sales discount, and the customer has sent a check for the full amount of the invoice. The amount received is recorded in the Cash Debit column and the Accounts Receivable Credit column.
- The entry for April 16 involves cash received from an additional investment by the owner. The debit part of the entry is recorded in the Cash Debit column. Since there is no special column for the Ann Lang, Capital account, the credit part of the entry must be made in the Other Accounts Credit column. Notice that it is necessary to write the name of the account to be credited when this column is used.
- The entries for April 17 and 24 involve cash received from credit customers who are paying invoices within the discount period. Thus each of these customers has deducted a sales discount from the total of the invoice. The

amount actually received is recorded in the Cash Debit column. The amount of the sales discount is recorded in the Sales Discount Debit column. The total of the invoice is recorded in the Accounts Receivable Credit column.

Notice that the essential facts about each transaction can be recorded on a single line in the cash receipts journal. Also notice that the debits and credits for the transactions are exactly the same as they were in the general journal.

Cash may come into a business in several forms: currency (paper money), coins, checks, and money orders. When cash is received, it is usually recorded on a source document and then deposited in the bank. Most businesses deposit their cash often in order to safeguard it.

Cash receipts may be currency, coins, checks, and money orders.

The source documents for cash receipts vary from business to business. Modern Appliance Distributors uses the following weekly cash received report to provide the necessary information for the journal entries.

CASH RECEIVED REPORT
FOR WEEK OF April 15-21 19 X1

CASH SALES

DATE	AMOUNT
4/15	$330
4/16	210
4/17	170
TOTAL	$1,350

CASH RECEIVED ON ACCOUNT

DATE	INVOICE NO.	AMOUNT OF CHECK	DISCOUNT	INVOICE TOTAL	NAME OF CUSTOMER
4/17	541	$245	$5	$250	Capitol Appliance Store
TOTAL		$245			

CASH FROM OTHER SOURCES

DATE	AMOUNT	SOURCE
4/16	$2,000	Additional investment by Ann Lang
TOTAL	$2,000	

SUMMARY
Cash Sales $1,350
Cash Received on Account 245
Cash From Other Sources 2,000
Total Cash Received $3,595

Other businesses use cash register tapes as source documents for cash sales and prepare a form called a *remittance slip* as a source document for each check received from a credit customer. Cash received reports, cash register tapes, and remittance slips are only a few of the possible source documents for cash receipts.

The columns in the cash receipts journal can also vary. Some businesses arrange the columns in a different order from the one shown for Modern Appliance Distributors. Other businesses use more or fewer columns, according to the number of accounts needed most often to record their cash receipts transactions.

Posting From the Cash Receipts Journal

During the month, each amount appearing in the Other Accounts Credit column of the cash receipts journal is posted individually to the account named in the entry. Thus the owner's additional investment of $2,000 was posted individually to the Ann Lang, Capital account in the general ledger on April 16. The number of this account (301) was then written in the journal next to the amount.

At the end of each month, all the money columns of the cash receipts journal are added. The totals are usually written in small pencil figures and checked for accuracy

Posting From Cash Receipts Journal
- *During month, post individual credits from Other Accounts column.*
- *At end of month, post totals of rest of columns.*

The Cash Receipts Journal 103

before being entered in ink. The checking is very simple. First, the totals of the debit columns are added together. Then, the totals of the credit columns are added together.

Debit Totals: $10,158 + $12 = $10,170
Credit Totals: $1,150 + $7,020 + $2,000 = $10,170

Cross-footing: Adding column totals to check accuracy.

If the sum of each group of column totals is the same, equal debits and credits were recorded during the month. This method of checking a journal is called *cross-footing*. After the equality of the debits and credits is proved, the column totals are written in regular-sized ink figures, and the cash receipts journal is ruled.

CASH RECEIPTS JOURNAL FOR MONTH OF April 19X1   PAGE 1

DATE	EXPLANATION	DEBITS CASH	DEBITS SALES DISCOUNT	✓	CREDITS ACCOUNTS RECEIVABLE	CREDITS SALES REVENUE	OTHER ACCOUNTS TITLE	POST. REF.	AMOUNT
19X1 Apr. 1	Balance on hand, $6,000								
7	Cash sales for first week	1800 00				1800 00			
8	Town Appliance Center – Inv. 540	550 00			550 00				
14	Cash sales for second week	2200 00				2200 00			
16	Additional investment by owner	2000 00					Ann Lang, Capital	301	2000 00
17	Capitol Appliance Store – Inv. 541	245 00	5 00		250 00				
21	Cash sales for third week	1350 00				1350 00			
24	Bristol Appliances – Inv. 542	343 00	7 00		350 00				
28	Cash sales for fourth week	1670 00				1670 00			
30	Totals	10158 00	12 00		1150 00	7020 00			2000 00
		(101)	(403)		(112)	(401)			(X)

Cash   NO. 101

DATE	EXPLANATION	POST. REF.	DEBIT	DATE	EXPLANATION	POST. REF.	CREDIT
19X1 Apr. 1		J1	6000 00				
30		CR1	10158 00				

Accounts Receivable   NO. 112

DATE	EXPLANATION	POST. REF.	DEBIT	DATE	EXPLANATION	POST. REF.	CREDIT
19X1 Apr. 1		J1	1000 00	19X1 Apr. 30		CR1	1150 00
30		S1	2760 00				

Ann Lang, Capital   NO. 301

DATE	EXPLANATION	POST. REF.	DEBIT	DATE	EXPLANATION	POST. REF.	CREDIT
				19X1 Apr. 1		J1	35000 00
				16		CR1	2000 00

104   Accounting Fundamentals

		Sales Revenue					NO. 401	
DATE	EXPLANATION	POST. REF.	DEBIT	DATE	EXPLANATION	POST. REF.	CREDIT	
				19X1 Apr. 30		S1	276000	
				30		CR1	702000	

		Sales Discount					NO. 403	
DATE	EXPLANATION	POST. REF.	DEBIT	DATE	EXPLANATION	POST. REF.	CREDIT	
19X1 Apr. 30		CR1	1200					

As each column total is posted to an account in the general ledger, the account number is written in parentheses below the total in the journal. The total of the Other Accounts Credit column is not posted. An *X* is therefore written in parentheses below this total. (Remember that the credit to the Ann Lang, Capital account was posted as an individual item.) The abbreviation *CR* and the journal page number are entered in the general ledger accounts to identify the postings from the cash receipts journal.

Remember that the general journal entries for these transactions required 18 separate postings. When a cash receipts journal is used, the same information can be transferred to the general ledger in four postings of column totals and one individual posting.

Posting Reference for Cash Receipts Journal: The letters *CR* and the journal page number.

Chapter Summary

- The cash receipts journal is a special journal in which all a business's cash receipts transactions can be recorded. It groups together the entries for cash receipts.
- The use of a cash receipts journal makes an accounting system more efficient. It eliminates repetition in the journalizing and posting of cash receipts.
- The cash receipts journal usually has several special money columns that simplify the recording of routine entries. These columns are for the accounts (such as Cash, Sales Discount, Accounts Receivable, and Sales Revenue) that a business uses most often in recording cash receipts. A column called Other Accounts is used for credits to accounts for which there are no special columns.
- A memorandum entry is made in the cash receipts journal to record the cash balance at the beginning of each month.
- The totals of the debits and credits must be equal for each transaction recorded in the cash receipts journal.
- The credits in the Other Accounts column are posted individually during the month to the general ledger accounts indicated in the journal entries. The totals of the rest of the columns are posted at the end of the month to the general ledger accounts named in the column headings.
- Before posting any column totals, it is necessary to check their accuracy. A process called cross-footing is used for this purpose.
- The form of the cash receipts journal may vary according to the needs of a business.

Checking Your Knowledge

BUSINESS APPLICATION

Problem 16-1. During the month of April, Atlantic Food Products, a wholesaler of groceries, had the cash receipts transactions listed at the right. Do the following work for the business.

1. Open general ledger accounts for Cash 101; Accounts Receivable 112; Office Equipment 120; Ray Koslo, Capital 301; Sales Revenue 401; and Sales Discount 403. Use the forms on page 65 of the workbook.
2. Enter the April 1 balances in the following accounts: Cash, $3,620.85; Accounts Receivable, $4,427.80; Office Equipment, $1,400.00; and Ray Koslo, Capital, $20,000.00.
3. Make a memorandum entry of the beginning cash balance in the cash receipts journal. Use the journal form on page 66 of the workbook.
4. Record each of the transactions in the cash receipts journal.
5. Post the items in the Other Accounts Credit column individually to the general ledger accounts named in the entries.
6. Pencil-foot the column totals of the cash receipts journal and prove their accuracy. (Use the cross-footing method.)
7. Enter the column totals and rule the cash receipts journal.
8. Post the column totals to the general ledger accounts that are affected.

Apr. 2 Received $130.50 in cash from Ben's Market for Invoice 845.
 4 Received $320.10 in cash from Gem Groceries for Invoice 848 ($330), less discount ($9.90).
 7 Sold merchandise for $792.75 in cash during the first week of April.
 9 Sold a used office file for $30 in cash.
 10 Received $236.45 in cash from Hanson's Diner for Invoice 844.
 12 Received $281.30 in cash from Dover Foods for Invoice 849 ($290), less discount ($8.70).
 14 Sold merchandise for $845.75 in cash during the second week of April.
 16 Received $192.35 in cash from Hanson's Diner for Invoice 846.
 18 Received $240.85 in cash from Lee's Coffee Shop for Invoice 847.
 20 Ray Koslo made an additional cash investment of $5,000 in the business.
 21 Sold merchandise for $690.25 in cash during the third week of April.
 24 Received $223.10 in cash from Dover Foods for Invoice 851 ($230), less discount ($6.90).
 27 Received $388 in cash from Top Food Mart for Invoice 852 ($400), less discount ($12).
 28 Sold merchandise for $820.95 in cash during the fourth week of April.
 30 Received $315.90 in cash from Hanson's Diner for Invoice 850.

MANAGERIAL ANALYSIS

Case 16. Diane Scott owns a retail store that sells sporting goods. Since the store is located in an area with many resort hotels, she also rents bicycles, golf clubs, and fishing gear to tourists. The business has been growing rapidly, and a good deal of cash is received each day.

Because it is now so time-consuming to record these transactions in the general journal, Diane Scott wants to set up a cash receipts journal. Her three regular sources of cash receipts are amounts from charge account customers, amounts from cash sales, and amounts from rentals of equipment. (All rentals are for cash.) No discounts are offered to charge account customers. There are separate accounts for sales revenue and rental revenue.

1. What column headings should be used in the cash receipts journal for this business?
2. Explain why the cash receipts journal for this business might be different from the one illustrated on page 101.

17

The Cash Payments Journal

Businesses must pay out cash for a number of reasons: to make cash purchases of equipment and supplies, to make cash purchases of merchandise, to settle invoices for credit purchases, and to take care of operating expenses such as wages, electricity, and telephone service. In addition, there may be regular cash withdrawals by the owner. Observe the following 15 entries for cash payments that were recorded in the general journal of Modern Appliance Distributors during April.

DATE	DESCRIPTION OF ENTRY	POST. REF.	DEBIT	CREDIT
19X1 Apr. 2	Warehouse Equipment	118	3000.00	
	Cash	101		3000.00
	Purchased bins, shelves, and conveyors.			
3	Office Equipment	120	600.00	
	Cash	101		600.00
	Purchased typewriter, electronic calculator, and postage meter.			
4	Accounts Payable	202	1400.00	
	Cash	101		1400.00
	Paid to Reliable Products for Invoice 82895.			
5	Supplies	115	320.00	
	Cash	101		320.00
	Purchased shipping cartons.			
9	Accounts Payable	202	1500.00	
	Cash	101		1455.00
	Purchases Discount	504		45.00
	Paid to Allied Manufacturing Co. for Invoice 1167 less discount.			

GENERAL JOURNAL PAGE 1

GENERAL JOURNAL
PAGE 2

DATE	DESCRIPTION OF ENTRY	POST. REF.	DEBIT	CREDIT
19X1 Apr.				
11	Merchandise Purchases	501	450 00	
	Cash	101		450 00
12	Truck Expense	511	90 00	
	Cash	101		90 00
	Paid for gasoline, oil, and repairs for the delivery truck.			
14	Miscellaneous Expense	512	50 00	
	Cash	101		50 00
	Paid electric bill.			
14	Miscellaneous Expense	512	35 00	
	Cash	101		35 00
	Paid telephone bill.			

GENERAL JOURNAL
PAGE 3

DATE	DESCRIPTION OF ENTRY	POST. REF.	DEBIT	CREDIT
19X1 Apr.				
17	Merchandise Purchases	501	1960 00	
	Cash	101		1960 00
19	Miscellaneous Expense	512	20 00	
	Cash	101		20 00
	Purchased pencils, pens, and typing paper.			
24	Accounts Payable	202	600 00	
	Cash	101		594 00
	Purchases Discount	504		6 00
	Paid to Arco Electric Products for Invoice 6281 less discount.			
25	Office Equipment	120	70 00	
	Cash	101		70 00
	Purchased a file cabinet.			
30	Wages Expense	513	1620 00	
	Cash	101		1620 00
	Paid monthly wages to truck driver and shipping clerk.			
30	Ann Lang, Drawing	302	900 00	
	Cash	101		900 00

108 Accounting Fundamentals

The general journal entries for cash payments during the month required 32 separate postings to general ledger accounts. Fifteen credits were posted to the Cash account, and two credits were posted to the Purchases Discount account. These credit amounts were offset by three debits to the Accounts Payable account, two debits to the Merchandise Purchases account, and ten debits to other general ledger accounts.

Cash — No. 101

Date	Explanation	Post. Ref.	Debit	Date	Explanation	Post. Ref.	Credit
				19X1 Apr. 2		J1	3000 00
				3		J1	60 00
				4		J1	1400 00
				5		J1	320 00
				9		J2	1455 00
				11		J2	450 00
				12		J2	90 00
				14		J2	50 00
				14		J2	35 00
				17		J3	1960 00
				19		J3	20 00
				24		J4	594 00
				25		J4	70 00
				30		J4	1620 00
				30		J4	900 00

Supplies — No. 115

Date	Explanation	Post. Ref.	Debit	Date	Explanation	Post. Ref.	Credit
19X1 Apr. 5		J1	320 00				

Warehouse Equipment — No. 118

Date	Explanation	Post. Ref.	Debit	Date	Explanation	Post. Ref.	Credit
19X1 Apr. 2		J1	3000 00				

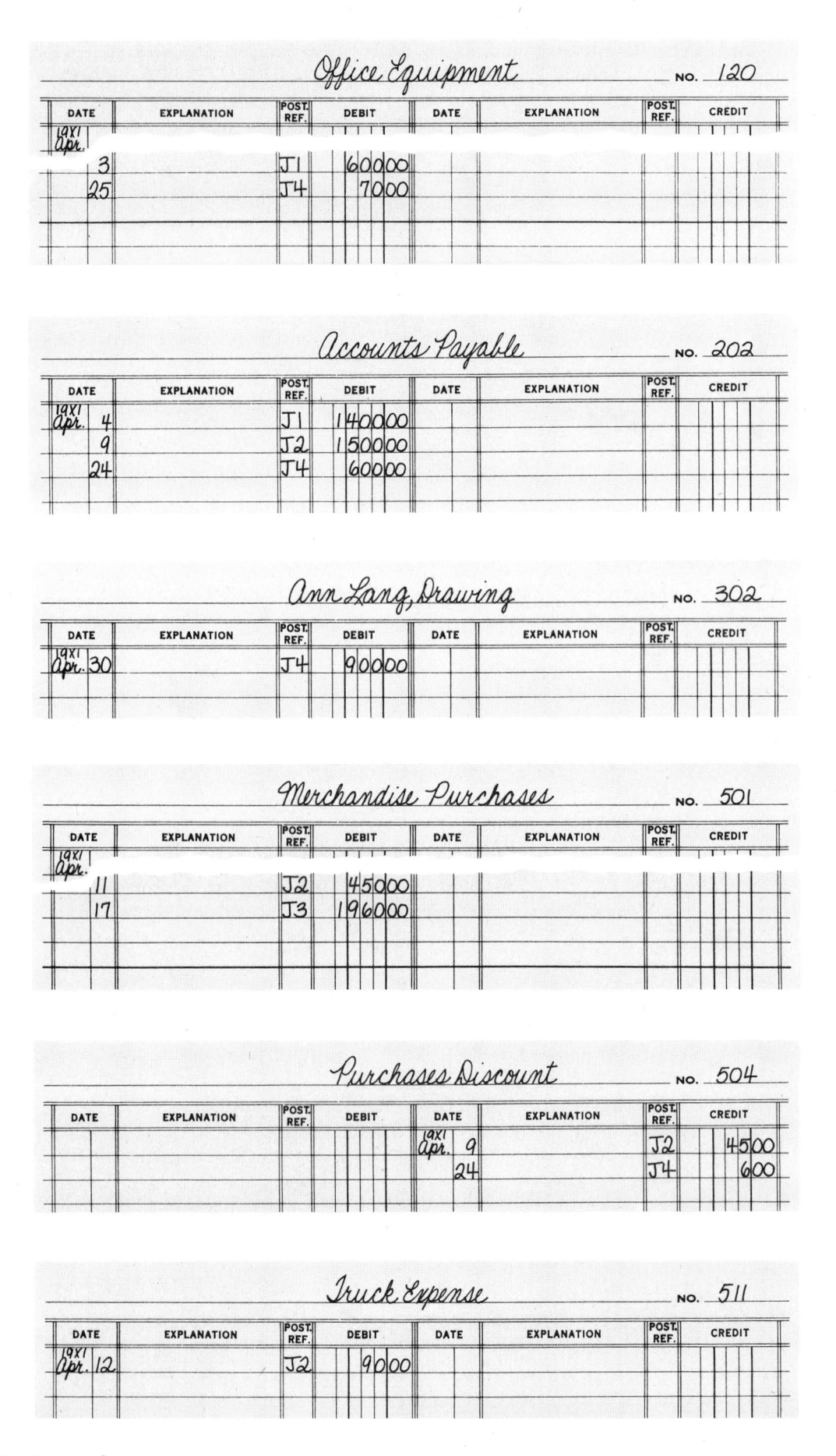

Office Equipment — NO. 120

DATE	EXPLANATION	POST. REF.	DEBIT	DATE	EXPLANATION	POST. REF.	CREDIT
19X1 Apr. 3		J1	600 00				
25		J4	70 00				

Accounts Payable — NO. 202

DATE	EXPLANATION	POST. REF.	DEBIT	DATE	EXPLANATION	POST. REF.	CREDIT
19X1 Apr. 4		J1	1400 00				
9		J2	1500 00				
24		J4	600 00				

Ann Lang, Drawing — NO. 302

DATE	EXPLANATION	POST. REF.	DEBIT	DATE	EXPLANATION	POST. REF.	CREDIT
19X1 Apr. 30		J4	900 00				

Merchandise Purchases — NO. 501

DATE	EXPLANATION	POST. REF.	DEBIT	DATE	EXPLANATION	POST. REF.	CREDIT
19X1 Apr. 11		J2	450 00				
17		J3	1960 00				

Purchases Discount — NO. 504

DATE	EXPLANATION	POST. REF.	DEBIT	DATE	EXPLANATION	POST. REF.	CREDIT
				19X1 Apr. 9		J2	45 00
				24		J4	6 00

Truck Expense — NO. 511

DATE	EXPLANATION	POST. REF.	DEBIT	DATE	EXPLANATION	POST. REF.	CREDIT
19X1 Apr. 12		J2	90 00				

Miscellaneous Expense — NO. 512

DATE	EXPLANATION	POST. REF.	DEBIT	DATE	EXPLANATION	POST. REF.	CREDIT
19X1 Apr. 14		J2	50 00				
14		J2	35 00				
19		J3	20 00				

Wages Expense — NO. 513

DATE	EXPLANATION	POST. REF.	DEBIT	DATE	EXPLANATION	POST. REF.	CREDIT
19X1 Apr. 30		J4	1 620 00				

Modern Appliance Distributors will further increase the efficiency of its accounting system by adding a special *cash payments journal*. This journal will provide the same kind of advantages as the other special journals. It will group together information about all of the business's cash payments, and it will eliminate repetition in the journalizing and posting of these transactions.

Cash Payments Journal: Chronological record of cash payments.

Setting Up a Cash Payments Journal

The cash payments journal that Modern Appliance Distributors will use is shown below. This journal was set up in a similar manner to the business's cash receipts journal. A special money column is provided for each account that will be used often in recording cash payments. The special money columns make it easier to enter transactions and permit the summary posting of totals at the end of each month.

CASH PAYMENTS JOURNAL FOR MONTH OF April 19 X1   PAGE 1

DATE	CHECK NO.	EXPLANATION	✓	ACCOUNTS PAYABLE (DR)	MERCHANDISE PURCHASES (DR)	OTHER ACCOUNTS — ACCOUNT TITLE	POST. REF.	AMOUNT	PURCHASES DISCOUNT (CR)	CASH (CR)
19X1 Apr. 2	101	Bins, shelves, conveyors				Warehouse Equipment	118	300 00		300 00
3	102	Typewriter, calculator, postage meter				Office Equipment	120	600 00		600 00
4	103	Reliable Products — Inv. 82895		1 400 00						1 400 00
5	104	Shipping cartons				Supplies	115	32 00		32 00
9	105	Allied Manufacturing Co. — Inv. 1167		1 500 00					45 00	1 455 00
11	106	Merchandise			450 00					450 00
12	107	Gasoline, oil, repairs for truck				Truck Expense	511	90 00		90 00
14	108	Electric bill				Miscellaneous Expense	512	50 00		50 00
14	109	Telephone bill				Miscellaneous Expense	512	35 00		35 00
17	110	Merchandise			1 960 00					1 960 00
19	111	Pencils, pens, typing paper				Miscellaneous Expense	512	20 00		20 00
24	112	Arco Electric Products — Inv. 6281		600 00					6 00	594 00
25	113	File cabinet				Office Equipment	120	70 00		70 00
30	114	Monthly wages				Wages Expense	513	1 620 00		1 620 00
30	115	Withdrawal by owner				Ann Lang Drawing	302	900 00		900 00
30		Totals		3 500 00	2 410 00			6 785 00	51 00	12 564 00
				(202)	(501)			(X)	(504)	(101)

The Cash Payments Journal 111

The Accounts Payable column is used to record the amounts of invoices for credit purchases that are being paid. The Merchandise Purchases column is used to record the amounts of cash purchases of merchandise. The debits to the Accounts Payable account and the Merchandise Purchases account are entered in these two columns during the month. (There were only two cash purchases of merchandise in April. However, the Merchandise Purchases column will be used more often in the future as the business expands.)

The Other Accounts column is used to record the debit entries for all other types of payments, such as payments for cash purchases of equipment or supplies and payments for expenses.

The Purchases Discount column is used to record the discounts taken on purchase invoices that are paid within the discount period. The Cash column is used to record the amounts of all the cash payments. The credits to the Purchases Discount account and the Cash account are entered in these two columns during the month.

Notice that the cash payments journal also includes a Check No. column. In a well-run business, payments are made by check. The checks have consecutive numbers, and these numbers are listed in the cash payments journal when the transactions are recorded. (The preparation of checks and the use of a checking account will be discussed in Chapter 23.)

Recording Transactions in the Cash Payments Journal

Observe the following about the entries in the cash payments journal of Modern Appliance Distributors.

- The entries for April 2, 3, and 25 involve payments for cash purchases of equipment. There was also a payment on April 5 for a cash purchase of supplies. The amount of each payment is recorded in the Other Accounts Debit column and the Cash Credit column. The Other Accounts Debit column must be used because there are no special columns for the Warehouse Equipment, Office Equipment, and Supplies accounts.
- The entries for April 4, 9, and 24 involve payments that were made to settle invoices owed for credit purchases. The payment on April 4 was made after the discount period. Since there was no discount, the amount is recorded in the Accounts Payable Debit column and the Cash Credit column. The payments on April 9 and 24 were made in time to take advantage of the discounts. The total of each of these invoices is recorded in the Accounts Payable Debit column. The amount of the discount is recorded in the Purchases Discount Credit column. The amount of cash actually paid is recorded in the Cash Credit column.
- The entries for April 11 and 17 involve payments for cash purchases of merchandise. The amounts are recorded in the Merchandise Purchases Debit column and the Cash Credit column.
- The entries for April 12, 14, 19, and 30 involve payments for expenses. The amounts are recorded in the Other Accounts Debit column (because there are no special columns for the expense accounts) and the Cash Credit column.
- The second entry for April 30 involves a payment for a cash withdrawal by the owner. The amount is recorded in the Other Accounts Debit column (since the journal does not include a special column for the Ann Lang, Drawing account) and the Cash Credit column.

Unlike the general journal, the cash payments journal makes it possible to enter each payment on a single line. However, the same accounts are used and equal debits and credits are still recorded for each payment.

The information needed to journalize cash payments usually comes from the checkbook of a business. For example, the following three check stubs provided the information for the entries of April 2, 3, and 4 in the cash payments journal of Modern Appliance Distributors.

The form of the cash payments journal varies from business to business. For example, some firms add columns for expense accounts that they use often in recording cash payments. The number of columns used and the headings must suit the needs of each business.

Posting From the Cash Payments Journal

During the month, the amounts in the Other Accounts Debit column are posted individually to the general ledger accounts named in the entries. The posting of the April 2 entry to the Warehouse Equipment account is shown below. The rest of the entries in the Other Accounts Debit column are posted in the same way.

At the end of each month, all the money columns of the cash payments journal are added and checked for accuracy.

Debit Totals: $3,500 + $2,410 + $6,705 = $12,615
Credit Totals: $51 + $12,564 = $12,615

After the equality of the debits and credits is proved, the column totals are entered and the cash payments journal is ruled. Then the totals are posted to the general ledger accounts named in the column headings. As these postings are made, the account numbers are written in parentheses below the totals in the journal. The total of the Other Accounts Debit column is, of course, not posted because the amounts were posted individually during the month. Thus an X is placed in parentheses below this total. The abbreviation CP and the journal page number are entered in the general ledger accounts to identify the postings from the cash payments journal.

Posting From Cash Payments Journal
- During month, post individual debits from Other Accounts column.
- At end of month, post totals of rest of columns.

The Cash Payments Journal 113

Cash — No. 101

DATE	EXPLANATION	POST. REF.	DEBIT	DATE	EXPLANATION	POST. REF.	CREDIT
19X1 Apr. 1		J1	6000.00	19X1 Apr. 30		CP1	12564.00
30		CR1	10158.00				

Accounts Payable — No. 202

DATE	EXPLANATION	POST. REF.	DEBIT	DATE	EXPLANATION	POST. REF.	CREDIT
19X1 Apr. 30		CP1	3500.00	19X1 Apr. 1		J1	2200.00
				30		P1	6850.00

Merchandise Purchases — No. 501

DATE	EXPLANATION	POST. REF.	DEBIT	DATE	EXPLANATION	POST. REF.	CREDIT
19X1 Apr. 30		P1	6850.00				
30		CP1	2410.00				

Purchases Discount — No. 504

DATE	EXPLANATION	POST. REF.	DEBIT	DATE	EXPLANATION	POST. REF.	CREDIT
				19X1 Apr. 30		CP1	51.00

Posting Reference for Cash Payments Journal: The letters *CP* and the journal page number.

Notice that four postings of column totals and ten individual postings were made to transfer the information from the cash payments journal to the general ledger. However, when the general journal was used for recording cash payments, 32 separate postings were needed.

The General Journal

The general journal is used for entries that cannot be made in the special journals.

Although Modern Appliance Distributors has set up special journals for sales, purchases, cash receipts, and cash payments, it will still keep the general journal. This journal will now be used for any entries that cannot be made in the special journals. For example, the opening entry and closing entries must be recorded in the general journal. Credit purchases and sales of permanent assets such as equipment must also be recorded in the general journal.

Chapter Summary

☐ The cash payments journal is a special journal that is used for recording a business's cash payments. It groups together all entries for these transactions.

☐ A cash payments journal increases the efficiency of an accounting system by eliminating repetitious journalizing and posting.

☐ The cash payments journal usually has several special money columns that simplify the recording of routine entries. These columns are for the accounts that a

114 Accounting Fundamentals

business uses most often to record its cash payments, such as Accounts Payable, Merchandise Purchases, Purchases Discount, and Cash. A column called Other Accounts is also set up for debits to accounts for which there are no special columns.
- ☐ The source of information for entries in the cash payments journal is usually the checkbook of a business.
- ☐ The totals of the debits and credits must be equal for each transaction recorded in the cash payments journal.
- ☐ The debits in the Other Accounts column are posted individually during the month to the general ledger accounts indicated in the journal entries. The totals of the rest of the columns are posted at the end of the month to the general ledger accounts named in the column headings.
- ☐ The accuracy of the column totals must be checked before they are posted.
- ☐ After special journals are added to an accounting system, there is still a need for the general journal. This journal must be used for any entries that cannot be made in the special journals.

Checking Your Knowledge

BUSINESS APPLICATION

Problem 17-1. During the month of July, the Garden Shop, a retailer of plants, had the cash payments transactions listed at the right. Do the following work for the business.

1. Open general ledger accounts for Cash 101; Supplies 114; Accounts Payable 202; Jane Gold, Drawing 302; Merchandise Purchases 501; Purchases Discount 504; Wages Expense 511; and Miscellaneous Expense 512. Use the forms on page 67 of the workbook.

2. Enter the July 1 balances in the following accounts: Cash, $7,892.65; Accounts Payable, $867.85.

3. Record each of the transactions in the cash payments journal. Use the journal form on page 68 of the workbook.

4. Post the items in the Other Accounts Debit column individually to the general ledger accounts named in the entries.

5. Pencil-foot the column totals of the cash payments journal and prove their accuracy. (Use the cross-footing method.)

6. Enter the column totals and rule the cash payments journal.

7. Post the column totals to the general ledger accounts that are affected.

July 2 Issued Check 464 for $235.85 to Plants, Inc. to pay Invoice 1026.
5 Issued Check 465 for $125.50 to make a cash purchase of wrapping paper. (Debit Supplies.)
6 Issued Check 466 for $400 to make a cash purchase of merchandise.
10 Issued Check 467 for $20 to pay the telephone bill. (Debit Miscellaneous Expense.)
12 Issued Check 468 for $97 to Drew & Hall to pay Invoice 721 ($100), less discount ($3).
15 Issued Check 469 for $800 for a cash withdrawal by Jane Gold, the owner.
20 Issued Check 470 for $990.25 to make a cash purchase of merchandise.
24 Issued Check 471 for $294 to Wong's Nursery to pay Invoice 589 ($300), less discount ($6).
25 Issued Check 472 for $37.50 to pay the electric bill. (Debit Miscellaneous Expense.)
28 Issued Check 473 for $7.35 to make a cash purchase of office supplies. (Debit Miscellaneous Expense.)
30 Issued Check 474 for $300 to make a cash purchase of merchandise.
31 Issued Check 475 for $500 to pay the monthly wages of the salesclerk.

MANAGERIAL ANALYSIS

Case 17. David Hoffman owns a wholesale business that sells building supplies. The accounting system of this business was recently converted to special journals. Hoffman would like to know why all purchases of merchandise are not recorded in the cash payments journal. He also does not understand why his accountant set up an Other Accounts column in the cash payments journal instead of providing special money columns for all accounts that might be used.

1. How would you explain why the cash payments journal cannot be used for recording all purchases of merchandise?

2. Why is it not practical for the cash payments journal to include special money columns for all accounts that might be used in recording the business's cash payments?

The Accounts Receivable Ledger

All the accounting systems discussed in previous chapters contained a single ledger—the general ledger. However, many businesses also use other types of ledgers. These ledgers do not replace the general ledger. They are intended to increase the efficiency of the accounting system and provide additional information to management.

During April, Modern Appliance Distributors made sales on credit to several customers. These transactions were recorded in the sales journal. When invoices became due during the month, the business received checks from credit customers. The amounts collected from credit customers were recorded in the cash receipts journal. At the end of April, after the totals of these two special journals were posted to the general ledger, the Accounts Receivable account showed the following information.

- The total amount owed by credit customers at the beginning of the month ($1,000).
- The total increase in accounts receivable as a result of sales made to credit customers during the month ($2,760). This amount was posted from the sales journal.
- The total decrease in accounts receivable as a result of cash collected from credit customers during the month ($1,150). This amount was posted from the cash receipts journal.
- The balance still owed by credit customers at the end of the month ($2,610). This amount is found by subtracting the total credits ($1,150) from the total debits ($3,760).

SALES JOURNAL FOR MONTH OF April 19X1					PAGE 1
DATE	INVOICE NO.	SOLD TO	TERMS	✓	AMOUNT
19X1 Apr. 30		Total	Debit 112 Credit 401	✓✓	2760 00

The Accounts Receivable Ledger **117**

CASH RECEIPTS JOURNAL FOR MONTH OF April 19 X1   PAGE 1

DATE	EXPLANATION	DEBITS CASH	DEBITS SALES DISCOUNT	✓	CREDITS ACCOUNTS RECEIVABLE	CREDITS SALES REVENUE	OTHER ACCOUNTS ACCOUNT TITLE	POST. REF.	AMOUNT
19X1 Apr. 30	Totals	10158 00	12 00		1150 00	7020 00			2000 00
		(101)	(403)		(112)	(401)			(X)

Accounts Receivable   NO. 112

DATE	EXPLANATION	POST. REF.	DEBIT	DATE	EXPLANATION	POST. REF.	CREDIT
19X1 Apr. 1		J1	1000 00	19X1 Apr. 30		CR1	1150 00
30	2,610.00	S1	2760 00				

Although the owner, Ann Lang, knows that $2,610 is the total amount still owed by credit customers, she does not know who owes this money. She also does not know how much each customer owes. To find this information, Ann Lang would have to look at all the entries in the sales journal and compute the total amount sold to each customer during the month. Then she would have to check through the cash receipts journal and compute the total amount collected from each customer. The difference between the two totals would be the amount still owed by each customer. This method is inefficient and time-consuming, and it can easily lead to errors.

A better way to know how much money is owed by credit customers is to use a separate account for each one. Most businesses do not keep these accounts in the general ledger. Instead, they place all accounts for credit customers in another ledger called the *accounts receivable ledger*. Since the general ledger is the business's main ledger, the accounts receivable ledger is referred to as a *subsidiary ledger*.

The accountant for Modern Appliance Distributors has set up an accounts receivable ledger for the business. One of the accounts from this ledger is shown below. Notice that a *balance ledger form* with three money columns is used. This form provides a continuous record of the account balance. Whenever a transaction is posted, the current balance is entered in the Balance column.

Accounts Receivable Ledger: Ledger that contains accounts for credit customers.

Subsidiary Ledger: Ledger used for a single group of accounts.

Balance Ledger Form: Form of ledger account that always shows the account balance.

NAME: Capitol Appliance Store
ADDRESS: 164 Bond Street
Austin, TX 78750   TERMS: 2/10, n/30

DATE	DESCRIPTION	POST. REF.	DEBIT	CREDIT	BALANCE
19X1 Apr. 7	Invoice 541	S1	250 00		250 00
17		CR1		250 00	— 00
29	Invoice 544	S1	880 00		880 00

118   Accounting Fundamentals

Posting to the Accounts Receivable Ledger

Entries are usually posted to the accounts receivable ledger on a daily basis so that the balances can be kept up to date. First, the entries from the sales journal are posted to this ledger. Then, the entries from the Accounts Receivable Credit column of the cash receipts journal are posted.

During April, the following journal entries were posted to the accounts receivable ledger of Modern Appliance Distributors.

SALES JOURNAL FOR MONTH OF April 19X1   PAGE 1

DATE	INVOICE NO.	SOLD TO	TERMS	✓	AMOUNT
19X1 Apr. 7	541	Capitol Appliance Store	2/10, n/30	✓	250 00
16	542	Bristol Appliances	2/10, n/30	✓	350 00
24	543	Economy Appliance Center	1/10, n/60	✓	1280 00
29	544	Capitol Appliance Store	2/10, n/30	✓	880 00
30		Total	Debit 112 Credit 401	✓✓	2760 00

CASH RECEIPTS JOURNAL FOR MONTH OF April 19X1   PAGE 1

DATE	EXPLANATION	CASH (Dr)	SALES DISCOUNT (Dr)	✓	ACCOUNTS RECEIVABLE (Cr)	SALES REVENUE (Cr)	OTHER ACCOUNTS - ACCOUNT TITLE	POST. REF.	AMOUNT
19X1 Apr. 1	Balance on hand, $6,000								
8	Town Appliance Center—Inv. 540	550 00		✓	550 00				
17	Capitol Appliance Store—Inv. 541	245 00	5 00	✓	250 00				
24	Bristol Appliances—Inv. 542	343 00	7 00	✓	350 00				
30	Totals	10 138 00	12 00		1 150 00	7 020 00			2 000 00
		(101)	(403)		(112)	(401)			(X)

The accounts receivable ledger contains four accounts, which are arranged in alphabetic order. As the business gains more credit customers, additional accounts will be placed in the accounts receivable ledger.

NAME: Bristol Appliances
ADDRESS: 3946 Duncan Expressway
Dallas, TX 75221   TERMS: 2/10, n/30

DATE	DESCRIPTION	POST. REF.	DEBIT	CREDIT	BALANCE
19X1 Apr. 16	Invoice 542	S1	350 00		350 00
24		CR1		350 00	— 00

The Accounts Receivable Ledger   **119**

NAME: Capitol Appliance Store
ADDRESS: 164 Bond Street
Austin, TX 78750
TERMS: 2/10, n/30

DATE	DESCRIPTION	POST. REF.	DEBIT	CREDIT	BALANCE
19X1 Apr. 7	Invoice 541	S1	250 00		250 00
17		CR1		250 00	— 00
29	Invoice 544	S1	880 00		880 00

NAME: Economy Appliance Center
ADDRESS: 24 Hilton Shopping Mall
San Antonio, TX 78201
TERMS: 1/10, n/60

DATE	DESCRIPTION	POST. REF.	DEBIT	CREDIT	BALANCE
19X1 Apr. 1	Balance	✓			450 00
24	Invoice 543	S1	1280 00		1730 00

NAME: Town Appliance Center
ADDRESS: 1919 South Fairfax Avenue
Waco, TX 76706
TERMS: 2/10, n/30

DATE	DESCRIPTION	POST. REF.	DEBIT	CREDIT	BALANCE
19X1 Apr. 1	Balance	✓			550 00
8		CR1		550 00	— 00

Observe the following about the accounts receivable ledger.

- When the ledger is set up, the name, address, and terms for each credit customer are recorded on a separate ledger sheet or card. If any of the customers owe money, an entry is made to record the amount owed. This is the opening balance for the customer's account. On April 1, two credit customers owed money to Modern Appliance Distributors. The Economy Appliance Center owed $450, and the Town Appliance Center owed $550. Look at the accounts for these customers to see how the balances were recorded. The same type of entry must be made when a ledger sheet is filled, and the customer's balance must be transferred to another sheet.
- Each transaction listed in the sales journal is posted individually to a customer's account in the accounts receivable ledger. For example, notice how the entry of April 7 was posted to the account for the Capitol Appliance Store. The date of the transaction (April 7) is written in the Date column of the account. The invoice number (541) is written in the Description column to identify the sale. The amount ($250) is entered in the Debit column. (Remember that sales on credit increase the asset Accounts Receivable. Increases in assets are recorded as debits.) Because the Capitol Appliance Store had no previous balance, the amount of the sale is also written in the Balance column. Thus the balance of this customer's account on April 7 is $250. The abbreviation *S* and the journal page number (1) are written in the Posting

Reference column of the account to identify the source of the entry. A check mark is placed in the sales journal to show that the transaction was posted.
- If a customer's account already has a balance when a sale on credit is posted, the amount of the sale must be added to the previous balance. For example, study the April 24 entry in the account for the Economy Appliance Center. The amount of the sale ($1,280) is recorded in the Debit column. Then, this amount is added to the previous balance to find the current balance ($1,280 + $450 = $1,730). The current balance is entered in the Balance column.
- Each transaction listed in the Accounts Receivable Credit column of the cash receipts journal is posted individually to a customer's account in the accounts receivable ledger. For example, notice how the entry of April 8 was posted to the account for the Town Appliance Center. The date of the transaction (April 8) is written in the Date column. The amount ($550) is entered in the Credit column. (Remember that cash received from credit customers decreases the asset Accounts Receivable. Decreases in assets are recorded as credits.) The amount of cash received is subtracted from the previous balance to find the current balance ($550 − $550 = $0). The current balance is entered in the Balance column. Because the customer paid in full, the current balance of this account is zero. The abbreviation *CR* and the journal page number (1) are written in the Posting Reference column of the account. A check mark is placed in the cash receipts journal to indicate that the transaction was posted.

Proving the Accounts Receivable Ledger

At the end of the month, the accounts receivable ledger must be proved. To do this, a *schedule of accounts receivable* is used.

1. The name and account balance for each customer with an unpaid balance are listed on the schedule form. This information is taken from the accounts receivable ledger.
2. The balances are added to find the total amount owed by all credit customers.
3. The total of the schedule of accounts receivable is compared with the balance of the Accounts Receivable account in the general ledger. The two amounts must be the same.

Schedule of Accounts Receivable: List of customers' accounts with unpaid balances.

Modern Appliance Distributors
Schedule of Accounts Receivable
April 30, 19X1

Customer	Balance
Capitol Appliance Store	880 00
Economy Appliance Center	1730 00
Total	2610 00

The Accounts Receivable Ledger

DATE	EXPLANATION	POST. REF.	DEBIT	DATE	EXPLANATION	POST. REF.	CREDIT
19X1 Apr. 1		J1	1 000 00	19X1 Apr. 30		CR1	1 150 00
30	2,610.00	S1	2 760 00				

Accounts Receivable — NO. 112

Control Account: General ledger account that summarizes the balances of accounts in a subsidiary ledger.

The Accounts Receivable account in the general ledger is known as a *control account* because its balance is the total amount owed by all credit customers. This account provides a link between the subsidiary ledger and the general ledger. Notice that the total of the schedule of accounts receivable prepared at Modern Appliance Distributors on April 30 agrees with the balance of the Accounts Receivable account on that date.

Preparing the Statements of Account

Statement of Account: A periodic statement sent to a customer to report the balance that the customer owes.

Most businesses send a *statement of account* to each credit customer at regular intervals. Usually, this statement is prepared monthly. Some statements of account show all transactions with the customer during the period and the balance at the end of the period. Other statements of account show only the customer's final balance. The information for preparing the statement of account is taken from the accounts receivable ledger. Some businesses simply make a photocopy of the customer's ledger account and mail it to the customer.

The following statement of account was prepared at Modern Appliance Distributors on April 30. Compare this statement with the ledger account for the Capitol Appliance Store on page 120.

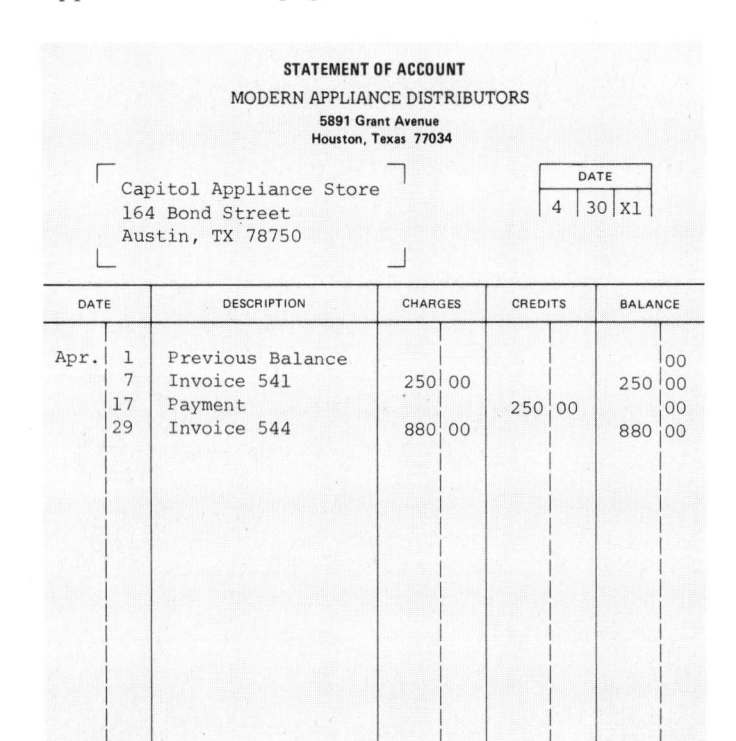

STATEMENT OF ACCOUNT
MODERN APPLIANCE DISTRIBUTORS
5891 Grant Avenue
Houston, Texas 77034

Capitol Appliance Store
164 Bond Street
Austin, TX 78750

DATE: 4 / 30 / X1

DATE	DESCRIPTION	CHARGES	CREDITS	BALANCE
Apr. 1	Previous Balance			00
7	Invoice 541	250 00		250 00
17	Payment		250 00	00
29	Invoice 544	880 00		880 00

122 Accounting Fundamentals

Aging the Accounts Receivable

The management of a business needs to know whether credit customers are paying their invoices on time. To obtain this information, some firms prepare a *schedule of accounts receivable by age* at the end of each month. The following procedure is used.

Schedule of Accounts Receivable by Age: List of customers' account balances classified according to age of unpaid invoices.

1. The name and account balance of each customer are listed on the schedule.
2. The entries in the accounts receivable ledger are examined to see which invoices are current and which are past due. The amounts of the current invoices are recorded in the Current column of the schedule.
3. The past-due invoices are classified according to how many days have gone by since the credit period ended. The amounts of these invoices are recorded in the Past Due columns of the schedule.
4. The columns of the schedule are added to find the total of the current invoices and the total of the past-due invoices in each age group.

Standard Auto Products
Schedule of Accounts Receivable by Age
November 30, 19X1

Account With	Balance	Current	Past Due 1-30 Days	Past Due 31-60 Days	Past Due Over 60 Days
Berger's Service Station	1335 00	910 00	425 00		
Elmwood Auto Service	250 00			150 00	100 00
Harry's Garage	770 00	770 00			
Paragon Auto Repairs	1100 00	800 00	100 00	200 00	
Totals	3455 00	2480 00	525 00	350 00	100 00

The schedule of accounts receivable by age shown above was prepared at Standard Auto Products, a distributor of auto parts and supplies. The information on this schedule helps management to control credit.

Chapter Summary

- The accounts receivable ledger is a subsidiary ledger that contains individual accounts for all credit customers.
- Transactions with the credit customers are posted to the accounts receivable ledger from the sales journal and the cash receipts journal. This posting work is usually done on a daily basis so that the balances can always be kept up to date.
- At the end of each month, the accounts receivable ledger is proved. First, a schedule of accounts receivable is prepared. Then, the total of the schedule is compared with the balance of the Accounts Receivable account in the general ledger. The two amounts should be the same.
- The Accounts Receivable account in the general ledger is a control account. It shows the total amount owed by all credit customers.
- A statement of account is sent to each credit customer. In most businesses, this is done monthly. The statement of account reports the balance due from the customer.
- Some businesses prepare a schedule of accounts receivable by age. This schedule shows whether customers are paying their invoices on time.

Checking Your Knowledge

BUSINESS APPLICATION

Problem 18-1. Sherman Hardware Distributors is setting up an accounts receivable ledger for its credit customers.

1. Open an account for Central Hardware Store, 110 Elm Street, Rockdale, IL 60436. The terms of sale are n/30. The balance on July 1 is $320. Use the ledger account form on page 69 of the workbook.

2. Assume that the sales journal and the cash receipts journal show the following transactions with Central Hardware Store during July and August. Enter these transactions in the customer's account. The posting references are S7 for the sales journal and CR10 for the cash receipts journal.

July 6 Sold merchandise for $250 on credit, Invoice 121.
10 Received $320 in cash on account.
15 Sold merchandise for $120 on credit, Invoice 205.
Aug. 1 Received $250 in cash for Invoice 121.
7 Sold merchandise for $475 on credit, Invoice 309.
12 Received $120 in cash for Invoice 205.
28 Sold merchandise for $200 on credit, Invoice 454.

Problem 18-2. The Chang Grocery Company is a distributor of food products. It has four credit customers. Do the following work for the business.

1. Open general ledger accounts for Cash 101, Accounts Receivable 111, Equipment 113, Sales Revenue 401, and Sales Discount 403. Use the forms on page 71 of the workbook.

2. Enter the February 1 balances in the following general ledger accounts: Cash, $5,000; Accounts Receivable, $755; and Equipment, $8,280.

3. Open accounts for the following credit customers in the accounts receivable ledger. The terms of sale are 2/20, n/60. Use the forms on pages 72 and 73 of the workbook.

Alvarez Grocery
125 West 15th Street
Greenville, PA 16125

Hill Supermarket
1520 Rodney Avenue
Greenville, PA 16125

Corner Food Mart
1630 Maple Street
Greenville, PA 16125

May's Grocery
1725 Adams Drive
Greenville, PA 16125

4. Enter the February 1 balances in the customers' accounts: Alvarez Grocery, $250; Corner Food Mart, $125; Hill Supermarket, $300; and May's Grocery, $80.

5. Make a memorandum entry of the beginning cash balance in the cash receipts journal. Use the journal form on page 70 of the workbook.

6. Record each of the transactions given below and on the next page in the sales journal or the cash receipts journal. Use the journal forms on pages 69 and 70 of the workbook.

7. Post the entries from the sales journal and from the Accounts Receivable Credit column of the cash receipts journal to the accounts receivable ledger.

8. Post the entries from the Other Accounts Credit column of the cash receipts journal to the general ledger.

9. Pencil-foot the cash receipts journal and prove its accuracy. Use the cross-footing method.

10. Total and rule the sales journal and the cash receipts journal.

11. Post the total of the sales journal and the totals of the cash receipts journal.

12. Prepare a schedule of accounts receivable, dated February 28. Use the form on page 73 of the workbook. Compare the total of the schedule with the balance of the Accounts Receivable account in the general ledger. The two amounts should be the same.

13. Prepare a detailed statement of account for May's Grocery as of February 28. Use the form on page 74 of the workbook.

Feb. 3 Sold merchandise for $200 on credit to Hill Supermarket, Invoice 76.
4 Received $245 in cash from Alvarez Grocery for Invoice 72 ($250), less discount ($5).
6 Sold merchandise for $100 on credit to May's Grocery, Invoice 77.
7 Sold merchandise for $1,562.30 in cash during the first week of February.
10 Sold merchandise for $90 on credit to Corner Food Mart, Invoice 78.
11 Sold merchandise for $180 on credit to Alvarez Grocery, Invoice 79.
12 Received $122.50 in cash from Corner Food Mart for Invoice 73 ($125), less discount ($2.50).

124 Accounting Fundamentals

Feb. 13 Sold merchandise for $210 on credit to May's Grocery, Invoice 80.

14 Sold merchandise for $1,240.62 in cash during the second week of February.

17 Received $294 in cash from Hill Supermarket for Invoice 74 ($300), less discount ($6).

18 Sold merchandise for $285 on credit to Corner Food Mart, Invoice 81.

18 Received $78.40 in cash from May's Grocery for Invoice 75 ($80), less discount ($1.60).

21 Sold merchandise for $981.20 in cash during the third week of February.

24 Sold a used typewriter for $65 in cash.

24 Sold merchandise for $200 on credit to Alvarez Grocery, Invoice 82.

Feb. 24 Received $98 in cash from May's Grocery for Invoice 77 ($100), less discount ($2).

25 Received $200 in cash from Hill Supermarket for Invoice 76.

26 Sold merchandise for $150 on credit to May's Grocery, Invoice 83.

27 Sold merchandise for $170 on credit to Hill Supermarket, Invoice 84.

27 Received $176.40 in cash from Alvarez Grocery for Invoice 79 ($180), less discount ($3.60).

28 Received $205.80 in cash from May's Grocery for Invoice 80 ($210), less discount ($4.20).

28 Sold merchandise for $1,142.15 in cash during the fourth week of February.

MANAGERIAL ANALYSIS

Case 18. Shortly after the end of June, the accountant for the Style Clothing Store found that the posting to the accounts receivable ledger was not up to date. As a result of the delay in posting, the monthly statements of account could not be prepared and mailed on time.

1. What kinds of problems may a business have if its accounts receivable ledger is not kept up to date?

2. Why is it important to send the statements of account promptly each month?

The Accounts Payable Ledger

The use of an accounts receivable ledger improves the efficiency of an accounting system. A record of all transactions with credit customers is available in one place. Also, the amount owed by each credit customer is always known. Similar benefits can be achieved for accounts payable by setting up an accounts payable ledger.

During April, Modern Appliance Distributors purchased merchandise on credit. The entries for these purchases were recorded in the purchases journal. The business made payments to creditors from time to time during the month. As checks were issued to creditors, the payments were recorded in the cash payments journal. At the end of April, after the totals were posted from these two special journals, the Accounts Payable account in the general ledger showed the following information.

- The total amount owed to creditors at the beginning of the month ($2,200).
- The total increase in accounts payable as a result of purchases made from creditors during the month ($6,850). This amount was posted from the purchases journal.
- The total decrease in accounts payable as a result of payments to creditors during the month ($3,500). This amount was posted from the cash payments journal.
- The balance owed to creditors at the end of the month ($5,550). This amount is found by subtracting the total debits ($3,500) from the total credits ($9,050).

Accounts Payable — No. 202

DATE	EXPLANATION	POST. REF.	DEBIT	DATE	EXPLANATION	POST. REF.	CREDIT
19X1 Apr. 30		CP1	3500 00	19X1 Apr. 1		J1	220 00
				30		P1	6850 00
					5,550.00		9050 00

It is important for Ann Lang, the owner, to know the total amount that the business owes to creditors. However, to manage operations effectively, she needs more information about the accounts payable. She must know which creditors the money is owed to and how much must be paid to each one. A good way to obtain such information is to keep separate accounts for the individual creditors. These accounts are usually placed in a subsidiary ledger called the *accounts payable ledger*.

The accountant for Modern Appliance Distributors has set up an accounts payable ledger for the business. The form used for these accounts is a balance ledger form with three money columns.

Accounts Payable Ledger: Ledger that contains accounts for creditors.

Posting to the Accounts Payable Ledger

Entries are usually posted to the accounts payable ledger on a daily basis so that the balances can be kept up to date. First, the entries from the purchases journal are posted to this ledger. Then, the entries from the Accounts Payable Debit column of the cash payments journal are posted.

During April, the following journal entries were posted to the accounts payable ledger of Modern Appliance Distributors.

PURCHASES JOURNAL for month of April 19X1 — PAGE 1

DATE	PURCHASED FROM	INVOICE NO.	INVOICE DATE	TERMS	✓	AMOUNT
19X1 Apr. 3	Allied Manufacturing Co.	1167	4/1/X1	3/10, n/60	✓	1500 00
18	Arco Electric Products	6281	4/16/X1	1/10, n/30	✓	600 00
24	Dow Industries	327	4/21/X1	3/10 EOM	✓	1750 00
30	Allied Manufacturing Co.	1191	4/23/X1	3/10, n/60	✓	3000 00
30	Total *Debit 501 / Credit 202*				✓	6850 00

CASH PAYMENTS JOURNAL for month of April 19X1 — PAGE 1

DATE	CHECK NO.	EXPLANATION	✓	ACCOUNTS PAYABLE	MERCHANDISE PURCHASES	ACCOUNT TITLE	POST. REF.	AMOUNT	PURCHASES DISCOUNT	CASH
19X1 Apr. 4	103	Reliable Products — Inv. B2895	✓	1400 00						1400 00
9	105	Allied Manufacturing Co. — Inv. 1167	✓	1500 00					45 00	1455 00
24	112	Arco Electric Products — Inv. 6281	✓	600 00					6 00	594 00
30		Totals		3500 00	2410 00			6705 00	51 00	12564 00
				(202)	(501)			(X)	(504)	(101)

The Accounts Payable Ledger 127

The accounts payable ledger contains four accounts, which are arranged alphabetically. As the business expands operations and deals with more creditors, additional accounts will be placed in the accounts payable ledger.

NAME: Allied Manufacturing Company
ADDRESS: 1268 Water Street
Chicago, IL 60628
TERMS: 3/10, n/60

DATE	DESCRIPTION	POST. REF.	DEBIT	CREDIT	BALANCE
19X1 Apr. 3	Invoice 1167, 4/1/X1	P1		1500 00	1500 00
9		CP1	1500 00		—00
30	Invoice 1191, 4/23/X1	P1		3000 00	3000 00

NAME: Arco Electric Products
ADDRESS: 129 Melbourne Street
Louisville, KY 40225
TERMS: 1/10, n/30

DATE	DESCRIPTION	POST. REF.	DEBIT	CREDIT	BALANCE
19X1 Apr. 18	Invoice 6281, 4/16/X1	P1		600 00	600 00
24		CP1	600 00		—00

NAME: Dow Industries
ADDRESS: 62 Bradshaw Avenue
San Antonio, TX 78201
TERMS: 3/10 EOM

DATE	DESCRIPTION	POST. REF.	DEBIT	CREDIT	BALANCE
19X1 Apr. 24	Invoice 327, 4/21/X1	P1		1750 00	1750 00

NAME: Reliable Products
ADDRESS: 3221 Lincoln Expressway
Dallas, TX 75207
TERMS: n/60

DATE	DESCRIPTION	POST. REF.	DEBIT	CREDIT	BALANCE
19X1 Apr. 1	Balance	✓			2200 00
4		CP1	1400 00		800 00

Observe the following about the accounts payable ledger.

- When the ledger is set up, each creditor's name, address, and terms are recorded on a separate ledger sheet or card. If the business owes money to any of the creditors, an entry is made to record the amount owed. This is the opening balance of the creditor's account. On April 1, Modern Appliance Distributors owed $2,200 to a creditor—Reliable Products. Look at the account for this creditor to see how the balance was recorded. The same type of

entry must be made when a ledger sheet is completed and the creditor's balance must be transferred to another sheet.
- Each transaction listed in the purchases journal is posted individually to a creditor's account in the accounts payable ledger. For example, notice how the entry of April 3 was posted to the account for Allied Manufacturing Company. The date of the transaction (April 3) is written in the Date column of the account. The invoice number (1167) and the invoice date (4/1/X1) are written in the Description column. This information identifies the purchase. The amount ($1,500) is entered in the Credit column of the account. (Remember that purchases on credit increase the liability Accounts Payable. Increases in liabilities are recorded as credits.) Because there was no previous balance for Allied Manufacturing Company, the amount of the purchase is also written in the Balance column. Thus the balance of this creditor's account on April 3 is $1,500. The abbreviation *P* and the journal page number (1) are written in the Posting Reference column of the account to identify the source of the entry. A check mark is placed in the purchases journal to show that the transaction was posted.
- If a creditor's account already has a balance when a purchase is posted, the amount of the purchase must be added to the previous balance. For example, suppose that a purchase of $1,000 is posted to the account of Dow Industries on May 1. The amount of the purchase would be recorded in the Credit column. Then this amount would be added to the previous balance to find the new balance ($1,750 + $1,000 = $2,750). The new balance would be entered in the Balance column.
- Each transaction listed in the Accounts Payable Debit column of the cash payments journal is posted individually to a creditor's account in the accounts payable ledger. For example, notice how the entry of April 4 was posted to the account for Reliable Products. The date of the transaction (April 4) is written in the Date column. The amount ($1,400) is entered in the Debit column. (Remember that payments to creditors decrease the liability Accounts Payable. Decreases in liabilities are recorded as debits.) The amount of the payment is subtracted from the previous balance to find the new balance ($2,200 − $1,400 = $800). The new balance is entered in the Balance column. The abbreviation *CP* and the journal page number (1) are written in the Posting Reference column of the account. A check mark is placed in the cash payments journal to show that the transaction was posted.

Proving the Accounts Payable Ledger

At the end of the month, the accounts payable ledger must be proved. A *schedule of accounts payable* is used to do this.

1. The name and account balance for each creditor with an unpaid balance are listed on the schedule form. This information is taken from the accounts payable ledger.
2. The balances are added to find the total amount owed to all creditors.
3. The total of the schedule of accounts payable is compared with the balance of the Accounts Payable account in the general ledger. The two amounts must be the same.

Schedule of Accounts Payable: List of creditors' accounts with unpaid balances.

The Accounts Payable account in the general ledger is a control account because its balance is the total amount owed to all creditors. This account provides a link between the subsidiary ledger and the general ledger. Notice that the total of the schedule of accounts payable prepared at Modern Appliance Distributors on April 30 agrees with the balance of the Accounts Payable account on that date.

Modern Appliance Distributors
Schedule of Accounts Payable
April 30, 19X1

Creditor	Balance
Allied Manufacturing Co.	3000 0
Dow Industries	1750 00
Reliable Products	800 00
Total	5550 00

Accounts Payable   NO. 202

DATE	EXPLANATION	POST. REF.	DEBIT	DATE	EXPLANATION	POST. REF.	CREDIT
19X1 Apr. 30		CP1	3500 00	19X1 Apr. 1		J1	220 00
				30	5,550.00	P1	6850 00
							9050 00

Chapter Summary

☐ The accounts payable ledger is a subsidiary ledger that contains individual accounts for all creditors.

☐ Transactions with the creditors are posted to the accounts payable ledger from the purchases journal and the cash payments journal. This posting is usually done on a daily basis so that the balances can be kept up to date.

☐ At the end of each month, the accounts payable ledger is proved. First, a schedule of accounts payable is prepared. Then, the total of the schedule is compared with the balance of the Accounts Payable account in the general ledger. The two amounts should be the same.

☐ The Accounts Payable account in the general ledger is a control account. It shows the total amount owed to all creditors.

Checking Your Knowledge

BUSINESS APPLICATION

Problem 19-1. Dawson's Furniture Store is setting up an accounts payable ledger for its creditors.

1. Open an account for Homecraft Manufacturing Company, 121 Clark Street, Mankato, MN 56001. The terms are n/30. The balance on September 1 is $562.85. Use the ledger account form on page 75 of the workbook.

2. Assume that the purchases journal and the cash payments journal show the following transactions with Homecraft Manufacturing Company during September and October. Enter these transactions in the creditor's account. The posting references are P9 for the purchases journal and CP12 for the cash payments journal.

Sept. 10 Purchased merchandise for $387 on credit; Invoice 4321, dated 9/8/X1.
     15 Paid $562.85 on account.
     26 Purchased merchandise for $720 on credit; Invoice 4537, dated 9/24/X1.
Oct. 3 Purchased merchandise for $693.45 on credit; Invoice 4762, dated 10/1/X1.
     5 Paid $387 for Invoice 4321.

Oct. 19 Purchased merchandise for $1,288.30 on credit; Invoice 5023, dated 10/17/X1.
21 Paid $720 for Invoice 4537.
28 Paid $693.45 for Invoice 4762.

Problem 19-2. Best Photo Products is a retail store that sells cameras and film. Most of the merchandise is purchased on credit from four suppliers. Do the following work for the business.

1. Open general ledger accounts for Cash 101; Equipment 113; Accounts Payable 202; Dale Wood, Drawing 302; Merchandise Purchases 501; and Purchases Discount 504. Use the forms on page 77 of the workbook.

2. Enter the September 1 balances in the following general ledger accounts: Cash, $8,760; Equipment, $2,550; and Accounts Payable, $1,875.

3. Open accounts for the following creditors in the accounts payable ledger. Use the forms on pages 78 and 79 of the workbook.

A & B Photo Supplies 2681 Wilson Street Chicago, IL 60614 Terms: 2/20, n/60	Santos Camera Company 237 Western Drive Camden, NJ 08106 Terms: 3/10, n/30
Nakata Corporation 1317 Eighth Avenue Greenville, PA 16125 Terms: n/30	Wayne Distributors 1816 Grand Avenue Des Moines, IA 50309 Terms: 2/10 EOM

4. Enter the September 1 balances in the creditors' accounts: A & B Photo Supplies, $350; Nakata Corporation, $475; Santos Camera Company, $650; and Wayne Distributors, $400.

5. Record each of the transactions given at the right in the purchases journal or the cash payments journal. Use the journal forms on pages 75 and 76 of the workbook.

6. Post the entries from the purchases journal and from the Accounts Payable Debit column of the cash payments journal to the accounts payable ledger.

7. Post the entries from the Other Accounts Debit column of the cash payments journal to the general ledger.

8. Pencil-foot the cash payments journal, and prove its accuracy. Use the cross-footing method.

9. Total and rule the purchases journal and the cash payments journal.

10. Post the total of the purchases journal and the totals of the cash payments journal.

11. Prepare a schedule of accounts payable, dated September 30. Use the form on page 79 of the workbook. Compare the total of the schedule with the balance of the Accounts Payable account in the general ledger. The two amounts should be the same.

Sept. 4 Purchased merchandise for $280 on credit from A & B Photo Supplies; Invoice 1361, dated 9/1/X1, terms 2/20, n/60.
4 Issued Check 221 for $630.50 to Santos Camera Company to pay Invoice 716 ($650), less discount ($19.50).
5 Issued Check 222 for $343 to A & B Photo Supplies to pay Invoice 1282 ($350), less discount ($7).
6 Purchased merchandise for $295 on credit from Nakata Corporation; Invoice 382, dated 9/4/X1, terms n/30.
8 Issued Check 223 for $392 to Wayne Distributors to pay Invoice 4512 ($400), less discount ($8).
10 Purchased merchandise for $600 on credit from Wayne Distributors; Invoice 4623, dated 9/8/X1, terms 2/10 EOM.
12 Issued Check 224 for $300 to make a cash purchase of merchandise.
13 Purchased merchandise for $175 on credit from Santos Camera Company; Invoice 797, dated 9/11/X1, terms 3/10, n/30.
15 Issued Check 225 for $285 to purchase a new typewriter for the office.
17 Purchased merchandise for $340 on credit from Nakata Corporation; Invoice 441, dated 9/15/X1, terms n/30.
18 Issued Check 226 for $475 to Nakata Corporation to pay Invoice 291.
19 Issued Check 227 for $274.40 to A & B Photo Supplies to pay Invoice 1361 ($280), less discount ($5.60).
20 Purchased merchandise for $330 on credit from A & B Photo Supplies; Invoice 1558, dated 9/18/X1, terms 2/20, n/60.
20 Issued Check 228 for $169.75 to Santos Camera Company to pay Invoice 797 ($175), less discount ($5.25).
22 Purchased merchandise for $718 on credit from Wayne Distributors; Invoice 4830, dated 9/20/X1, terms 2/10 EOM.
25 Purchased merchandise for $467 on credit from Nakata Corporation; Invoice 506, dated 9/23/X1, terms n/30.
26 Purchased merchandise for $222 on credit from Santos Camera Company; Invoice 882, dated 9/24/X1, terms 3/10, n/30.
27 Issued Check 229 for $200 to make a cash purchase of merchandise.
29 Issued Check 230 for $950 for a cash withdrawal by Dale Wood, the owner.
30 Issued Check 231 for $295 to Nakata Corporation to pay Invoice 382.

The Accounts Payable Ledger **131**

MANAGERIAL ANALYSIS

Case 19. The manager of the Olympic Ski Shop has learned that the business's accounting clerk has not been paying invoices within the discount period. In some cases, the accounting clerk does not issue checks for invoices until several days after the end of the credit period.

1. What problems will these payment procedures cause for the business?
2. What steps could be taken to make sure that invoices are paid on time?

SUMMARY PROBLEM III

Chapters 12–19. On February 1, 19X1, John Rossi opened the Star Lumber Company. The chart of accounts for this business is shown below. Mr. Rossi sells on credit to five local builders. He also makes cash sales to individuals who need lumber for home repairs and improvements. Most of the merchandise is purchased on credit from four suppliers. Do the following work for the business.

1. Make the opening entry in the general journal. Use the journal form on page 81 of the workbook. Mr. Rossi's investment consisted of the following items: Cash, $9,000; Merchandise Inventory, $17,000; Office Equipment, $1,250; and Warehouse Equipment, $2,500. Post the opening entry. The general ledger accounts appear on pages 85–89 of the workbook. These accounts have already been opened.

2. Make a memorandum entry of the cash balance in the cash receipts journal. Use the journal form on page 82 of the workbook.

3. Record each of the transactions given on page 133 in the proper journal. The business has a general journal and special journals for sales, purchases, cash receipts, and cash payments. The journal forms appear on pages 81–84 of the workbook.

4. Post individual entries to the subsidiary ledgers as follows. Post to the accounts receivable ledger from the sales journal and the Accounts Receivable Credit column of the cash receipts journal. Post to the accounts payable ledger from the purchases journal and the Accounts Payable Debit column of the cash payments journal. The subsidiary ledger accounts appear on pages 90 and 91 of the workbook.

5. Post individual entries to the general ledger from the Other Accounts Credit column of the cash receipts journal and the Other Accounts Debit column of the cash payments journal.

STAR LUMBER COMPANY
Chart of Accounts

Assets
101	Cash
112	Accounts Receivable
114	Merchandise Inventory
115	Supplies
116	Office Equipment
117	Accum. Depr.—Office Equip.*
118	Warehouse Equipment
119	Accum. Depr.—Warehouse Equip.*

Liabilities
202	Accounts Payable

Owner's Equity
301	John Rossi, Capital
302	John Rossi, Drawing
399	Revenue and Expense Summary*

Revenue
401	Sales Revenue
403	Sales Discount

Costs and Expenses
501	Merchandise Purchases
504	Purchases Discount
511	Advertising Expense
512	Delivery Expense
513	Depr. Exp.—Office Equip.*
514	Depr. Exp.—Warehouse Equip.*
515	Miscellaneous Expense
516	Rent Expense
517	Supplies Expense*
518	Utilities Expense
519	Wages Expense

*These accounts will be used in Summary Problem IV.

6. At the end of the month, pencil-foot the cash receipts journal and the cash payments journal. Then, prove the accuracy of these journals. Use the cross-footing method.

7. At the end of the month, total and rule the sales journal, the purchases journal, the cash receipts journal, and the cash payments journal.

8. Post the totals from the journals.

9. Prepare a schedule of accounts receivable and a schedule of accounts payable. Use the forms on page 92 of the workbook. Compare the totals of the schedules with the balances of the control accounts in the general ledger. The amounts should be the same.

10. Prepare a trial balance. Use the form on page 93 of the workbook.

11. Save all working papers for use in Summary Problem IV, which follows Chapter 22.

Feb. 1 Issued Check 101 for $450 to pay monthly rent for the building in which the business is located.

2 Sold merchandise for $875 on credit to Jensen Builders; Invoice A1, terms 2/10, n/30.

2 Issued Check 102 for $137.50 to pay for supplies that will be used in the business.

3 Purchased merchandise for $1,300 on credit from Mountain Lumber Company; Invoice 1364, dated 2/1/X1, terms 3/20, n/60.

3 Sold merchandise for $862.50 on credit to Warren Developers; Invoice A2, terms 1/10, n/60.

5 Purchased merchandise for $773.50 on credit from Delta Forest Products; Invoice 3176, dated 2/3/X1, terms 2/10, n/30.

5 Issued Check 103 for $10.75 to pay for typewriter repairs. (Debit Miscellaneous Expense.)

6 Issued Check 104 for $150 to pay for a newspaper advertisement.

6 Sold merchandise for $972.55 in cash during the first week of February.
Be sure to post the individual entries as specified in Parts 4 and 5 of the instructions for this problem.

8 Sold merchandise for $645.80 on credit to Betterbilt Homes; Invoice A3, terms 2/10, n/30.

10 Received $857.50 in cash from Jensen Builders for Invoice A1 ($875), less discount ($17.50).

11 Sold merchandise for $256.50 on credit to Cross Company; Invoice A4, terms 2/10, n/30.

11 Issued Check 105 for $758.03 to Delta Forest Products for Invoice 3176 ($773.50), less discount ($15.47).

13 Received $853.87 in cash from Warren Developers for Invoice A2 ($862.50), less discount ($8.63).

13 Sold merchandise for $993.30 in cash during the second week of February.
Be sure to post the individual entries.

15 Purchased merchandise for $725 on credit from Lane Building Materials; Invoice 1738, dated 2/13/X1, terms n/30.

15 Issued Check 106 for $750 to pay wages of employees for the first half of the month.

17 Sold merchandise for $1,250 on credit to Williams Construction Company; Invoice A5, terms 1/10, n/60.

18 Issued Check 107 for $1,261 to Mountain Lumber Company for Invoice 1364 ($1,300), less discount ($39).

19 Issued Check 108 for $110 to purchase an electronic calculator for the office.

20 Received $251.37 in cash from Cross Company for Invoice A4 ($256.50), less discount ($5.13).

20 Sold merchandise for $1,464.80 in cash during the third week of February.
Be sure to post the individual entries.

22 Issued Check 109 for $30 to pay for cleaning service. (Debit Miscellaneous Expense.)

22 Sold a used file cabinet for $20 in cash.

22 Issued Check 110 for $680.20 to make a cash purchase of merchandise.

23 Purchased merchandise for $465 on credit from Doral Lumber Company; Invoice 786, dated 2/20/X1, terms 2/10 EOM.

24 Purchased merchandise for $875 on credit from Delta Forest Products; Invoice 3285, dated 2/22/X1, terms 2/10, n/30.

25 Sold merchandise for $330.45 on credit to Betterbilt Homes; Invoice A6, terms 2/10, n/30.

25 Issued Check 111 for $410 to make a cash purchase of merchandise.

26 Purchased merchandise for $923.75 on credit from Lane Building Materials; Invoice 1801, dated 2/24/X1, terms n/30.

27 Issued Check 112 for $165 to pay for delivery service during the month.

27 Issued Check 113 for $75 to pay the electric bill.

27 Issued Check 114 for $48.52 to pay the telephone bill.

27 Issued Check 115 for $750 to pay wages of employees for the second half of the month.

27 Issued Check 116 for $1,000 for a cash withdrawal by John Rossi, the owner.

27 Sold merchandise for $1,410 in cash during the fourth week of February.
Be sure to post the individual entries.

Worksheet Adjustments

Worksheet: Form used to plan the preparation of financial statements.

Worksheet Adjustments: Amounts entered on the worksheet to provide information not yet recorded in the general ledger.

During each accounting period, journal entries are posted to the subsidiary ledgers and the general ledger. At the end of the period, the accuracy of the ledgers must be checked. First, the accounts receivable ledger and the accounts payable ledger are proved. Then, a trial balance is prepared to verify the equality of the debits and credits in the general ledger. The trial balance is usually entered on a *worksheet*.

Certain information about a business's operations does not appear in the general ledger at the time the trial balance is prepared. For example, the value of supplies used at Modern Appliance Distributors during April has not yet been recorded. *Adjustments* are entered on the worksheet to provide such information for the financial statements.

This chapter deals with adjustments for supplies used, expired insurance, and depreciation of fixed assets. The adjustment for merchandise inventory is discussed in the next chapter.

The Need for Adjustments

Matching Principle: All revenues earned and all expenses incurred during an accounting period must be used to determine the net income or net loss.

It is important that the financial statements present a complete picture of the results of operations and the condition of the business. For example, the income statement should report all revenues earned and all expenses incurred during the accounting period. The revenues and expenses for the period must be matched in order to accurately determine the net income or net loss. This is the *matching principle* of accounting.

The trial balance prepared at Modern Appliance Distributors on April 30 does not include the amounts of several expenses incurred during April—the expenses for supplies and for depreciation of the delivery equipment, the warehouse equipment, the office equipment, and the building. (Refer to the trial balance on page 137.) Worksheet adjustments must be recorded so that these expenses can be shown on the income statement and subtracted from the revenues for the month.

The Adjustment for Supplies Used

On April 5, Modern Appliance Distributors bought shipping cartons for $320. Because these supplies were expected to last for several months, their cost was debited to an asset account—the Supplies account. During April, some of the cartons were used to send goods to customers. A count was made of the remaining cartons on April 30. This figure was multiplied by the unit cost of the cartons to find the amount of supplies on hand. The amount of supplies used was then determined as shown below.

Cost of supplies bought during month	$320
Less: inventory of supplies at end of month	240
Cost of supplies used during the month	$ 80

134 Accounting Fundamentals

The cost of supplies used is an expense for the business. An adjustment must therefore be made to transfer this amount from the Supplies account to the Supplies Expense account. Look at the worksheet on page 137. Notice that it has a special section for adjustments. The adjustment for supplies used is recorded in this section by entering a debit of $80 on the line for the Supplies Expense account and a credit of $80 on the line for the Supplies account. The letter *A* is placed next to both of the $80 figures to identify the two parts of the adjustment.

The Adjustment for Expired Insurance

Many businesses buy insurance to protect their property. The amount paid for insurance usually covers a year or several years. For this reason, the amount is debited to an asset account—the Prepaid Insurance account. At the end of each accounting period, part of the insurance protection is used up. An adjustment must be made to charge the cost of the expired insurance to the operations of the period. This adjustment consists of a debit to the Insurance Expense account and a credit to the Prepaid Insurance account.

Modern Appliance Distributors does not yet have any insurance. However, suppose that the owner pays $600 on May 1 for an insurance policy that covers a year. At the end of each month during the year, an adjustment of $50 will be made for expired insurance: $600 ÷ 12(months) = $50.

The Adjustment for Depreciation

Businesses usually own certain types of property that will be used for a number of years. Land, buildings, machinery, and equipment are examples of such property. These items are called *fixed assets*, or *plant assets*.

All fixed assets except land eventually wear out, become obsolete, or become inadequate. They have a limited *useful life*. When a fixed asset is purchased, an estimate is made of its useful life. This estimate is usually based on the previous experience of the business, common practices in its industry, and guidelines published by the Internal Revenue Service.

Fixed assets are used in operating a business. They provide services that the business needs to function effectively and earn revenues. The cost of each fixed asset must therefore be charged to operations. During the useful life of the fixed asset, every accounting period bears part of the cost. The amount that is charged to operations is called *depreciation*.

Adjustments are made on the worksheet to record depreciation. Modern Appliance Distributors has four types of fixed assets. Information about the depreciation of these fixed assets is given in the following table.

Fixed Assets: Property that will be used for a number of years.

Useful Life: Estimated number of years that a fixed asset will be used in a business.

Depreciation: Part of the cost of a fixed asset that is charged to operations.

Purchase Date	Description	Original Cost	−	Disposal Value	=	Total Depreciation	÷	Estimated Useful Life	=	Yearly Depreciation	÷ 12 =	Monthly Depreciation
19X1 April 1	Delivery Equipment	$ 4,000	−	$ 640	=	$ 3,360	÷	7 years	=	$480	÷ 12 =	$40
1	Warehouse Equipment	$ 1,000	−	$ 100	=	$ 900	÷	15 years	=	$ 60	÷ 12 =	$ 5
2	Warehouse Equipment	3,000	−	300	=	2,700	÷	15 years	=	180	÷ 12 =	15
		$ 4,000								$240		$20
1	Office Equipment	$ 200	−	$ 20	=	$ 180	÷	5 years	=	$ 36	÷ 12 =	$ 3
3	Office Equipment	600	−	120	=	480	÷	10 years	=	48	÷ 12 =	4
25	Office Equipment	70	−	10	=	60	÷	5 years	=	12	÷ 12 =	1*
		$ 870								$ 96		$ 8**
1	Building	$20,000	−	$2,000	=	$18,000	÷	25 years	=	$720	÷ 12 =	$60

*During April, no depreciation can be taken on this item because it was purchased after April 15.
**The monthly depreciation recorded for office equipment in April is $7.

Disposal Value: Amount that a business expects to receive when a fixed asset is traded in or scrapped.

To determine the depreciation for a fixed asset, it is necessary to consider its cost, its disposal value, and its estimated useful life. The *disposal value* is the amount that the business expects to receive when the fixed asset is traded in or scrapped. The computation of monthly depreciation for the delivery equipment owned by Modern Appliance Distributors is shown below.

Depreciation of Delivery Equipment

$4,000 (original cost) − $640 (disposal value) = $3,360 (total depreciation)
$3,360 (total depreciation) ÷ 7 (estimated years of useful life) = $480 (yearly depreciation)
$480 (yearly depreciation) ÷ 12 (months) = $40 (monthly depreciation)

Straight-Line Method: Method of computing depreciation in which an equal amount is assigned to each period.

There are several methods of computing depreciation. The one used by Modern Appliance Distributors is called the *straight-line method*. With this method, an equal amount of depreciation is assigned to each accounting period.

Depreciation is an expense. When the adjustments for depreciation are recorded, the amount for each fixed asset is debited to a separate expense account. Look at the worksheet on page 137. The adjustments for depreciation are identified by the letters *B* through *E*. Notice that there is also a separate accumulated depreciation account for each fixed asset. This account is credited for the amount of depreciation.

Book Value: Portion of the original cost of a fixed asset that has not yet been depreciated.

The accumulated depreciation account will provide a record of the total depreciation taken on the fixed asset. The *book value* of the fixed asset can be computed at any time by subtracting the total depreciation from the original cost. For example, the book value of the delivery equipment owned by Modern Appliance Distributors is $3,960 after the depreciation for April is recorded. The Delivery Equipment account shows an original cost of $4,000. The Accumulated Depreciation—Delivery Equipment account shows total depreciation of $40.

Contra Account: Account used to record deductions from the balance of a related account.

The accumulated depreciation account is called a *contra account* because it has a credit balance, which is contrary to the normal balance for an asset account. As you have seen, the credit balance of the accumulated depreciation account is subtracted from the debit balance of the related fixed asset account to determine book value.

After the adjustments for depreciation are entered on the worksheet of Modern Appliance Distributors, the Adjustments section can be completed. (The adjustment for merchandise inventory will not appear in this section of the worksheet.) The amounts in the two columns of the Adjustments section are added. The total of the Debit column should equal the total of the Credit column.

The Adjusted Trial Balance Section

Notice that Modern Appliance Distributors uses a worksheet with ten money columns. This worksheet provides a special section for preparing an adjusted trial balance. The amounts in the Adjustments section must be combined with the amounts in the Trial Balance section to determine the new account balances. The following procedure is used to complete the Adjusted Trial Balance section.

- If an account has a debit in the Trial Balance section and no adjustment, the same debit is entered in the Adjusted Trial Balance section. Refer to the following accounts on the worksheet of Modern Appliance Distributors: Cash; Accounts Receivable; Merchandise Inventory; Delivery Equipment; Warehouse Equipment; Office Equipment; Building; Ann Lang, Drawing; Sales Discount; Merchandise Purchases; Miscellaneous Expense; Truck Expense; and Wages Expense.
- If an account has a debit in the Trial Balance section and a debit in the Adjustments section, the two amounts are added. The total is entered in the Debit column of the Adjusted Trial Balance section. This does not occur on the worksheet of Modern Appliance Distributors.

136 Accounting Fundamentals

Modern Appliance Distributors
Worksheet
Month Ended April 30, 19X1

ACCT. NO.	ACCOUNT NAME	TRIAL BALANCE DR.	TRIAL BALANCE CR.	ADJUSTMENTS DR.	ADJUSTMENTS CR.	ADJUSTED TRIAL BALANCE DR.	ADJUSTED TRIAL BALANCE CR.	INCOME STATEMENT DR.	INCOME STATEMENT CR.	BALANCE SHEET DR.	BALANCE SHEET CR.
101	Cash	3594.00				3594.00					
112	Accts. Receivable	2610.00				2610.00					
114	Mdse. Inventory	5000.00				5000.00					
115	Supplies	320.00			(A) 80.00	240.00					
116	Delivery Equip.	4000.00				4000.00					
117	Accum Depr.-Del. Eq.				(B) 40.00		40.00				
118	Warehouse Equip.	4000.00				4000.00					
119	Accum Depr.-Whse. Eq.				(C) 20.00		20.00				
120	Office Equip.	870.00				870.00					
121	Accum Depr.-Off. Eq.				(D) 7.00		7.00				
122	Building	20000.00				20000.00					
123	Accum. Depr.-Bldg.				(E) 60.00		60.00				
202	Accts. Payable		5550.00				5550.00				
301	A. Lang, Capital		3700.00				3700.00				
302	A. Lang, Drawing	900.00				900.00					
401	Sales Revenue		9780.00				9780.00				
403	Sales Discount	12.00				12.00					
501	Mdse. Purchases	9260.00				9260.00					
504	Purchases Discount		51.00				51.00				
511	Misc. Expense	105.00				105.00					
512	Truck Expense	90.00				90.00					
513	Wages Expense	1620.00				1620.00					
514	Supplies Expense			(A) 80.00		80.00					
515	Depr. Exp.-Del. Eq.			(B) 40.00		40.00					
516	Depr. Exp.-Whse. Eq.			(C) 20.00		20.00					
517	Depr. Exp.-Off. Eq.			(D) 7.00		7.00					
518	Depr. Exp.-Bldg.			(E) 60.00		60.00					
	Totals	52381.00	52381.00	207.00	207.00	52508.00	52508.00				

- If an account has a debit in the Trial Balance section and a credit in the Adjustments section, the amount of the credit is subtracted from the amount of the debit. The difference is entered in the Debit column of the Adjusted Trial Balance section. Refer to the worksheet of Modern Appliance Distributors. The Supplies account had a debit balance of $320 when the trial balance was prepared. This account was credited for $80 to record the adjustment for supplies used. There is now a debit balance of $240 ($320 − $80 = $240).
- If an account has no balance in the Trial Balance section and a debit in the Adjustments section, the same debit is entered in the Adjusted Trial Balance section. Refer to the Supplies Expense account and all the depreciation expense accounts on the worksheet of Modern Appliance Distributors.
- If an account has a credit in the Trial Balance section and no adjustment, the same credit is entered in the Adjusted Trial Balance section. Refer to the following accounts on the worksheet of Modern Appliance Distributors: Accounts Payable; Ann Lang, Capital; Sales Revenue; and Purchases Discount.
- If an account has a credit in the Trial Balance section and a credit in the Adjustments section, the two amounts are added. The total is entered in the

Credit column of the Adjusted Trial Balance section. This does not occur on the worksheet of Modern Appliance Distributors.
- If an account has a credit in the Trial Balance section and a debit in the Adjustments section, the amount of the debit is subtracted from the amount of the credit. The difference is entered in the Credit column of the Adjusted Trial Balance section. This does not occur on the worksheet of Modern Appliance Distributors.
- If an account has no balance in the Trial Balance section and a credit in the Adjustments section, the same credit is entered in the Adjusted Trial Balance section. Refer to the accumulated depreciation accounts on the worksheet of Modern Appliance Distributors.

After all account balances are recorded in the Adjusted Trial Balance section, the columns are added to prove the equality of the debits and credits.

Chapter Summary

☐ At the end of the accounting period, certain information about operations does not appear in the general ledger. Adjustments must be entered on the worksheet to provide this information for the financial statements.

☐ The financial statements should present a complete picture of the results of operations and the condition of the business. The revenues and expenses for the accounting period must be matched in order to determine the net income or net loss accurately.

☐ An adjustment must be made for the amount of supplies used during the accounting period. The Supplies Expense account is debited, and the Supplies account is credited.

☐ When insurance is purchased, the amount paid is debited to an asset account—the Prepaid Insurance account. At the end of each accounting period, an adjustment must be made for expired insurance. The Insurance Expense account is debited, and the Prepaid Insurance account is credited.

☐ The cost of a fixed asset must be charged to operations during its estimated useful life. Each accounting period must bear part of the cost. The amount charged to operations is called depreciation.

☐ An adjustment must be made to record depreciation for each fixed asset at the end of the accounting period. A depreciation expense account is debited, and an accumulated depreciation account is credited.

☐ An accumulated depreciation account provides a record of the total depreciation taken on a fixed asset. The balance of this account is subtracted from the balance of the related fixed asset account to find the book value of the fixed asset.

☐ The ten-column worksheet has special sections for recording adjustments and preparing an adjusted trial balance. The amounts in the Trial Balance section and the Adjustments section are combined. The resulting account balances are entered in the Adjusted Trial Balance section.

Checking Your Knowledge

BUSINESS APPLICATION

Problem 20-1. Jane Peck started Valley Furniture Wholesalers on March 1, 19X1. At the end of the first month's operations, the general ledger accounts had the balances shown on page 139.

Account No.	Account Name	Balance
101	Cash	$ 4,500
112	Accounts Receivable	1,750
114	Merchandise Inventory	20,000
115	Supplies	350
116	Delivery Equipment	8,500
117	Accum. Depr.—Delivery Equip.	
118	Warehouse Equipment	3,000
119	Accum. Depr.—Warehouse Equip.	
202	Accounts Payable	2,700
301	Jane Peck, Capital	36,080
302	Jane Peck, Drawing	1,000
401	Sales Revenue	18,860
403	Sales Discount	310
501	Merchandise Purchases	16,000
504	Purchases Discount	290
511	Depr. Expense—Delivery Equip.	
512	Depr. Expense—Warehouse Equip.	
513	Rent Expense	800
514	Supplies Expense	
515	Wages Expense	1,500
516	Utilities Expense	220

1. Set up the worksheet for the month ended March 31, 19X1. Enter the heading, the account numbers, and the account names. Use the form on page 95 of the workbook.

2. Prepare the Trial Balance section of the worksheet.

3. Prepare the Adjustments section of the worksheet. During the month, supplies costing $90 were used. The depreciation for the delivery equipment is $75, and the depreciation for the warehouse equipment is $40.

4. Prepare the Adjusted Trial Balance section of the worksheet. Make sure that the debits and credits are equal.

5. Save the worksheet for use in Problem 21-1.

Problem 20-2. Roy McVay owns Southern Toy Distributors. The business uses a quarterly accounting period. On December 31, 19X1, the general ledger accounts had the balances shown below.

1. Set up the worksheet for the quarter ended December 31, 19X1. Enter the heading, the account numbers, and the account names. Use the form on page 96 of the workbook.

2. Prepare the Trial Balance section of the worksheet.

3. Prepare the Adjustments section of the worksheet. The supplies on hand total $280. (Compute the amount of supplies used during the quarter.) The depreciation for the office equipment is $30, and the depreciation for the warehouse equipment is $90.

4. Prepare the Adjusted Trial Balance section of the worksheet. Make sure that the debits and credits are equal.

5. Save the worksheet for use in Problem 21-2.

Account No.	Account Name	Balance
101	Cash	$ 3,575
112	Accounts Receivable	2,140
114	Merchandise Inventory	18,600
115	Supplies	420
116	Office Equipment	1,960
117	Accum. Depr.—Office Equip.	210
118	Warehouse Equipment	6,000
119	Accum. Depr.—Warehouse Equip.	630
202	Accounts Payable	1,760
301	Roy McVay, Capital	28,325
302	Roy McVay, Drawing	3,200
401	Sales Revenue	34,000
403	Sales Discount	620
501	Merchandise Purchases	22,500
504	Purchases Discount	430
511	Depr. Expense—Office Equip.	
512	Depr. Expense—Warehouse Equip.	
513	Rent Expense	1,950
514	Supplies Expense	
515	Wages Expense	3,840
516	Utilities Expense	550

MANAGERIAL ANALYSIS

Case 20. The Fleet Delivery Service has six trucks. Paul Lazlo, the owner of the business, cannot understand why it is necessary to record depreciation for the trucks. He also cannot understand why the cost of a one-year insurance policy that he purchased recently was debited to the Prepaid Insurance account rather than the Insurance Expense account.

1. How would you explain why depreciation should be recorded for the trucks?

2. How would you explain why the Prepaid Insurance account is used for recording the purchase of the insurance policy?

21

Inventory, Cost of Goods Sold, and Statements

When the trial balance is prepared, the general ledger shows the amount of merchandise inventory that was on hand at the start of the accounting period. However, changes occurred in this inventory during the period because goods were purchased and sold. Before the worksheet can be completed, it is necessary to update the information about merchandise inventory. An adjustment must be made to record the amount on hand at the end of the period.

Updating the Merchandise Inventory

On April 1, Modern Appliance Distributors had a merchandise inventory totaling $5,000. This amount was the *beginning inventory* for the period. Remember that no entries are made in the Merchandise Inventory account during an accounting period. For this reason, the balance of the account is still $5,000 on April 30 when the business's trial balance is prepared. The following steps must be taken to determine the amount of the *ending inventory*.

1. An actual count is made of all merchandise on hand. This count is called a *physical inventory*.
2. Information about each item is listed on an *inventory sheet*. This information includes the stock number, description, quantity, and unit cost.
3. The total cost for each item is computed. The unit cost is multiplied by the quantity. The resulting amount is entered on the inventory sheet.
4. The total cost for the merchandise on hand is computed. This is done by adding the costs of all the items. The overall total is recorded at the bottom of the last inventory sheet.

The following inventory sheet shows that Modern Appliance Distributors had an ending inventory of $7,500 on April 30.

The Merchandise Inventory account must now be adjusted on the worksheet. The balance of the account must be updated so that it will show the ending inventory

Beginning Inventory: Merchandise on hand at the start of an accounting period.

Ending Inventory: Merchandise on hand at the end of an accounting period.

Physical Inventory: An actual count of merchandise on hand.

Inventory Sheet: Form listing information about a physical inventory.

STOCK NO.	DESCRIPTION	QUANTITY	UNIT COST	TOTAL
3624 L	Ace microwave oven	8	130 00	1,040 00
2376 X	Mason food processor	24	23 50	564 00
			TOTAL	7,500 00

INVENTORY SHEET April 30, 19X1 No. 6
COUNTED BY GS   COMPUTED BY JR
LISTED BY RV   CHECKED BY AL

for the period. This is done in two steps. (Refer to the worksheet below after you read each step.)

1. The amount of the beginning inventory ($5,000) is charged to the period's operations by recording it in the Debit column of the Income Statement section. The entry is made on the line for the Merchandise Inventory account.
2. The amount of the ending inventory ($7,500) is included in the period's figures by recording it in the Credit column of the Income Statement section and the Debit column of the Balance Sheet section. This entry also appears on the line for the Merchandise Inventory account. The two parts of the entry are identified by the letter *F*.

The amounts of the beginning inventory and the ending inventory are needed to determine the cost of goods sold for the accounting period. This information is shown on the income statement. (The cost of goods sold is discussed later in this chapter.)

Completing the Ten-Column Worksheet

After the adjustment for merchandise inventory is made, the worksheet can be completed.

Modern Appliance Distributors
Worksheet
Month Ended April 30, 19X1

ACCT. NO.	ACCOUNT NAME	TRIAL BALANCE DR.	TRIAL BALANCE CR.	ADJUSTMENTS DR.	ADJUSTMENTS CR.	ADJUSTED TRIAL BALANCE DR.	ADJUSTED TRIAL BALANCE CR.	INCOME STATEMENT DR.	INCOME STATEMENT CR.	BALANCE SHEET DR.	BALANCE SHEET CR.
101	Cash	3594 00				3594 00				3594 00	
112	Accts. Receivable	2610 00				2610 00				2610 00	
114	Mdse. Inventory	5000 00				5000 00		5000 00	(F) 7500 00	(F) 7500 00	
115	Supplies	320 00			(A) 80 00	240 00				240 00	
116	Delivery Equip.	4000 00				4000 00				4000 00	
117	Accum. Depr.-Del. Eq.				(B) 40 00		40 00				40 00
118	Warehouse Equip.	4000 00				4000 00				4000 00	
119	Accum. Depr.-Whse. Eq.				(C) 20 00		20 00				20 00
120	Office Equip.	870 00				870 00				870 00	
121	Accum. Depr.-Off. Eq.				(D) 7 00		7 00				7 00
122	Building	20000 00				20000 00				20000 00	
123	Accum. Depr.-Bldg.				(E) 60 00		60 00				60 00
202	Accts. Payable		5550 00				5550 00				5550 00
301	A. Lang, Capital		37000 00				37000 00				37000 00
302	A. Lang, Drawing	900 00				900 00				900 00	
401	Sales Revenue		9780 00				9780 00		9780 00		
403	Sales Discount	12 00				12 00		12 00			
501	Mdse. Purchases	9260 00				9260 00		9260 00			
504	Purchases Discount		51 00				51 00		51 00		
511	Misc. Expense	105 00				105 00		105 00			
512	Truck Expense	90 00				90 00		90 00			
513	Wages Expense	1620 00				1620 00		1620 00			
514	Supplies Expense			(A) 80 00		80 00		80 00			
515	Depr. Exp.-Del. Eq.			(B) 40 00		40 00		40 00			
516	Depr. Exp.-Whse. Eq.			(C) 20 00		20 00		20 00			
517	Depr. Exp.-Off. Eq.			(D) 7 00		7 00		7 00			
518	Depr. Exp.-Bldg.			(E) 60 00		60 00		60 00			
	Totals	52381 00	52381 00	207 00	207 00	52508 00	52508 00	16294 00	17331 00	43714 00	42677 00
	Net Income							1037 00			1037 00
								17331 00	17331 00	43714 00	43714 00

Inventory, Cost of Goods Sold, and Statements

The following procedures are used to prepare the last two sections of the worksheet—the Income Statement section and the Balance Sheet section.

1. The balances of the asset, liability, and owner's equity accounts shown in the Adjusted Trial Balance section are recorded in the proper columns of the Balance Sheet section. The only exception is the balance of the Merchandise Inventory account. The Balance Sheet section already contains the ending inventory as a result of the adjustment.
2. The balances of the revenue, cost, and expense accounts shown in the Adjusted Trial Balance section are recorded in the proper columns of the Income Statement section. The beginning inventory and the ending inventory also appear in this section because of the adjustment. (The inclusion of the inventory figures makes it possible to compute the net income.)
3. The columns of the Income Statement section and the Balance Sheet section are totaled.
4. The total of the Debit column in the Income Statement section is subtracted from the total of the Credit column ($17,331 − $16,294 = $1,037). The difference is the net income for the period. This amount is entered below the total of the Debit column. (There is a net income because the revenue exceeds the costs and expenses. However, if the total of the Debit column is greater than the total of the Credit column, the business has a net loss. The costs and expenses exceed the revenue.)
5. The total of the Credit column in the Balance Sheet section is subtracted from the total of the Debit column ($43,714 − $42,677 = $1,037). The difference is the same as the net income. This amount is entered below the total of the Credit column.
6. The columns of the Income Statement section and the Balance Sheet section are totaled again. In each section, the debits and credits should be equal.

Preparing the Financial Statements

The completed worksheet provides the information needed for the financial statements.

The Income Statement. The income statement shown on page 143 was prepared at Modern Appliance Distributors. It reports the results of operations for the month ended April 30.

The income statement for Modern Appliance Distributors consists of five sections.

- The Operating Revenue section shows information about the revenue that the business earned from selling merchandise during the accounting period. The sales discount is subtracted from the sales revenue to find the net sales ($9,780 − $12 = $9,768).
- The Cost of Goods Sold section shows information about the cost that the business incurred for the merchandise it sold during the accounting period. The beginning inventory and the net purchases are added to find the total merchandise that was available for sale ($5,000 + $9,209 = $14,209). Then, the ending inventory is subtracted from the total merchandise available for sale to find the cost of goods sold ($14,209 − $7,500 = $6,709).
- The Gross Profit on Sales section contains a single figure. This figure is the difference between the revenue earned from selling merchandise and the cost of that merchandise. The amount of gross profit on sales for the accounting period is computed by subtracting the cost of goods sold from the net sales ($9,768 − $6,709 = $3,059).
- The Operating Expenses section shows information about the expenses the

business incurred to conduct its operations during the accounting period. The amounts of the individual expenses are added to find the total operating expenses ($2,022).
- The Net Income section contains a single figure. This figure is the business's profit for the accounting period. The total of the operating expenses is subtracted from the gross profit on sales to find the net income ($3,059 − $2,022 = $1,037).

```
                    Modern Appliance Distributors
                           Income Statement
                      Month Ended April 30, 19X1


Operating Revenue
    Sales Revenue                                          $ 9,780
    Less Sales Discount                                         12
    Net Sales                                                            $9,768
Cost of Goods Sold
    Merchandise Inventory, April 1, 19X1                   $ 5,000
    Merchandise Purchases                        $9,260
    Less Purchases Discount                          51
    Net Purchases                                            9,209
    Total Merchandise Available for Sale                   $14,209
    Less Merchandise Inventory, April 30, 19X1               7,500
      Cost of Goods Sold                                              6,709
Gross Profit on Sales                                                 $3,059
Operating Expenses
    Miscellaneous Expense                                  $   105
    Truck Expense                                               90
    Wages Expense                                            1,620
    Supplies Expense                                            80
    Depreciation Expense--Delivery Equipment                    40
    Depreciation Expense--Warehouse Equipment                   20
    Depreciation Expense--Office Equipment                       7
    Depreciation Expense--Building                              60
      Total Operating Expenses                                        2,022
Net Income                                                            $1,037
```

Notice that the income statement for a merchandising business is more complex than the income statement for a service business. A merchandising business must report cost of goods sold and gross profit on sales as well as revenue, expenses, and net income or net loss.

The Statement of Owner's Equity. After the income statement is completed, the statement of owner's equity is prepared. Remember that this financial report shows the changes in owner's equity that occur during an accounting period. The following statement of owner's equity was prepared at Modern Appliance Distributors. It covers the month ended April 30.

The amount of capital at the start of the month ($35,000) and the additional investment made during the month ($2,000) are taken from the capital account in the general ledger. The net income for the month ($1,037) and the owner's withdrawals ($900) come from the worksheet. The rest of the amounts are computed on the statement of owner's equity.

```
                    Modern Appliance Distributors
                      Statement of Owner's Equity
                       Month Ended April 30, 19X1


    Ann Lang, Capital, April 1, 19X1              $35,000
    Additional Investment                           2,000
       Total Investment                           $37,000
    Net Income                          $1,037
    Less Withdrawals                       900
       Net Increase in Owner's Equity                 137
    Ann Lang, Capital, April 30, 19X1             $37,137
```

The Balance Sheet. The following balance sheet was prepared at Modern Appliance Distributors on April 30. It shows the financial position of the business at the end of the accounting period.

```
                    Modern Appliance Distributors
                            Balance Sheet
                           April 30, 19X1

                                Assets

    Current Assets
       Cash                                         $3,594
       Accounts Receivable                           2,610
       Merchandise Inventory                         7,500
       Supplies                                        240
          Total Current Assets                              $13,944

    Fixed Assets
       Delivery Equipment             $ 4,000
       Less Accumulated Depreciation       40   $ 3,960
       Warehouse Equipment            $ 4,000
       Less Accumulated Depreciation       20     3,980
       Office Equipment               $   870
       Less Accumulated Depreciation        7       863
       Building                       $20,000
       Less Accumulated Depreciation       60    19,940
          Total Fixed Assets                               28,743
    Total Assets                                          $42,687


                    Liabilities and Owner's Equity

    Current Liabilities
       Accounts Payable                                    $ 5,550

    Owner's Equity
       Ann Lang, Capital                                    37,137
    Total Liabilities and Owner's Equity                   $42,687
```

144 Accounting Fundamentals

The amounts of the assets and liabilities are taken from the worksheet. The amount of capital comes from the statement of owner's equity. This amount ($37,137) is the capital on April 30 after the net income has been added and the withdrawals have been subtracted.

In accounting, assets are usually classified into two groups: current assets and fixed assets (or plant assets). Liabilities are also classified into two groups: current liabilities and long-term liabilities. Modern Appliance Distributors uses a *classified balance sheet*. This type of balance sheet shows assets and liabilities in groups.

Current assets consist of cash, property that will be turned into cash within a year, and property that will be used up within a year. Modern Appliance Distributors has the following current assets on April 30: cash, accounts receivable, merchandise inventory, and supplies. The accounts receivable will be turned into cash as customers pay their bills. The merchandise inventory will be turned into cash as goods are sold. The supplies will be used up in operations.

As discussed in Chapter 20, *fixed assets* consist of property that a business uses for a number of years. Modern Appliance Distributors has the following fixed assets on April 30: delivery equipment, warehouse equipment, office equipment, and a building. Notice that the balance sheet shows three amounts for each fixed asset: the original cost, the accumulated depreciation, and the book value. The book value is computed on the balance sheet.

Current liabilities are debts that must be paid within a year. Modern Appliance Distributors has a single current liability on April 30: accounts payable.

Long-term liabilities are debts that extend for more than a year. Modern Appliance Distributors does not have any long-term liabilities on April 30. However, suppose that the business had a 20-year mortgage on its building. This debt would be listed on the balance sheet as a long-term liability.

The classified balance sheet helps management to judge the *solvency* of the business—the ability of the business to pay its debts when they become due. For example, management compares the amounts of the current assets and the current liabilities. The current assets will provide the money needed to pay the current liabilities. On April 30, Modern Appliance Distributors has accounts payable of $5,550. However, the cash, accounts receivable, and merchandise inventory total $13,704. Thus the business should be able to pay its debts without difficulty.

Classified Balance Sheet: Type of balance sheet that shows assets and liabilities in groups.

Current Assets: Cash, property that will be turned into cash within a year, and property that will be used up within a year.

Fixed Assets: Property that will be used for a number of years.

Current Liabilities: Debts that must be paid within a year.

Long-Term Liabilities: Debts that extend for more than a year.

Solvency: Ability of a business to pay its debts.

Chapter Summary

- Before the worksheet can be completed, information about the merchandise inventory must be updated. An adjustment must be made to record the ending inventory.
- Determining the ending inventory involves counting all merchandise on hand, listing information about the merchandise on inventory sheets, computing the cost of each item, and computing the total cost of all merchandise.
- The adjustment for merchandise inventory is recorded on the worksheet as follows. First, the amount of the beginning inventory is entered in the Debit column of the Income Statement section. Then, the amount of the ending inventory is entered in the Credit column of the Income Statement section and the Debit column of the Balance Sheet section.
- After the merchandise inventory is adjusted on the worksheet, the Income Statement section and the Balance Sheet section are prepared. The balances for all accounts except the Merchandise Inventory account are transferred from the Adjusted Trial Balance section. The net income is entered below the totals of the Debit column in the Income Statement section and the Credit column in the Balance Sheet section. Then, these sections are totaled again.
- The completed worksheet provides the information needed to prepare the financial statements.

- The income statement for a merchandising business shows cost of goods sold and gross profit on sales as well as revenue, expenses, and net income or net loss.
- The cost of goods sold is computed in the following way. The beginning inventory and the net purchases are added to find the total merchandise available for sale. Then, the ending inventory is subtracted from the total merchandise available for sale.
- The gross profit on sales is computed by subtracting the cost of goods sold from the net sales.
- Assets are classified into two groups. Current assets consist of cash, property that will be turned into cash within a year, and property that will be used up within a year. Fixed assets consist of property that a business will use for a number of years.
- Liabilities are also classified into two groups. Current liabilities are debts that must be paid within a year. Long-term liabilities are debts that extend for more than a year.
- The classified balance sheet shows assets and liabilities in groups.

Checking Your Knowledge

BUSINESS APPLICATION

Problem 21-1. Perform the following activities for Valley Furniture Wholesalers.

1. Complete the worksheet that you started in Problem 20-1. The merchandise inventory on March 31 is $21,325.
2. Prepare an income statement for the month ended March 31, 19X1. Use the form on page 97 of the workbook.
3. Prepare a statement of owner's equity for the month ended March 31, 19X1. Use the form on page 98 of the workbook. The balance of the capital account on March 1 was $33,080. The owner made an additional investment of $3,000 during the month.
4. Prepare a classified balance sheet dated March 31, 19X1. Use the form on page 99 of the workbook.
5. Save the worksheet for use in Problem 22-1.

Problem 21-2. Perform the following activities for Southern Toy Distributors.

1. Complete the worksheet that you started in Problem 20-2. The merchandise inventory on December 31 is $17,390.
2. Prepare an income statement for the quarter ended December 31, 19X1. Use the form on page 100 of the workbook.
3. Prepare a statement of owner's equity for the quarter ended December 31, 19X1. Use the form on page 101 of the workbook. The balance of the capital account on October 1 was $23,325. The owner made an additional investment of $5,000 during the quarter.
4. Prepare a classified balance sheet dated December 31, 19X1. Use the form on page 102 of the workbook.
5. Save the worksheet for use in Problem 22-2.

Problem 21-3. A worksheet for the Delmar Wholesale Grocery Company is shown on page 103 of the workbook. This worksheet contains the trial balance prepared on March 31, 19X1. Perform the following activities for the business.

1. Prepare the Adjustments section of the worksheet. During March, supplies costing $130 were used, and insurance costing $60 expired. The depreciation for the delivery equipment is $150, and the depreciation for the warehouse equipment is $30.
2. Prepare the Adjusted Trial Balance, Income Statement, and Balance Sheet sections of the worksheet. The merchandise inventory on March 31 is $9,800.

MANAGERIAL ANALYSIS

Case 21. Angela Diaz recently opened the Active Sportswear Shop. After the merchandise inventory was counted and computed at the end of the first month, she examined the inventory sheets. She found that the salesclerks had used the selling price of each item rather than the cost price in making their calculations for the merchandise inventory.

1. What effect would this error have on the income statement?

2. What effect would this error have on the balance sheet?

22

Adjusting and Closing the General Ledger

After the financial statements are prepared, adjusting entries must be journalized and posted. The purpose of these entries is to make the amounts in the general ledger agree with the amounts reported on the financial statements. It is also necessary to journalize and post closing entries so that the general ledger will be ready to receive transactions for the next period.

Recording the Adjusting Entries

Adjusting the General Ledger: Making the amounts in the general ledger agree with the amounts on the financial statements.

A business must have a permanent record of the adjustments that appear on the worksheet. The required entries are made in the general journal and then posted to the proper general ledger accounts.

The following general journal shows the adjusting entries recorded at Modern Appliance Distributors on April 30. The amounts were obtained from the Adjustments section of the worksheet. (Refer to the worksheet on page 141.)

GENERAL JOURNAL PAGE 2

DATE	DESCRIPTION OF ENTRY	POST. REF.	DEBIT	CREDIT
19X1 Apr. 30	Supplies Expense	514	80 00	
	Supplies	115		80 00
	Cost of supplies used during April.			
30	Depreciation Expense—Delivery Equipment	515	40 00	
	Accum. Depr.—Delivery Equipment	117		40 00
	Depreciation for April.			
30	Depreciation Expense—Warehouse Equipment	516	20 00	
	Accum. Depr.—Warehouse Equipment	119		20 00
	Depreciation for April.			
30	Depreciation Expense—Office Equipment	517	7 00	
	Accum. Depr.—Office Equipment	121		7 00
	Depreciation for April.			
30	Depreciation Expense—Building	518	60 00	
	Accum. Depr.—Building	123		60 00
	Depreciation for April.			

Accounting Fundamentals

Study the general ledger accounts on pages 150 through 155 to see how the adjusting entries are posted.

Recording the Closing Entries

After the adjusting entries are posted, closing entries must be recorded. These entries reduce the balances of the temporary accounts to zero and transfer the results of operations to the capital account. Also, in many businesses, the Merchandise Inventory account is updated during the closing process.

Closing the General Ledger: Making the general ledger ready to receive the next period's transactions.

The general journal shown below contains the closing entries recorded at Modern Appliance Distributors on April 30. The procedure for making these entries is explained on page 150.

GENERAL JOURNAL — PAGE 2

DATE	DESCRIPTION OF ENTRY	POST. REF.	DEBIT	CREDIT
19X1 Apr. 30	Merchandise Inventory	114	7500.00	
	Sales Revenue	401	9780.00	
	Purchases Discount	504	51.00	
	Revenue and Expense Summary	399		17331.00
	To record ending inventory and close temporary accounts with credit balances.			
30	Revenue and Expense Summary	399	16294.00	
	Merchandise Inventory	114		5000.00
	Sales Discount	403		12.00
	Merchandise Purchases	501		9260.00
	Miscellaneous Expense	511		105.00
	Truck Expense	512		90.00
	Wages Expense	513		1620.00
	Supplies Expense	514		80.00
	Depr. Expense—Delivery Equipment	515		40.00
	Depr. Expense—Warehouse Equipment	516		20.00
	Depr. Expense—Office Equipment	517		7.00
	Depr. Expense—Building	518		60.00
	To transfer beginning inventory and close temporary accounts with debit balances.			
30	Revenue and Expense Summary	399	1037.00	
	Ann Lang, Drawing	302		1037.00
	To close summary account and transfer net income to drawing account.			
30	Ann Lang, Drawing	302	137.00	
	Ann Lang, Capital	301		137.00
	To close drawing account and transfer net increase in owner's equity to capital account.			

Adjusting and Closing the General Ledger

- The first step is to record the ending merchandise inventory and close the temporary accounts with credit balances. The worksheet provides the necessary information. The amounts to be debited in the journal entry are taken from the Income Statement Credit column of the worksheet. The total of these amounts is credited to the Revenue and Expense Summary account. Study the worksheet on page 141 and the first closing entry on page 149.
- The second step is to transfer the beginning merchandise inventory and close the temporary accounts with debit balances. The worksheet again provides the necessary information. The amounts to be credited in this journal entry are obtained from the Income Statement Debit column of the worksheet. The total of these amounts is debited to the Revenue and Expense Summary account. Study the worksheet on page 141 and the second closing entry on page 149.
- The third step is to close the Revenue and Expense Summary account and transfer the net income to the drawing account. The worksheet shows the net income for the period. The Revenue and Expense Summary account is debited for this amount. The offsetting credit is to the drawing account. Study the third closing entry on page 149. (If there is a net loss, this entry must be made differently. It is necessary to debit the drawing account and credit the Revenue and Expense Summary account.)
- The fourth step is to close the drawing account and transfer the net increase in owner's equity to the capital account. Remember that the net increase in owner's equity is computed by subtracting the withdrawals from the net income. The drawing account is debited for the net increase in owner's equity. The offsetting credit is to the capital account. Study the fourth closing entry on page 149. (If there is a net decrease in owner's equity, this entry must be made differently. It is necessary to debit the capital account and credit the drawing account.)

After the closing entries are posted, the revenue, cost, expense, summary, and drawing accounts have no balances. Only the permanent accounts are still open. (Refer to the general ledger accounts below and on pages 151 through 155.)

Ruling and Balancing the Accounts

Most of the general ledger accounts must be ruled to separate the entries of the present period from the entries that will be posted in the next period. Some of the permanent accounts also require balancing. The balances of these accounts must be brought forward to prepare for the next period. (The procedures for ruling and balancing accounts were explained on pages 59 and 60.)

Cash   NO. 101

DATE	EXPLANATION	POST. REF.	DEBIT	DATE	EXPLANATION	POST. REF.	CREDIT
19X1 Apr. 1		J1	6000.00	19X1 Apr. 30		CP1	12564.00
30	3,594.00	CR1	10158.00	30	Carried Forward	✓	3594.00
			16158.00				16158.00
19X1 May 1	Brought Forward	✓	3594.00				

150   Accounting Fundamentals

Accounts Receivable — NO. 112

DATE	EXPLANATION	POST. REF.	DEBIT	DATE	EXPLANATION	POST. REF.	CREDIT
19X1 Apr. 1		J1	1000.00	19X1 Apr. 30		CR1	1150.00
30	2,610.00	S1	2760.00	30	Carried Forward	✓	2610.00
			3760.00				3760.00
19X1 May 1	Brought Forward	✓	2610.00				

Merchandise Inventory — NO. 114

DATE	EXPLANATION	POST. REF.	DEBIT	DATE	EXPLANATION	POST. REF.	CREDIT
19X1 Apr. 1		J1	5000.00	19X1 Apr. 30	Closing	J2	5000.00
30	Closing 7,500.00	J2	7500.00	30	Carried Forward	✓	7500.00
			12500.00				12500.00
19X1 May 1	Brought Forward	✓	7500.00				

Supplies — NO. 115

DATE	EXPLANATION	POST. REF.	DEBIT	DATE	EXPLANATION	POST. REF.	CREDIT
19X1 Apr. 5	240.00	CP1	320.00	19X1 Apr. 30	Adjusting	J2	80.00
				30	Carried Forward	✓	240.00
			320.00				320.00
19X1 May 1	Brought Forward	✓	240.00				

Delivery Equipment — NO. 116

DATE	EXPLANATION	POST. REF.	DEBIT	DATE	EXPLANATION	POST. REF.	CREDIT
19X1 Apr. 1		J1	4000.00				

Accumulated Depreciation — Delivery Equipment — NO. 117

DATE	EXPLANATION	POST. REF.	DEBIT	DATE	EXPLANATION	POST. REF.	CREDIT
				19X1 Apr. 30	Adjusting	J2	40.00

Warehouse Equipment — NO. 118

DATE	EXPLANATION	POST. REF.	DEBIT	DATE	EXPLANATION	POST. REF.	CREDIT
19X1 Apr. 1		J1	1000.00	19X1 Apr. 30	Carried Forward	✓	4000.00
2		CP1	3000.00				
			4000.00				4000.00
19X1 May 1	Brought Forward	✓	4000.00				

Adjusting and Closing the General Ledger

Accumulated Depreciation—Warehouse Equipment — NO. 119

DATE	EXPLANATION	POST. REF.	DEBIT	DATE	EXPLANATION	POST. REF.	CREDIT
				19X1 Apr. 30	Adjusting	J2	20 00

Office Equipment — NO. 120

DATE	EXPLANATION	POST. REF.	DEBIT	DATE	EXPLANATION	POST. REF.	CREDIT
19X1 Apr. 1		J1	200 00	19X1 Apr. 30	Carried Forward	✓	870 00
3		CP1	600 00				
25		CP1	70 00				
			870 00				870 00
19X1 May 1	Brought Forward	✓	870 00				

Accumulated Depreciation—Office Equipment — NO. 121

DATE	EXPLANATION	POST. REF.	DEBIT	DATE	EXPLANATION	POST. REF.	CREDIT
				19X1 Apr. 30	Adjusting	J2	7 00

Building — NO. 122

DATE	EXPLANATION	POST. REF.	DEBIT	DATE	EXPLANATION	POST. REF.	CREDIT
19X1 Apr. 1		J1	20,000 00				

Accumulated Depreciation—Building — NO. 123

DATE	EXPLANATION	POST. REF.	DEBIT	DATE	EXPLANATION	POST. REF.	CREDIT
				19X1 Apr. 30	Adjusting	J2	60 00

Accounts Payable — NO. 202

DATE	EXPLANATION	POST. REF.	DEBIT	DATE	EXPLANATION	POST. REF.	CREDIT
19X1 Apr. 30		CP1	3,500 00	19X1 Apr. 1		J1	2,200 00
30	Carried Forward	✓	5,550 00	30		P1	6,850 00
			9,050 00		5,550.00		9,050 00
				19X1 May 1	Brought Forward	✓	5,550 00

152   Accounting Fundamentals

Ann Lang, Capital — NO. 301

DATE	EXPLANATION	POST. REF.	DEBIT	DATE	EXPLANATION	POST. REF.	CREDIT
19X1 Apr. 30	Carried Forward	✓	37137 00	19X1 Apr. 1		J1	35000 00
				16		CR1	2000 00
				30	From Drawing	J2	137 00
			37137 00				37137 00
				19X1 May 1	Brought Forward	✓	37137 00

Ann Lang, Drawing — NO. 302

DATE	EXPLANATION	POST. REF.	DEBIT	DATE	EXPLANATION	POST. REF.	CREDIT
19X1 Apr. 30		CP1	900 00	19X1 Apr. 30	Net Income	J2	1037 00
30	To Capital	J2	137 00				
			1037 00				1037 00

Revenue and Expense Summary — NO. 399

DATE	EXPLANATION	POST. REF.	DEBIT	DATE	EXPLANATION	POST. REF.	CREDIT
19X1 Apr. 30	Closing	J2	16294 00	19X1 Apr. 30	Closing	J2	17331 00
30	Net Income	J2	1037 00				
			17331 00				17331 00

Sales Revenue — NO. 401

DATE	EXPLANATION	POST. REF.	DEBIT	DATE	EXPLANATION	POST. REF.	CREDIT
19X1 Apr. 30	Closing	J2	9780 00	19X1 Apr. 30		S1	2760 00
				30		CR1	7020 00
			9780 00				9780 00

Sales Discount — NO. 403

DATE	EXPLANATION	POST. REF.	DEBIT	DATE	EXPLANATION	POST. REF.	CREDIT
19X1 Apr. 30		CR1	12 00	19X1 Apr. 30	Closing	J2	12 00

Merchandise Purchases — NO. 501

DATE	EXPLANATION	POST. REF.	DEBIT	DATE	EXPLANATION	POST. REF.	CREDIT
19X1 Apr. 30		P1	6850 00	19X1 Apr. 30	Closing	J2	9260 00
30		CP1	2410 00				
			9260 00				9260 00

Adjusting and Closing the General Ledger

Purchases Discount — No. 504

DATE	EXPLANATION	POST. REF.	DEBIT	DATE	EXPLANATION	POST. REF.	CREDIT
19X1 Apr. 30	Closing	J2	51 00	19X1 Apr. 30		CP1	51 00

Miscellaneous Expense — No. 511

DATE	EXPLANATION	POST. REF.	DEBIT	DATE	EXPLANATION	POST. REF.	CREDIT
19X1 Apr. 14		CP1	50 00	19X1 Apr. 30	Closing	J2	105 00
14		CP1	35 00				
19		CP1	20 00				
			105 00				105 00

Truck Expense — No. 512

DATE	EXPLANATION	POST. REF.	DEBIT	DATE	EXPLANATION	POST. REF.	CREDIT
19X1 Apr. 12		CP1	90 00	19X1 Apr. 30	Closing	J2	90 00

Wages Expense — No. 513

DATE	EXPLANATION	POST. REF.	DEBIT	DATE	EXPLANATION	POST. REF.	CREDIT
19X1 Apr. 30		CP1	162 00	19X1 Apr. 30	Closing	J2	162 00

Supplies Expense — No. 514

DATE	EXPLANATION	POST. REF.	DEBIT	DATE	EXPLANATION	POST. REF.	CREDIT
19X1 Apr. 30	Adjusting	J2	80 00	19X1 Apr. 30	Closing	J2	80 00

Depreciation Expense—Delivery Equipment — No. 515

DATE	EXPLANATION	POST. REF.	DEBIT	DATE	EXPLANATION	POST. REF.	CREDIT
19X1 Apr. 30	Adjusting	J2	40 00	19X1 Apr. 30	Closing	J2	40 00

Depreciation Expense—Warehouse Equipment — No. 516

DATE	EXPLANATION	POST. REF.	DEBIT	DATE	EXPLANATION	POST. REF.	CREDIT
19X1 Apr. 30	Adjusting	J2	20 00	19X1 Apr. 30	Closing	J2	20 00

Depreciation Expense – Office Equipment NO. 517

DATE	EXPLANATION	POST. REF.	DEBIT	DATE	EXPLANATION	POST. REF.	CREDIT
19X1 Apr. 30	Adjusting	J2	7 00	19X1 Apr. 30	Closing	J2	7 00

Depreciation Expense – Building NO. 518

DATE	EXPLANATION	POST. REF.	DEBIT	DATE	EXPLANATION	POST. REF.	CREDIT
19X1 Apr. 30	Adjusting	J2	60 00	19X1 Apr. 30	Closing	J2	60 00

Preparing the Postclosing Trial Balance

Before work is started for the next period, it is necessary to check the equality of the debits and credits in the open accounts. For this reason, the following postclosing trial balance was prepared at Modern Appliance Distributors on April 30. The accounts that appear on the postclosing trial balance are the asset, liability, and owner's capital accounts.

Modern Appliance Distributors
Postclosing Trial Balance
April 30, 19X1

Acct. No.	Account Name	Debit	Credit
101	Cash	3,594 00	
112	Accounts Receivable	2,610 00	
114	Merchandise Inventory	7,500 00	
115	Supplies	240 00	
116	Delivery Equipment	4,000 00	
117	Accumulated Depreciation – Delivery Equipment		40 00
118	Warehouse Equipment	4,000 00	
119	Accumulated Depreciation – Warehouse Equipment		20 00
120	Office Equipment	870 00	
121	Accumulated Depreciation – Office Equipment		7 00
122	Building	20,000 00	
123	Accumulated Depreciation – Building		60 00
202	Accounts Payable		5,550 00
301	Ann Lang, Capital		37,137 00
	Totals	42,814 00	42,814 00

Chapter Summary

- Adjusting entries must be journalized and posted so that the amounts in the general ledger will agree with the amounts reported on the financial statements.
- Adjusting entries are recorded in the general journal and then posted to the proper general ledger accounts. The information for these entries comes from the Adjustments section of the worksheet.
- After the adjusting entries are completed, it is necessary to journalize and post closing entries. These entries make the general ledger ready to receive transactions for the next period.

- The first closing entry is used to record the ending merchandise inventory and close the temporary accounts with credit balances. The necessary information comes from the Income Statement Credit column of the worksheet.
- The second closing entry is used to transfer the beginning merchandise inventory and close the temporary accounts with debit balances. The necessary information comes from the Income Statement Debit column of the worksheet.
- The third closing entry is used to close the Revenue and Expense Summary account and transfer the net income or net loss to the drawing account.
- The fourth closing entry is used to close the drawing account and transfer the net increase or net decrease in owner's equity to the capital account.
- After the closing entries are posted, it is necessary to rule most of the general ledger accounts. The ruling procedure separates the entries of the present period from the entries that will be posted in the next period. It is also necessary to balance some of the permanent accounts.
- A postclosing trial balance is prepared to check the equality of the debits and credits in the accounts that remain open.

Checking Your Knowledge

BUSINESS APPLICATION

Problem 22-1. Do the following tasks for Valley Furniture Wholesalers. Obtain the necessary information from the worksheet that you prepared in Problems 20-1 and 21-1.

1. Record adjusting entries in the general journal. Use the journal form on page 105 of the workbook.

2. Assume that the adjusting entries have been posted. Record closing entries in the general journal. Use the journal forms on pages 105 and 106 of the workbook.

Problem 22-2. Do the following tasks for Southern Toy Distributors. Obtain the necessary information from the worksheet that you prepared in Problems 20-2 and 21-2.

1. Record adjusting entries in the general journal. Use the journal form on page 107 of the workbook.

2. Post the adjusting entries to the general ledger accounts given on pages 109–112 of the workbook. (Only the final balance as of December 31 is shown in each account to save space.)

3. Record closing entries in the general journal. Use the journal forms on pages 107 and 108 of the workbook.

4. Post the closing entries to the general ledger accounts.

5. Rule the closed accounts.

6. Rule and balance any open account that has two or more entries.

7. Prepare a postclosing trial balance. Use the form on page 113 of the workbook.

MANAGERIAL ANALYSIS

Case 22. Donald Wilson owns a store that sells paint and wallpaper. To save time and labor, Wilson has suggested to his accountant that the journalizing of adjusting and closing entries be eliminated. Wilson feels that the information can be posted directly from the worksheet to the general ledger accounts.

How would you convince Wilson that the adjusting and closing entries should be recorded in the general journal?

SUMMARY PROBLEM IV

Chapters 20–22. Perform the following end-of-period activities for the Star Lumber Company. Use the worksheet and general ledger accounts from Summary Problem III.

1. Record the adjustments on the worksheet. Then complete the worksheet.
A. Supplies used during February amounted to $37.50.
B. Depreciation on the office equipment is $15.
C. Depreciation on the warehouse equipment is $30.
D. The merchandise inventory on February 28 is $18,500.

    2. Prepare an income statement for the month ended February 28, 19X1. Use the form on page 115 of the workbook.

    3. Prepare a statement of owner's equity for the month ended February 28, 19X1. Use the form on page 116 of the workbook. (Refer to the general ledger to find the capital on February 1. Note that there was no additional investment during the month.)

    4. Prepare a classified balance sheet dated February 28, 19X1. Use the form on page 117 of the workbook.

    5. Record the adjusting entries in the general journal. Use the journal form on page 118 of the workbook.

    6. Post the adjusting entries to the general ledger accounts.

    7. Record the closing entries in the general journal. Use the journal forms on pages 118 and 119 of the workbook.

    8. Post the closing entries to the general ledger accounts.

    9. Rule all closed accounts.

    10. Rule and balance any open account that has two or more entries.

    11. Prepare a postclosing trial balance. Use the form on page 120 of the workbook.

Banking Procedures

A well-run business uses a checking account for its cash transactions. The business deposits all its cash receipts in a bank and makes all cash payments by check. This is done for safety and as an aid to good recordkeeping.

Opening a Checking Account

One of the first things that the owner of a new business must do is open a checking account. The owner fills out various bank forms and deposits some money. The bank requires that the owner and any other persons who will be signing checks for the business write their names on a *signature card*. This card is kept on file at the bank to verify signatures on checks whenever necessary.

Signature Card: Form containing the depositor's signature, which is used by the bank to verify signatures on checks.

The bank assigns a number to each checking account. This number is printed on the checks and deposit slips that the business receives. Most firms request that their name and address also be printed for easy identification.

Making Bank Deposits

Bank deposits should be made often to protect cash receipts. For this reason, many businesses deposit their cash receipts daily.

Remember that cash receipts usually include coins, currency (paper money), and cash substitutes such as checks and money orders. The following procedure is used to prepare these items for deposit.

- The coins and currency are counted. A note is made of the totals. Then the cash is recounted to verify the totals. If the amount is large, it is usually necessary to sort the coins and currency by denomination and place them in coin wrappers and currency bands supplied by the bank.
- All checks and money orders are endorsed. An *endorsement* legally transfers the right to collect payment on a check or money order. Endorsements are written or stamped on the backs of these items. (Many businesses use a rubber stamp to speed up the process of making endorsements.) Three types of endorsements are shown on page 159. A *blank endorsement* consists of only the name of the endorser. The check or money order is then payable to anyone holding it. A *full endorsement* includes the name of the person or business to whom the check or money order is being transferred. A *restrictive endorsement* limits the use of the check or money order to the purpose stated in the endorsement. This is the safest type of endorsement.

Endorsement: Signature or stamp on the back of a check or money order, which legally transfers the right to collect payment.

158 Accounting Fundamentals

Modern Appliance Distributors

*Pay to the Order of
Security National Bank
Modern Appliance Distributors*

*Pay to the Order of
Security National Bank
For Deposit Only
Modern Appliance Distributors*

BLANK ENDORSEMENT **FULL ENDORSEMENT** **RESTRICTIVE ENDORSEMENT**

Every bank deposit must be accompanied by a form called a *deposit slip*. The following deposit slip was prepared at Modern Appliance Distributors on April 8. Notice that the amount of each check being deposited is listed separately. (If the checks are too numerous to enter on the deposit slip, they can be recorded on an adding machine tape. The total of the checks is written on the deposit slip, and the adding machine tape is attached to provide a detailed listing.)

Deposit Slip: Form used to list items to be deposited in the bank.

Deposited in
Security National Bank
Houston, Texas

Date April 8, 19X1

Deposit to Account of

MODERN APPLIANCE DISTRIBUTORS
5891 GRANT AVENUE
HOUSTON, TEXAS 77034

242 ⑈ 27720 ⑈

		Dollars	Cents
Currency		225	00
Coin		14	25
Checks	1	608	60
(List separately)	2	212	15
	3	456	70
	4	283	30
	5		
	6		
	7		
TOTAL		1,800	00

This deposit accepted under and subject to the provisions of the Uniform Commercial Code.

The deposit slip, along with the coins, currency, and checks, is given to a bank teller, who provides a receipt for the deposit. This receipt is often a copy of the deposit slip, which the bank teller has stamped or initialed. (Many deposit slip forms consist of an original and one or more copies.)

The bank adds the amount of the deposit to the balance of the checking account.

Writing Checks

After a business opens a checking account, it may withdraw money by issuing checks. A *check* gives written authorization for the bank to pay a stated amount of money from the business's account.

It is essential that the account contain sufficient funds to cover all checks issued. To make sure of this, the business must have an up-to-date record of the account balance. Every deposit must be added to the balance, and every check must be subtracted. This information is usually shown on *check stubs* or in a *check register*.

The following procedures should be used when issuing checks. Refer to the check stub and check on page 160 as you study these procedures.

Check: Written authorization for the bank to pay a stated amount of money from an account.

Check Stubs or Check Register: Record of deposits, checks, and the account balance.

- Checks should be numbered consecutively to make it easier to keep track of them. (Many banks now provide checks that are printed with consecutive numbers.)
- The check stub or check register entry should be completed before the check is written. All the important facts about the payment must be recorded.

Banking Procedures 159

Preparing the check stub or check register entry first makes it less likely that this task will be forgotten.
- Checks should be prepared in ink, typewritten, or prepared by data processing equipment. Pencil should never be used in writing a check.
- There must be no alterations or erasures on a check. If an error is made, the word *VOID* is written in large letters across the face of the check and also on the check stub. The check is then placed in a check file. (This file is discussed in the next section.)
- Checks must be carefully prepared to prevent later changes in the amount or the name of the party being paid (the payee). It is a good practice to use a line to fill any space after the name and after the amount in words. It is also a good practice to write the amount in figures close to the dollar sign.
- Checks must have an authorized signature. Only a signature shown on the signature card is valid.

Drawer: Person or business that issues a check.

Payee: Person or business that will receive payment.

The person or business that issues (draws) a check is known as the *drawer*. The person or business that will receive payment is called the *payee*.

Check 105 issued by Modern Appliance Distributors is shown below. The check stub remains in the business's checkbook and is used to record the transaction in the cash payments journal.

The payee (Allied Manufacturing Company) deposits the check in its own bank account. The check is then forwarded to the bank where Modern Appliance Distributors has its account. This bank deducts the money from the account of Modern Appliance Distributors and places the check in a folder with other checks issued by the business. The bank keeps the checks until the end of the month and then returns them to the business.

Reconciling the Business's Records With the Bank Statement

Bank Statement: Form provided by the bank at regular intervals to report checking account transactions.

Canceled Checks: Checks that the bank has paid.

Service Charge: The charge a bank makes for maintaining a customer's checking account.

The owner of Modern Appliance Distributors receives a *bank statement* every month. This form shows the business's transactions with the bank. For example, the bank statement on page 161 reports the deposits and checks that the bank processed for Modern Appliance Distributors in April. *Canceled checks* accompany the bank statement. These are the checks paid from the business's account during the month.

Examine the bank statement for Modern Appliance Distributors. The first two columns list all the items deducted from the account balance—paid checks and a *service charge*. The service charge is identified by the letters *SC*. The third column of the bank statement shows the deposits, which were added to the account balance. The fourth column gives the dates of the transactions. The fifth column lists the account balance after the completion of each day's transactions. Notice that the balance on April 30 is $3,413 according to the bank statement.

160 Accounting Fundamentals

Security National Bank
Houston, Texas

MODERN APPLIANCE DISTRIBUTORS ACCOUNT NUMBER 242-27720
5891 GRANT AVENUE
HOUSTON, TX 77034 PERIOD ENDING APRIL 30, 19X1

Checks	Checks	Deposits	Date	Balance
		6,000.00	APRIL 1	6,000.00
3,000.00			4	3,000.00
600.00			5	2,400.00
1,400.00	320.00	1,800.00	8	2,480.00
		550.00	9	3,030.00
450.00			14	2,580.00
90.00	1,455.00	2,200.00	15	3,235.00
35.00	50.00	2,000.00	17	5,150.00
		245.00	18	5,395.00
20.00		1,350.00	22	6,725.00
		343.00	25	7,068.00
1,960.00	70.00		28	5,038.00
1,620.00	5.00SC		30	3,413.00

Beginning Balance	Total Amount of Deposits	Total Amount of Checks Paid	Total Charges	Ending Balance
.00	14,488.00	11,070.00	5.00	3,413.00

Number of Deposits Made	Number of Checks Paid	Number of Other Charges
8	13	1

Codes: CC Certified Check   OD Overdrawn
       DM Debit Memorandum   RI   Returned Item
       EC Error Correction   SC Service Charge

Please examine this statement upon receipt and report at once if you find any difference. If no error is reported in ten days, the account will be considered correct. All items are subject to final payment.

It is necessary to compare the bank statement with the business's own records. In most cases, the final balances will differ. For example, the checkbook of Modern Appliance Distributors shows a balance of $3,594 on April 30. This amount agrees with the balance of the Cash account in the general ledger.

The factors causing the difference between the bank statement balance and the checkbook balance must be determined. Then the two balances can be brought into agreement. This procedure is known as *reconciling the bank statement*.

The reconciliation form on page 162 was prepared at Modern Appliance Distributors. This form is printed on the back of the bank statement. (Many bank statements contain similar forms.)

The steps needed to reconcile the bank statement are as follows.

1. List the bank statement balance and the checkbook balance on the reconciliation form.
2. Identify any deposits not recorded on the bank statement. The deposits shown on the bank statement must be compared with the deposits shown in the checkbook. Any unrecorded deposits are then listed on the reconciliation form. Modern Appliance Distributors made a deposit of $1,670 on April 29. This deposit appears in the checkbook. However, the bank did not complete the processing of the deposit in time to enter it on the April 30 bank statement. The amount of this unrecorded deposit must be added to the bank statement balance.

Reconciling the Bank Statement: Finding the factors that cause the bank statement balance and the checkbook balance to differ.

Banking Procedures   **161**

Outstanding Checks: Checks that the drawer has issued but the bank has not yet paid.

3. Compare the canceled checks with the amounts of the paid checks shown on the bank statement. It is necessary to make sure that the bank recorded these checks correctly and returned all the canceled checks.
4. Identify any *outstanding checks*—checks that the drawer has issued but the bank has not yet paid. The canceled checks must be arranged in numeric order and compared with the information in the checkbook. Any outstanding checks are then listed on the reconciliation form. Modern Appliance Distributors had two outstanding checks on April 30: Check 112 for $594 and Check 115 for $900. The total of these checks must be subtracted from the bank statement balance.
5. Identify any service charge or other bank charges not yet recorded in the checkbook. The bank statement must be examined for such charges. These charges are then listed on the reconciliation form. Modern Appliance Distributors had a service charge of $5, which the bank imposed for handling the business's account during April. The amount of this service charge must be subtracted from the checkbook balance.
6. Compare the adjusted bank statement balance and the adjusted checkbook balance. As a result of the previous steps, each side of the reconciliation form contains an adjusted balance. The two amounts should be the same.

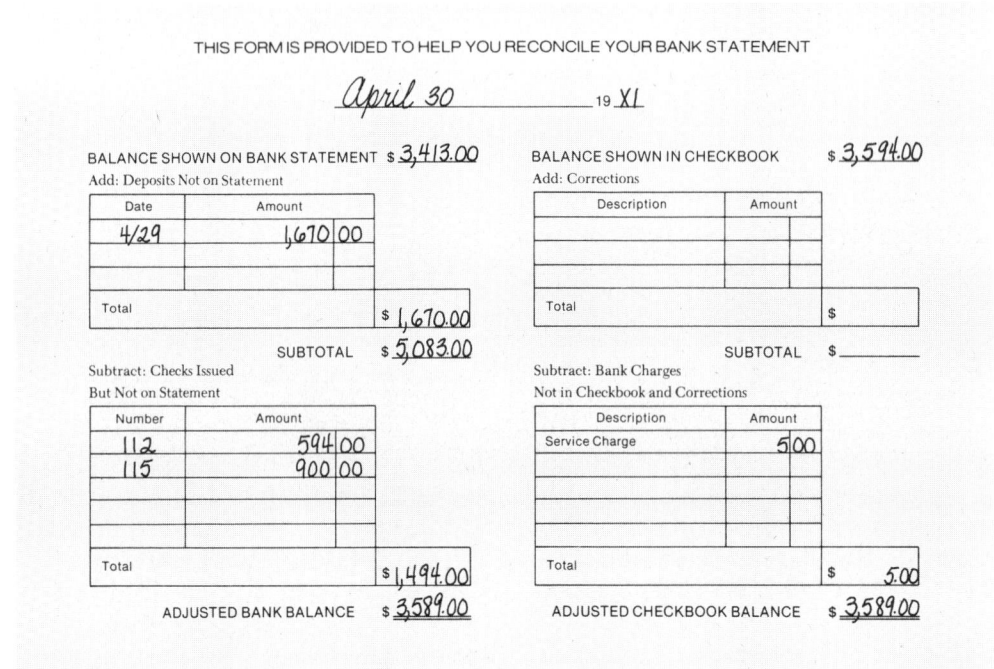

THIS FORM IS PROVIDED TO HELP YOU RECONCILE YOUR BANK STATEMENT

April 30 19 *XI*

BALANCE SHOWN ON BANK STATEMENT $3,413.00
Add: Deposits Not on Statement

Date	Amount
4/29	1,670.00

Total $1,670.00

SUBTOTAL $5,083.00

Subtract: Checks Issued But Not on Statement

Number	Amount
112	594.00
115	900.00

Total $1,494.00

ADJUSTED BANK BALANCE $3,589.00

BALANCE SHOWN IN CHECKBOOK $3,594.00
Add: Corrections

Description	Amount

Total $

SUBTOTAL $

Subtract: Bank Charges Not in Checkbook and Corrections

Description	Amount
Service Charge	5.00

Total $5.00

ADJUSTED CHECKBOOK BALANCE $3,589.00

After the bank statement is reconciled, it may be necessary to update the business's records. For example, at Modern Appliance Distributors, the Cash account and the checkbook do not yet reflect the April service charge. The following entries are therefore made in the cash payments journal and the checkbook.

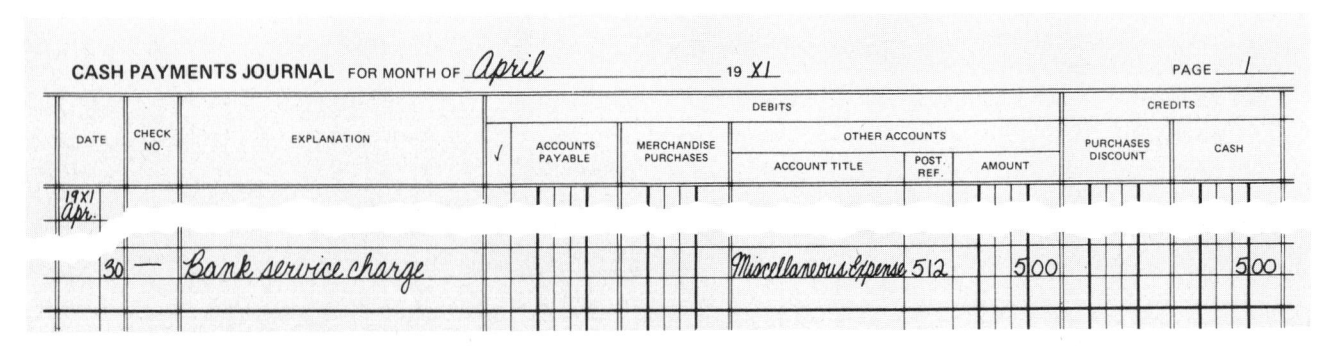

CASH PAYMENTS JOURNAL FOR MONTH OF *April* 19 *XI* PAGE 1

DATE	CHECK NO.	EXPLANATION	✓	ACCOUNTS PAYABLE	MERCHANDISE PURCHASES	ACCOUNT TITLE	POST. REF.	AMOUNT	PURCHASES DISCOUNT	CASH
19X1 Apr. 30	—	Bank service charge				Miscellaneous Expense	512	5.00		5.00

162 Accounting Fundamentals

Notice that the journal entry for the service charge consists of a debit to Miscellaneous Expense and a credit to Cash. A line is drawn in the Check No. column to show that no check was issued. The checkbook entry is made on the latest check stub. The effect of these two entries is to bring the Cash account and the checkbook into agreement with the adjusted checkbook balance on the reconciliation form.

It is considered a good accounting practice to delay the end-of-period work until the bank statement has been reconciled. This makes it possible for any resulting changes in the Cash account to be shown in the current period's records.

The canceled checks should be stored in a check file. It is important to keep these checks because they provide proof of payment.

In the future, the procedure for reconciling the bank statement at Modern Appliance Distributors may be more complex. For example, the business may need to make corrections for errors in checkbook computations. There may also be several different types of bank charges.

Other Bank Services

Banks provide a variety of services besides the ones already discussed. For example, some banks lend money to businesses. A firm that has established a good reputation with its bank may be able to arrange short-term loans. Another service offered by some banks is the processing of sales that businesses make with bank credit cards such as Visa and Master Charge. (The handling of these sales is explained in Chapter 26.)

Many retail businesses need to make deposits after the bank is closed so that they can safeguard their cash receipts. Banks often provide a *night depository* for this purpose.

If a check is lost or stolen, the drawer can ask the bank to stop payment on the check. It is necessary to notify the bank quickly and fill out a bank form called a *stop payment order*.

In certain transactions, a business may be required to use a *certified check*. The drawer writes a check in the usual way and then takes it to the bank. A bank teller stamps the word *Certified* on the face of the check. The amount is immediately deducted from the account and set aside for payment of the check. Thus, the payee has a guarantee that the necessary funds are available to cover the check.

Banks usually charge a fee for services such as stopping payment on checks and certifying checks.

Night Depository: Vault located in a wall of the bank, which can be used to make deposits when the bank is closed.

Stop Payment Order: Form instructing the bank not to pay a check.

Certified Check: Check on which the bank guarantees payment.

Chapter Summary

- A well-run business deposits all its cash receipts in a bank and makes all cash payments by check.
- Bank deposits should be made often to protect cash receipts. A deposit slip must accompany the coins, currency, and checks that are deposited.
- Every check must be endorsed before it is deposited. An endorsement legally transfers the right to collect payment on a check.
- A business must have a record of its checks, deposits, and account balance. This information is usually shown on check stubs or in a check register. The check stub or check register entry should be completed before a check is written.
- It is important that all checks be prepared with care and accuracy.
- At regular intervals, the bank provides information about the checking account transactions it has processed. This information is given on the bank statement. The bank sends canceled checks along with the bank statement.
- It is necessary to reconcile the business's records with the bank statement. The factors causing the difference between the bank statement balance and the checkbook balance must be determined. Then the two balances can be brought into agreement.

- After the reconciliation procedure is completed, any unrecorded bank charges must be entered in the cash payments journal and the checkbook.
- The canceled checks should be stored in a check file.
- Banks provide a variety of services that are useful to businesses.

Checking Your Knowledge

BUSINESS APPLICATION

Problem 23-1. Kay's Music Center is a retail store that sells stereo records and tapes. On March 15, 19X1, the business had the following items to be deposited in its account at the Mountain National Bank.

Four $20 bills, nine $10 bills, six $5 bills, seventeen $1 bills, seven half-dollars, fifteen quarters, eighteen dimes, twenty-one nickels, and eleven pennies.

Checks for $48.95, $24.72, and $56.40.

    1. Show the various ways that the checks could be endorsed. Prepare a blank endorsement, a full endorsement, and a restrictive endorsement. Use the partial checks on page 121 of the workbook.

    2. Prepare the deposit slip needed to accompany the bank deposit. Use the form on page 121 of the workbook.

    3. Record the deposit in the checkbook. Use the check stub on page 122 of the workbook.

Problem 23-2. On March 16, 19X1, Kay's Music Center bought some store equipment from Apex Corporation. Issue Check 514 for $1,026.80 to pay the bill. Leave the signature line blank. The owner will sign the check. Remember to prepare the check stub first. The necessary check stub and check are given on page 122 of the workbook.

Problem 23-3. On August 3, 19X1, the Delmar Garden Supply Store received its bank statement and canceled checks for July. Use the following information to reconcile the business's records with the bank statement. The necessary reconciliation form is given on page 122 of the workbook.

    A. The bank statement balance as of July 31 is $1,288.68.

    B. The checkbook balance as of July 31 is $1,573.63.

    C. The checkbook shows a deposit of $422.60 that does not appear on the bank statement. This deposit was made on July 30.

    D. The following checks are outstanding: Check 868 for $18.76, Check 870 for $45.97, Check 872 for $12.30, and Check 873 for $64.82.

    E. The bank statement shows a service charge of $4.20.

MANAGERIAL ANALYSIS

Case 23. Carl Wagner owns and operates a drugstore. After closing the business every evening, he counts the day's cash receipts and writes a blank endorsement on any checks. He then takes the coins, currency, and checks home with him for safekeeping. In the morning, he deposits these items in the bank.

    1. What are the weaknesses in Wagner's procedures for handling the cash receipts of his business?

    2. What procedures would you suggest that Wagner use?

24

Petty Cash and Other Special Cash Procedures

You have already learned that a well-run business deposits all cash receipts in the bank and pays all bills by check. However, most businesses need a small amount of money on hand to take care of items that cannot conveniently be paid by check. Examples of such items are carfare for messengers, purchases of postage stamps, supper money for employees who work overtime, and purchases of minor amounts of supplies. The use of a *petty cash fund* provides a way of handling small cash payments.

Petty Cash Fund: Money kept on hand to make small cash payments.

Setting Up the Petty Cash Fund

The size of the petty cash fund is determined by the needs of each business. Usually, the amount chosen is large enough to take care of petty cash needs for several weeks or a month. The fund is set up by issuing a check payable to Petty Cash for the required amount. The bank will cash such a check for any authorized person after the check is endorsed. The money is taken in various denominations of currency and coins.

On May 1, Ann Lang decided to set up a petty cash fund of $50 for Modern Appliance Distributors. She issued Check 116 for this amount. The entry for the transaction is made in the cash payments journal as shown below.

CASH PAYMENTS JOURNAL FOR MONTH OF May 19 X1 PAGE 2

DATE	CHECK NO.	EXPLANATION	✓	DEBITS — ACCOUNTS PAYABLE	MERCHANDISE PURCHASES	OTHER ACCOUNTS — ACCOUNT TITLE	POST. REF.	AMOUNT	CREDITS — PURCHASES DISCOUNT	CASH
19X1 May 1	116	Set up petty cash fund				Petty Cash	102	50 00		50 00

A new asset account called Petty Cash is debited, and Cash is credited. Now, the business has two cash accounts: Cash (in the form of a checking account at the bank) and Petty Cash (in the form of currency and coins in a petty cash box at the office). The Petty Cash account immediately follows the Cash account in the general ledger. These accounts also appear on the balance sheet in that order.

The balance of the Petty Cash account should always reflect the original amount of the fund ($50) unless the fund is permanently increased or decreased to meet operating needs. No further entries are made in this account unless the amount of the fund is changed.

Petty Cash and Other Special Cash Procedures

Using the Petty Cash Fund

The petty cash fund is put into the care of a responsible office employee who usually keeps it in a locked strongbox. This employee must make sure that no unauthorized person has access to the money and that it is safely locked away at night. In a large business, there may be many petty cash funds. Each fund will be under the care of a different employee such as a department secretary.

Petty Cash Voucher: Form that explains and authorizes a petty cash payment.

To obtain a payment from the fund, it is necessary to fill out a form called a *petty cash voucher*. This form should be prepared in ink or typewritten to prevent later changes. The petty cash voucher used by Modern Appliance Distributors is shown below. Notice that it has space for writing the name of the account to be charged. Spaces are also provided for the signature of the person to whom payment is made and the signature of the person who approves the payment.

PETTY CASH VOUCHER   NO. 1

DESCRIPTION OF EXPENDITURE	CHARGE TO ACCOUNT	AMOUNT
Supper money	Miscellaneous Expense	7 50
	TOTAL	7 50

RECEIVED *Paul Sanchez* DATE 5/2/X1 APPROVED BY *Ann Lang* DATE 5/2/X1

Any bill or receipt that verifies the payment is stapled to the petty cash voucher. The voucher is then placed in the petty cash box.

Proving the Petty Cash Fund

Proving Petty Cash: Making sure that the total of the money and the vouchers in the petty cash box equals the amount of the fund.

At any time, the person who is in charge of the petty cash fund should be able to account for the amount of the fund. This is done by *proving petty cash*. The money in the petty cash box is counted. Then the amounts of the petty cash vouchers in the box are added to find out how much was spent. The total cash on hand and the total of the vouchers should equal the original amount of the fund.

On May 31, the petty cash box at Modern Appliance Distributors contained $14.20 in cash and five vouchers. The form at the top of page 167 shows how the amounts were proved.

Replenishing the Petty Cash Fund

Replenishing Petty Cash: Restoring the petty cash fund to its original amount.

The petty cash fund is restored to its original amount at the end of each month and at any other time when the money in the box is low. This procedure is known as *replenishing petty cash*. The steps to be followed are listed below.

1. The petty cash fund is proved.
2. The vouchers are sorted according to the nature of the expenses. The amount spent for each kind of expense is then determined. This information is listed on a memorandum or some other type of form. (See the form in the middle of page 167.)

166   Accounting Fundamentals

```
              Proof of Petty Cash Fund
                   May 31, 19X1


Cash on hand
  $5 bills                    x   2   =   $10.00
   1 bills                    x   3   =     3.00
  Quarters          .25       x   2   =      .50
  Dimes             .10       x   4   =      .40
  Nickels           .05       x   5   =      .25
  Pennies           .01       x   5   =      .05
    Total cash                               $14.20

Vouchers on hand
  1  Supper money (Miscellaneous Expense)   $ 7.50
  2  Carfare (Miscellaneous Expense)          2.00
  3  Gasoline for truck (Truck Expense)       5.30
  4  Stamps (Miscellaneous Expense)          14.00
  5  Gasoline for truck (Truck Expense)       7.00
    Total vouchers                           35.80

Total cash and vouchers                     $50.00
Amount of fund                               50.00
Cash short or over                             —
```

3. The proof of the fund, the vouchers, and the supporting bills and receipts are given to the accounting clerk along with a request for replenishment.
4. The accounting clerk cancels the vouchers by writing the word *PAID* across each of them or by perforating them. This is done to make sure that the vouchers are not used again. The accounting clerk then gives a check to the person in charge of the petty cash fund. This check is for the total amount spent (which is the total of all the vouchers submitted). The person in charge of the fund cashes the check and puts the money in the petty cash box.
5. The accounting clerk makes an entry in the cash payments journal to record the replenishment of the petty cash fund.

On May 31, the person in charge of the petty cash fund at Modern Appliance Distributors prepared the following request for replenishment of the fund.

```
Request for Replenishment of Petty Cash Fund
              May 31, 19X1


Original amount of fund              $50.00

Vouchers 1-5 (attached):
  Miscellaneous Expense              $23.50
  Truck Expense                       12.30
    Total spent                      $35.80
    Cash on hand                      14.20
Total accounted for                  $50.00

Amount requested                     $35.80
```

The journal entry shown below was made when the petty cash fund was replenished on May 31. After the amounts in this entry are posted, there is a record of all the expenses paid from the fund during May.

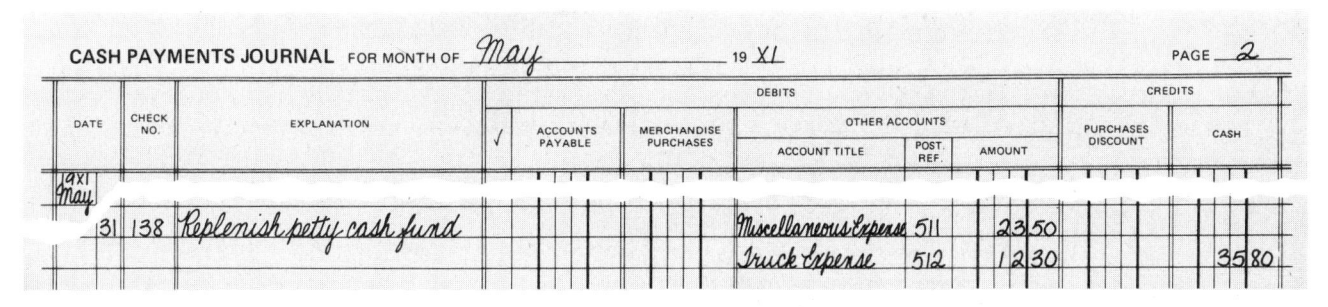

DATE	CHECK NO.	EXPLANATION	✓	ACCOUNTS PAYABLE	MERCHANDISE PURCHASES	ACCOUNT TITLE	POST. REF.	AMOUNT	PURCHASES DISCOUNT	CASH
19X1 May 31	138	Replenish petty cash fund				Miscellaneous Expense	511	23 50		
						Truck Expense	512	12 30		35 80

CASH PAYMENTS JOURNAL FOR MONTH OF May 19 X1 PAGE 2

Petty Cash and Other Special Cash Procedures

It is important to replenish the petty cash fund at the end of each month. In this way, the expenses can be recorded in the month they are incurred and the money in the petty cash box can be brought into agreement with the balance of the Petty Cash account.

Other Cash Funds

Travel Advances: Cash given to employees for business trips.

Change Fund: Money kept on hand to make change when customers pay cash.

The type of petty cash fund described above always remains at the same level and is replenished for the exact amount that has been spent. This system has other uses besides providing money for small office expenses. For example, some firms set up a cash fund to provide *travel advances* to employees who must go on out-of-town business trips.

Many retail stores have a *change fund*. This fund consists of currency and coins that are always kept on hand to make change when customers pay cash. The change fund is placed in the cash register every morning. At the end of the day, the fund is separated from the cash receipts and placed in an office safe. The cash receipts are deposited in the bank. The amount of the fund is shown in an asset account called Change Fund.

Cash Shortages and Overages

Cash Short: Less cash on hand than there should be.

Cash Over: More cash on hand than there should be.

Because dishonesty or errors are always possible in the handling of cash, all cash funds should be proved often. Petty cash funds are proved as described earlier in this chapter. When there are cash sales, the money in the cash register must be proved against the audit tape prepared by the register.

Sometimes the amount of money in the cash register will not agree with the amount that should be there. If less cash is on hand than there should be, cash is *short*. If more cash is on hand than there should be, cash is *over*. In businesses that have cash sales, some shortages and overages can be expected because of errors in making change. However, large or frequent shortages or overages should be investigated. They may be a sign of poor cash handling procedures or dishonesty.

For proper control of cash, amounts short and over must be recorded. An account called Cash Short or Over is used. This account is debited for cash shortages and credited for cash overages. Entries for cash shortages are made in the cash payments journal. Entries for cash overages are made in the cash receipts journal.

The Cash Short or Over account may be considered either as an expense or as revenue according to its balance at the end of the accounting period. If the account has a debit balance (shortages exceed overages), it appears on the income statement as an expense. If the account has a credit balance (overages exceed shortages), it appears on the income statement as revenue.

Chapter Summary

- The petty cash fund is used for small cash payments. A petty cash voucher must be prepared to explain each payment.
- When the petty cash fund is set up, an asset account called Petty Cash is debited. The balance of this account always reflects the original amount of the fund unless the fund is permanently increased or decreased.
- The petty cash fund is replenished at the end of each month and at any other time when the money is low. A check is issued for the total amount spent. Then, an entry is made in the cash payments journal. This entry involves debits to the various expense accounts affected by the petty cash payments. The Cash account is credited for the total amount.
- The petty cash fund is one common type of cash fund. Other types used by many businesses are funds for giving travel advances and funds for making change.

- All cash funds should be proved often. It is also necessary to prove the cash receipts in a cash register.
- Cash shortages and overages must be recorded. The Cash Short or Over account is used for this purpose.

Checking Your Knowledge

BUSINESS APPLICATION

Problem 24-1. On June 1, 19X1, the owner of the Fiesta Gift Shop set up a petty cash fund of $75. She issued Check 134 for this purpose. During June, the following four payments were made from the fund.

Paid $6.78 for pens and pencils (Office Expense); Voucher 1.

Paid $12.22 for mailing packages (Delivery Expense); Voucher 2.

Paid $5.80 for file folders (Office Expense); Voucher 3.

Paid $6.92 for supper money (Miscellaneous Expense); Voucher 4.

At the end of the month, the currency and coins in the petty cash box consisted of two $10 bills, two $5 bills, ten $1 bills, nine quarters, eight dimes, three nickels, and eight pennies.

1. Make an entry in the cash payments journal to record the establishment of the petty cash fund. The necessary journal is given on page 124 of the workbook.

2. Prove the petty cash fund as of June 30, 19X1. The necessary form is given on page 123 of the workbook.

Problem 24-2. Do the following additional work for the Fiesta Gift Shop.

1. Prepare a request for replenishment of the petty cash fund as of June 30, 19X1. Obtain the amounts from Problem 24-1. The necessary form is given on page 125 of the workbook.

2. Make an entry in the cash payments journal to record the replenishment of the petty cash fund. Assume that Check 154 was issued for this transaction. The necessary journal form is given on page 126 of the workbook.

MANAGERIAL ANALYSIS

Case 24. John Hogan owns a hardware store. Whenever he or one of his employees must make a small cash payment, the money is taken from the cash register. No record of the payment is prepared.

Hogan's accountant has advised him to set up a petty cash fund. However, Hogan feels that he does not need such a fund.

1. What is wrong with the business's current procedure for handling small cash payments?

2. How would you convince Hogan that he should have a petty cash fund?

Payroll Records

Most businesses have employees. By law, these businesses must keep accurate, complete payroll records and perform certain payroll procedures. For example, they are required to compute employee earnings, deduct taxes from these earnings, compute their own tax contributions, send all taxes to the proper government agencies, and prepare payroll tax reports for the government. Businesses are also responsible for providing employees with information about earnings and deductions. The employees need this information in order to file income tax returns.

Pay Plans

Gross Earnings:
Total amount an employee earns.

The total amount an employee earns is known as *gross earnings*. This amount can be determined in various ways, depending on the type of pay plan used for the employee. The most common pay plans are explained in this section.

Salary Plan:
$$\text{Salary} = \overset{\text{Gross}}{\text{Earnings}}$$
$225 = $225

Salary Plan. Under the *salary plan*, employees earn a fixed amount for each pay period. (Pay periods vary from business to business. However, they are usually on a weekly, biweekly, semimonthly, or monthly basis.) Most office employees, supervisors, and managers are paid according to the salary plan.

Hourly-Rate Plan:
$$\text{Hours} \times \text{Rate} = \overset{\text{Gross}}{\text{Earnings}}$$
40 × $5 = $200

Hourly-Rate Plan. When the *hourly-rate plan* is used, employees earn a fixed amount for each hour they work. The number of hours an employee worked during a pay period is multiplied by the employee's hourly rate to find the gross earnings. Production employees in factories and service employees in retail businesses are often paid according to the hourly-rate plan.

Piece-Rate Plan:
$$\text{Items} \times \text{Rate} = \overset{\text{Gross}}{\text{Earnings}}$$
1,900 × $.10 = $190

Piece-Rate Plan. Under the *piece-rate plan*, employees earn a fixed amount for each item they produce. At the end of the pay period, the number of items completed is multiplied by the rate per item to determine an employee's gross earnings. The piece-rate plan is referred to as an *incentive plan* because employees can increase their earnings by producing more. Some factories use the piece-rate plan.

Commission Plan. The *commission plan* is an incentive plan for salespeople. In some businesses, the amount that such employees earn is based on the amount of goods they sell. At the end of the pay period, the amount of goods sold is multiplied by the commission rate to find the gross earnings. The commission rate is a percentage.

Commission Plan

Sales	×	Rate (Percentage)	=	Gross Earnings
$12,000	×	0.02	=	$240

Accounting Fundamentals

Salary-Commission Plan. In the *salary-commission plan*, salespeople receive a salary as well as a commission on the goods they sell. The salary and the commission are added to determine the gross earnings for a pay period.

Salary-Commission Plan

Salary	+	Commission	=	Gross Earnings
$100	+	($12,000 × 0.01)	=	$220
$100	+	$120	=	$220

Computing Gross Earnings

Gross earnings may include both regular earnings and overtime earnings. Many employees are subject to the federal Fair Labor Standards Act. One section of this law specifies that employees must receive extra pay for *overtime*—all time worked beyond 40 hours a week. The rate paid for overtime hours must be at least $1\frac{1}{2}$ times the regular rate.

There are a number of methods for keeping track of the hours that employees work. Some businesses use a form called a *time sheet*. Daily arrival and departure times are recorded on this sheet by the employees or by their supervisor, depending on the policy of the firm. Other businesses use a *time clock* and *time cards*. When employees enter or leave their work area, they place the cards in the time clock. This device prints the time on each card.

At the end of the pay period, it is necessary to total the hours recorded on the time sheet or time cards. Then the gross earnings of each employee can be computed. Study the time card shown below. (No deductions were made for lateness because the firm allows lateness of up to 5 minutes without penalty.)

Overtime: All time worked beyond 40 hours a week.

Time Sheets and Time Cards: Records showing hours worked by employees.

Time Clock: Device used to print arrival and departure times on time cards.

Simplex Time Recorder Company
TIME CLOCK

Payroll Records **171**

Notice how the gross earnings are computed on the time card.

1. The regular hours worked are multiplied by the employee's regular hourly rate to find the regular earnings (40 hours × $5 = $200).
2. The overtime hours worked are multiplied by the employee's overtime rate to find the overtime earnings (4 hours × $7.50 = $30). The overtime rate is 1½ times the regular rate of $5.
3. The regular earnings and the overtime earnings are added to find the gross earnings ($200 + $30 = $230).

The example given here is for an employee who is on the hourly-rate plan. However, some salaried employees also have overtime earnings as well as regular earnings.

Determining Employee Deductions

The amount of pay that employees actually receive is usually less than their gross earnings. Most employees are subject to deductions for federal income tax and social security (FICA) tax. These deductions are required by law. Other required deductions in some areas are state income tax, city income tax, state disability tax, and state unemployment tax. If employees belong to a union, they may have a required deduction for union dues. Many employees also have voluntary deductions for items such as medical insurance, savings bonds, and pension plan contributions.

The procedures for determining the federal income tax deduction and the social security (FICA) tax deduction are discussed in this section.

Federal Income Tax Withholding. At the end of each pay period, a business must withhold federal income tax from the earnings of its employees. The amount to be withheld for any employee depends on three factors: the employee's gross earnings, marital status, and withholding allowances.

When employees are hired, the business must obtain information about the number of withholding allowances they are claiming. Each employee is therefore asked to fill out a government form called an *Employee's Withholding Allowance Certificate* (*Form W-4*). This form is placed in the business's payroll files after the employee completes it.

The easiest way to find the proper amount of federal income tax withholding for an employee is to use the tax tables in the *Employer's Tax Guide,* which is published by the Internal Revenue Service. (This booklet is also known as *Circular E.*) There are separate tax tables for different pay periods. For example, the partial tax tables given on page 173 cover a weekly pay period. Notice that one of these tables is for single persons and the other is for married persons.

To use an income tax withholding table, look at the first two columns and select the line that covers the employee's gross earnings. Then follow the line across the table until you reach the column for the number of withholding allowances the employee claims. The figure shown at this point in the table is the amount of income tax to be withheld.

According to the time card on page 171, David Clark earned $230 during the week ended May 22. Clark is married and claims two withholding allowances. The table for married persons given on page 173 shows that $24.60 should be deducted from his gross earnings for federal income tax withholding.

States and cities that have an income tax provide tables similar to those for federal income tax.

Social Security (FICA) Tax. The Federal Insurance Contributions Act (FICA) specifies that a tax must be deducted from the earnings of most employees to support the

SINGLE Persons — WEEKLY Payroll Period

And the wages are—		And the number of withholding allowances claimed is—									
At least	But less than	0	1	2	3	4	5	6	7	8	9	10 or more
		The amount of income tax to be withheld shall be—									
$135	$140	$19.00	$15.30	$11.90	$8.40	$5.50	$2.10	$0	$0	$0	$0	$0
170	180	26.80	22.80	18.80	15.10	11.70	8.20	4.80	2.00	0	0	0
180	190	28.90	24.90	20.90	16.90	13.50	10.00	6.50	3.50	.60	0	0
190	200	31.00	27.00	23.00	18.90	15.30	11.80	8.30	5.00	2.10	0	0
200	210	33.60	29.10	25.10	21.00	17.10	13.60	10.10	6.70	3.60	.70	0
210	220	36.20	31.20	27.20	23.10	19.10	15.40	11.90	8.50	5.10	2.20	0
220	230	38.80	33.80	29.30	25.20	21.20	17.20	13.70	10.30	6.80	3.70	.80
230	240	41.40	36.40	31.40	27.30	23.30	19.20	15.50	12.10	8.60	5.20	2.30
240	250	44.00	39.00	34.00	29.40	25.40	21.30	17.30	13.90	10.40	6.90	3.80
250	260	46.60	41.60	36.60	31.60	27.50	23.40	19.40	15.70	12.20	8.70	5.30
260	270	49.20	44.20	39.20	34.20	29.60	25.50	21.50	17.50	14.00	10.50	7.10

MARRIED Persons — WEEKLY Payroll Period

And the wages are—		And the number of withholding allowances claimed is—									
At least	But less than	0	1	2	3	4	5	6	7	8	9	10 or more
		The amount of income tax to be withheld shall be—									
$0	$46	$0	$0	$0	$0	$0	$0	$0	$0	$0	$0	$0
				15.50	12.10	8.20	6.30	3.40	.90	0	0	0
170	180	20.80	17.30	13.80	10.70	7.80	4.90	2.00	0	0	0	0
180	190	22.60	19.10	15.60	12.20	9.30	6.40	3.50	.60	0	0	0
190	200	24.40	20.90	17.40	14.00	10.80	7.90	5.00	2.10	0	0	0
200	210	26.20	22.70	19.20	15.80	12.30	9.40	6.50	3.60	.80	0	0
210	220	28.10	24.50	21.00	17.60	14.10	10.90	8.00	5.10	2.30	0	0
220	230	30.20	26.30	22.80	19.40	15.90	12.50	9.50	6.60	3.80	.90	0
230	240	32.30	28.30	24.60	21.20	17.70	14.30	11.00	8.10	5.30	2.40	0
240	250	34.40	30.40	26.40	23.00	19.50	16.10	12.60	9.60	6.80	3.90	1.00
250	260	36.50	32.50	28.50	24.80	21.30	17.90	14.40	11.10	8.30	5.40	2.50
260	270	38.60	34.60	30.60	26.60	23.10	19.70	16.20	12.70	9.80	6.90	4.00
270	280	40.70	36.70	32.70	28.60	24.90	21.50	18.00	14.50	11.30	8.40	5.50

social security program. This program provides retirement, survivors, and disability benefits and health insurance for the aged (Medicare).

The rate of the FICA tax changes periodically. The chart given in the margin shows the planned rate levels through 1990. (These rate levels may be revised by Congress.)

At the end of the pay period, the amount of the FICA deduction for each employee can be found by multiplying the employee's gross earnings by the current tax rate. For example, with a rate of 6.13 percent, David Clark's FICA deduction for the week ended May 22 would be computed as follows: $230 × 0.0613 = $14.10.

To simplify the process of determining FICA deductions, many businesses use a tax table. The *Employer's Tax Guide* (*Circular E*) contains such a table.

In any calendar year (January 1 to December 31), only a certain amount of gross earnings is subject to FICA tax. When an employee's earnings reach the maximum amount (called the *tax base*), no further FICA deductions are made during that year. Like the FICA tax rate, the tax base changes periodically. The planned amounts through 1987 are shown in the margin.

Businesses must contribute to the social security program by paying an employer's FICA tax. This tax is equal to the amount of FICA tax deducted from the earnings of the employees.

Schedule of FICA Tax Rates for Employees:
1980	6.13%
1981	6.65
1982–1984	6.70
1985	7.05
1986–1989	7.15
1990	7.65

Schedule for FICA Tax Bases:
1980	$25,900
1981	29,700
1982	30,000
1983	31,800
1984	33,600
1985	35,400
1986	37,500
1987	39,600

Computing Net Pay

After all deductions for an employee have been determined, the amounts are added. The total of the deductions is then subtracted from the employee's gross earnings for the period. The resulting figure is the employee's *net pay* or *take-home pay*. This is the amount that the employee actually receives.

Net Pay: Amount that an employee receives after deductions are subtracted from gross earnings.

David Clark had two deductions for the week ended May 22: federal income tax withholding and FICA tax. The total of these two deductions is $38.70 ($24.60 + $14.10 = $38.70). Thus, Clark's net pay for the period is $191.30 ($230 − $38.70 = $191.30).

Preparing Payroll Records

Government regulations make it necessary for businesses to keep records showing detailed information about payroll. Many firms use a payroll register and employee earnings records to satisfy these regulations.

Payroll Register: Record showing hours worked, gross earnings, deductions, and net pay of all employees for a pay period.

Payroll Register. At the end of the pay period, the hours worked, gross earnings, deductions, and net pay of all employees are entered in the *payroll register*. For employees on the hourly-rate plan, this information is taken from the time cards. An example of a payroll register is given below. Notice that the beginning and ending dates of the pay period are shown at the top of the payroll register sheet.

PAYROLL REGISTER

WEEK BEGINNING May 16 19 X1 AND ENDING May 22 19 X1 PAID May 25 19 X1

EMP. NO.	NAME	WITH. ALLOW.	MARITAL STATUS	HOURS WORKED REG.	HOURS WORKED OVER-TIME	REG. HRLY. RATE	OVER-TIME RATE	EARNINGS REGULAR	EARNINGS OVERTIME	EARNINGS TOTAL	DEDUCTIONS INCOME TAX	DEDUCTIONS FICA TAX	DEDUCTIONS OTHER	DEDUCTIONS TOTAL	NET PAY AMOUNT	NET PAY CHECK NO.
1	Clark, David	2	M	40	4	5 00	7 50	200 00	30 00	230 00	24 60	14 10		38 70	191 30	131
2	Diaz, Paul	5	M	40	4	5 50	8 25	220 00	33 00	253 00	17 90	15 51		33 41	219 59	132
3	Foley, Irene	3	M	40	2	5 00	7 50	200 00	15 00	215 00	17 60	13 18		30 78	184 22	133
4	Hall, Steven	1	S	40	4	4 50	6 75	180 00	27 00	207 00	29 10	12 69		41 79	165 21	134
5	Kowalski, Jane	1	M	40	2	5 00	7 50	200 00	15 00	215 00	24 50	13 18		37 68	177 32	135
	Totals							1000 00	120 00	1120 00	113 70	68 66		182 36	937 64	

The payroll register should be totaled and proved before the employees are paid. The cross-footing method is used to verify the accuracy of the amounts.

1. The totals of the Regular Earnings column and the Overtime Earnings column are added. The sum of these amounts must equal the total of the Total Earnings column.
2. The totals of the Income Tax column and the FICA Tax column are added. The sum of these amounts must equal the total of the Total Deductions column.
3. The total of the Total Deductions column is subtracted from the total of the Total Earnings column. The resulting figure must equal the total of the Net Pay column.

When the payroll checks are issued, the date of payment and the check numbers are entered in the payroll register.

Employee Earnings Record: Record showing complete payroll information for an employee during a year.

Year-to-Date Earnings: An employee's gross earnings from the beginning of the year to the current date.

Employee Earnings Records. The information in the payroll register is transferred to *employee earnings records*. A separate earnings record is set up for each employee at the beginning of the year. Entries are made in this record throughout the year as each pay period ends. Thus, the earnings record contains complete payroll information for the employee. An example of this type of record is shown on page 175.

Notice that there is a column for entering the *year-to-date earnings*—the employee's gross earnings from the beginning of the year to the current date. This column makes it easy to see whether the employee has reached the maximum amount of yearly earnings subject to FICA tax.

174 Accounting Fundamentals

EMPLOYEE EARNINGS RECORD FOR THE YEAR 19 XI

NAME David Clark
ADDRESS 2761 Pinewood Avenue
Houston, Texas 77047
SOCIAL SECURITY NO. 224-08-9572
MARITAL STATUS Married
POSITION Delivery Truck Driver
WITHHOLDING ALLOWANCES 2

PERIOD ENDING	RATE REG.	OVER-TIME	HOURS REG.	OT	EARNINGS REGULAR	OVERTIME	TOTAL	YEAR-TO-DATE EARNINGS	DEDUCTIONS INCOME TAX	FICA TAX	OTHER	TOTAL	NET PAY
Jan. 7	5.00	7.50	40		200 00		200 00	200 00	19 20	12 26		31 46	168 54
May 22	5.00	7.50	40	4	200 00	30 00	230 00	5125 00	24 60	14 10		38 70	191 30

Paying the Employees

There are several different methods for paying employees. The most common practice is to prepare a check for each employee. However, some businesses make cash payments. Each employee is given a pay envelope containing currency and coins. Other businesses have their bank place each employee's net pay in his or her checking account. The money is transferred from the firm's account.

Many businesses provide each employee with a *pay statement* listing the hours worked, gross earnings, deductions, and net pay. This statement is usually attached to the payroll check, or it appears on the front of the pay envelope. The necessary information is obtained from the payroll register.

Pay Statement: A form listing payroll information, which is given to an employee at the end of a pay period.

Recording the Payroll

After the payroll is computed, it must be recorded in the general journal. The amounts needed for this entry come from the payroll register.

GENERAL JOURNAL PAGE 10

DATE	DESCRIPTION OF ENTRY	POST. REF.	DEBIT	CREDIT
19X1 May 22	Wages Expense	513	1120 00	
	Employee Income Taxes Payable	221		113 70
	FICA Taxes Payable	222		68 66
	Wages Payable	225		937 64
	Payroll for week ended May 22.			

The total of the employee earnings represents an expense for the business and is debited to the Wages Expense account. The taxes deducted from employee earnings are liabilities until the money is sent to the government. The totals of these taxes are credited to the Employee Income Taxes Payable account and the FICA Taxes Payable account. The total of the net pay is a liability until the employees are paid. It is therefore credited to the Wages Payable account.

When the payroll checks are issued, an entry must be made in the cash payments journal. The total of the net pay is debited to the Wages Payable account and credited to the Cash account.

Payroll Records 175

CASH PAYMENTS JOURNAL FOR MONTH OF May 19 X1										PAGE 5
			DEBITS					**CREDITS**		
DATE	CHECK NO.	EXPLANATION	✓	ACCOUNTS PAYABLE	MERCHANDISE PURCHASES	OTHER ACCOUNTS			PURCHASES DISCOUNT	CASH
						ACCOUNT TITLE	POST. REF.	AMOUNT		
19X1 May										
25	131-135	May 22 payroll				Wages Payable	225	937 64		937 64

If the employees are paid in cash, a single check is drawn in order to obtain the necessary currency and coins for the pay envelopes. The entry recorded in the cash payments journal is the same as the one shown above except that only one check number is listed.

Recording the Employer's Payroll Taxes

Most businesses are subject to several payroll taxes—the employer's FICA tax, federal unemployment tax, and state unemployment tax. Remember that businesses must contribute to the social security program by paying a FICA tax equal to the amount deducted from employee earnings. In addition, the federal and state governments impose unemployment taxes on businesses. The money from these taxes is used to provide benefits for jobless workers.

Unemployment tax rates and regulations vary somewhat among the states. Also, the federal and state governments increase their rates from time to time. Another factor that determines the state tax to be paid is the merit-rating system. Under this system, businesses that give steady employment pay a reduced rate. Most states have such a system.

The payroll register on page 174 lists total employee earnings of $1,120 for the weekly pay period ended May 22. Let's assume that the business has the following payroll taxes: employer's FICA tax of 6.13 percent on a base of $25,900, federal unemployment tax of 0.7 percent on a base of $6,000, and state unemployment tax of 2.7 percent on a base of $6,000. (Remember that the tax base is the maximum amount of each employee's yearly earnings on which tax is paid.) If all earnings from the May 22 pay period are taxable, the business's payroll taxes would be computed as follows.

Employer's FICA Tax	$1,120 × 0.0613 =	$ 68.66
Federal Unemployment Tax	1,120 × 0.007 =	7.84
State Unemployment Tax	1,120 × 0.027 =	30.24
Total		$106.74

After these payroll taxes are computed, they must be recorded in the general journal.

GENERAL JOURNAL				PAGE 10
DATE	DESCRIPTION OF ENTRY	POST. REF.	DEBIT	CREDIT
19X1 May 22	Payroll Taxes Expense	521	106 74	
	FICA Taxes Payable	222		68 66
	Federal Unemployment Taxes Payable	223		7 84
	State Unemployment Taxes Payable	224		30 24
	Employer's taxes on May 22 payroll.			

Accounting Fundamentals

Payroll taxes represent an expense for the business and are therefore debited to the Payroll Taxes Expense account. The amount owed for each type of tax is a liability until it is paid to the proper government agency. Thus, three liability accounts are credited: FICA Taxes Payable, Federal Unemployment Taxes Payable, and State Unemployment Taxes Payable.

Federal and state laws specify when a business must pay taxes. The dates for submitting federal income tax withholdings, FICA taxes, and federal unemployment taxes vary according to the amounts owed. State unemployment taxes are usually paid quarterly. After a check is issued for taxes, the following type of entry is made in the cash payments journal. Notice that the tax liability account is debited and the Cash account is credited.

CASH PAYMENTS JOURNAL FOR MONTH OF July 19 X1 PAGE 7

DATE	CHECK NO.	EXPLANATION	✓	ACCOUNTS PAYABLE	MERCHANDISE PURCHASES	ACCOUNT TITLE	POST. REF.	AMOUNT	PURCHASES DISCOUNT	CASH
19X1 July 3	164	Taxes for second quarter				State Unempl. Taxes Pay.	224	321 88		321 88

Preparing Payroll Tax Forms

The federal government requires businesses to prepare a number of payroll tax forms. For example, at the end of each quarter, it is necessary to submit an *Employer's Quarterly Federal Tax Return* (*Form 941*) to the Internal Revenue Service. This form reports the federal income tax withholdings and FICA taxes for the quarter.

In January of each year, the business must prepare a *Wage and Tax Statement* (*Form W-2*) for each employee, showing the employee's earnings, federal income tax withheld, and FICA tax withheld during the previous year. If there are state and city income taxes, these amounts are also shown on Form W-2. The employee receives two or more copies of this form. The business also sends a copy of each employee's Form W-2 to the Internal Revenue Service along with a *Transmittal of Income and Tax Statements* (*Form W-3*).

Another tax form that must be filed in January of each year is the *Employer's Annual Federal Unemployment Tax Return* (*Form 940*). This form reports the business's federal unemployment tax for the previous year.

Businesses usually pay federal income tax withholdings and FICA taxes (both employee's and employer's contributions) by depositing them in a bank that the Internal Revenue Service has authorized to receive these taxes. Each payment must be accompanied by a *Federal Tax Deposit* (*Form 501*).

State and city tax agencies may also require a variety of payroll tax forms.

- ☐ The total amount an employee earns is known as gross earnings. This amount can be computed in various ways according to the pay plan used. There are a number of different pay plans.
- ☐ Gross earnings may include both regular earnings and overtime earnings. By law, many employees are entitled to receive overtime pay for all time worked in excess of 40 hours a week. The overtime rate must be at least $1\frac{1}{2}$ times the regular rate. Businesses must keep records such as time sheets or time cards in order to determine the number of regular hours and overtime hours.
- ☐ Net pay is usually less than gross earnings because most employees have deductions. Some deductions such as federal income tax withholding and FICA tax are required. Other deductions are voluntary.

Chapter Summary

- The amount of federal income tax withheld for each employee depends on the employee's gross earnings, marital status, and number of withholding allowances. The FICA tax is a percentage of the employee's gross earnings. If these earnings reach a certain maximum amount in any year, no further deductions for FICA tax are made during that year.
- By law, businesses must keep detailed records of the hours worked, gross earnings, deductions, and net pay of their employees. For this reason, many businesses prepare a payroll register and employee earnings records.
- After the payroll is computed, it must be recorded in the general journal. When the employees are paid, an entry is made in the cash payments journal.
- Most businesses are subject to several payroll taxes—the employer's FICA tax, federal unemployment tax, and state unemployment tax. After the payroll amounts are determined, these taxes are computed and recorded in the general journal. As checks are issued to send the payroll taxes to the proper agencies, entries are made in the cash payments journal.
- Businesses must prepare a number of payroll tax forms for the federal government. Other payroll tax forms may be required by state and city tax agencies.

Checking Your Knowledge

BUSINESS APPLICATION

Problem 25-1. Rosemary Dunn is employed by the United Electronics Company. She is single and claims one withholding allowance. Her time card for the week ended June 30, 19X1, is given on page 127 of the workbook. Complete the time card as follows.

1. Determine and enter the number of hours worked each day. Also enter the regular hours, overtime hours, and total hours for the week. (The normal work day is from 8 a.m. to 12 noon and from 1 to 5 p.m. Don't count differences of 5 minutes or less from these times.)
2. Determine and enter the regular earnings, overtime earnings, and gross earnings. The hourly rates are shown on the time card.
3. Determine and enter the deductions. Use the proper tax table on page 173 of the text to find the amount of federal income tax to be withheld. Compute the FICA tax at the rate of 6.13 percent. This employee also has voluntary deductions of $3.50 for medical insurance and $10 for savings bonds. Be sure to record the total deductions.
4. Determine and enter the net pay.

Problem 25-2. Payroll information for the Dayton Auto Parts Company is shown below. The hours worked cover the week of March 24–30, 19X1.

1. Determine the earnings, deductions, and net pay for each employee. Use the income tax tables on page 173 of the text. Assume a FICA rate of 6.13 percent. In addition to federal income tax and FICA tax, each employee has a deduction of $4 for medical insurance.
2. Complete the payroll register given on page 128 of the workbook. Use the cross-footing method to prove the totals.

Employee No.	Name	Withholding Allowances	Marital Status	Hours Worked Regular	Hours Worked Overtime	Hourly Rate Regular	Hourly Rate Overtime
1	Clay, John	4	M	40	5	$5.00	$7.50
2	Fong, Alan	2	S	40	7	4.50	6.75
3	Hill, Wayne	5	M	40	3	4.60	6.90
4	Massi, Janet	1	S	40	2	4.80	7.20
5	Nye, George	6	M	40	4	4.90	7.35
6	Soto, Alice	3	M	40	9	4.50	6.75

Problem 25-3. The following information comes from the payroll register of Century Tool Distributors. This information is for the week of June 22–28, 19X1.

Total Earnings	$876.20
Total Income Tax Deductions	91.60
Total FICA Tax Deductions	53.71
Total Net Pay	730.89

1. Record the payroll in the general journal given on page 129 of the workbook.
2. Determine the business's payroll taxes—the employer's FICA tax, federal unemployment tax, and state unemployment tax. Assume a rate of 0.7 percent for federal unemployment tax and a rate of 2.7 percent for state unemployment tax.
3. Record the payroll taxes in the general journal given on page 129 of the workbook.

Problem 25-4. Do the following tasks for the Stanley Office Supply Store. Use the cash payments journal given on page 130 of the workbook.

1. Record the payment of the payroll for the biweekly period ended March 31, 19X1. Check 594 for $517.80 was issued to obtain the necessary cash on April 2.
2. Record the payment of state unemployment taxes for the quarter ended March 31, 19X1. Check 595 for $191.30 was issued on April 4.
3. Record the payment of federal income taxes and FICA taxes for the month ended March 31, 19X1. The general ledger showed a balance of $283.45 in the Employee Income Taxes Payable account and a balance of $169.20 in the FICA Taxes Payable account. Check 596 for the total taxes owed was issued on April 6.

MANAGERIAL ANALYSIS

Case 25. Helen Montoya owns a clothing factory. She would like to reduce the amount of payroll work for the business. Up to now, she has been paying her employees in cash on a weekly basis. Her accountant is suggesting that the business adopt a biweekly (two-week) pay period and issue checks to the employees.

1. Do you think that the accountant's suggestions will reduce the business's payroll work? Why or why not?
2. Do you think that the new procedures may cause any problems for the business?

26

Special Procedures Related to Sales

Businesses try to sell merchandise that will please their customers. However, sometimes a customer will return merchandise or request an allowance. The merchandise may be damaged, or it may be unsatisfactory for some other reason. This chapter discusses procedures for handling sales returns and allowances as well as other special procedures related to sales.

Sales Returns and Allowances

When a customer returns merchandise or receives an allowance, there is a decrease in the business's revenue from sales. This decrease can be recorded by debiting the Sales Revenue account. However, most businesses prefer to use a separate account called the Sales Returns and Allowances account. Having a separate account makes it easy to determine the total amount of sales returns and allowances for each period. This information helps management to judge customer satisfaction.

Returns and Allowances on Cash Sales. When merchandise is sold for cash, many businesses provide a cash refund if the customer returns the goods or asks for an allowance. For example, Modern Appliance Distributors sold merchandise for $250 in cash on May 1. An item costing $50 was damaged in delivery. The customer returned this item on May 4 and was given a check for $50. The necessary entry is made in the cash payments journal. The Sales Returns and Allowances account is debited, and the Cash account is credited.

CASH PAYMENTS JOURNAL FOR MONTH OF May 19 X1 PAGE 2

DATE	CHECK NO.	EXPLANATION	✓	ACCOUNTS PAYABLE	MERCHANDISE PURCHASES	OTHER ACCOUNTS ACCOUNT TITLE	POST. REF.	AMOUNT	PURCHASES DISCOUNT	CASH
19X1 May 4	117	Cash refund for return				Sales Ret. and Allow.	402	50 00		50 00

Sales Returns and Allowances NO. 402

DATE	EXPLANATION	POST. REF.	DEBIT	DATE	EXPLANATION	POST. REF.	CREDIT
19X1 May 4	Return	CP2	50 00				

180 Accounting Fundamentals

Returns and Allowances on Credit Sales. The procedure for handling returns and allowances on credit sales involves the use of a form called a *credit memorandum,* or *credit slip.* This form shows that the seller will deduct the amount of the return or allowance from the customer's account balance. The credit memorandum consists of an original and at least one copy. The seller sends the original to the customer. The copy provides the information that the seller needs to journalize the transaction.

Modern Appliance Distributors issued the following credit memorandum to the Economy Appliance Center on May 6. The return is entered in the general journal. Then postings are made to the general ledger and the accounts receivable ledger.

Credit Memorandum: Form showing the deduction from a customer's account for a return or allowance.

MODERN APPLIANCE DISTRIBUTORS
5891 Grant Avenue
Houston, Texas 77034

To Economy Appliance Center   Credit Memorandum No. 1
    24 Hilton Shopping Mall
    San Antonio, TX 78201   Date 5/6/X1

We have credited your account as follows:

Quantity	Stock No.	Description	Unit Price	Amount
2	C128	Arco broilers sold on Invoice 543	$40.00	$80.00

Explanation Arrived in damaged condition.

GENERAL JOURNAL PAGE 3

DATE	DESCRIPTION OF ENTRY	POST. REF.	DEBIT	CREDIT
19X1 May 6	Sales Returns and Allowances	402	80 00	
	Accounts Receivable/Economy Appliance Center	112/✓		80 00
	Issued Credit Memorandum 1 for the return of merchandise sold on Invoice 543.			

Sales Returns and Allowances   NO. 402

DATE	EXPLANATION	POST. REF.	DEBIT	DATE	EXPLANATION	POST. REF.	CREDIT
19X1 May 4	Return	CP2	50 00				
6	Return, CM1	J3	80 00				

Accounts Receivable   NO. 112

DATE	EXPLANATION	POST. REF.	DEBIT	DATE	EXPLANATION	POST. REF.	CREDIT
19X1 May 1	Brought Forward	✓	2610 00	19X1 May 6	Return, CM1	J3	80 00

Special Procedures Related to Sales

NAME:	Economy Appliance Center
ADDRESS:	24 Hilton Shopping Mall
	San Antonio, TX 78201

TERMS: 1/10, n/60

DATE	DESCRIPTION	POST. REF.	DEBIT	CREDIT	BALANCE
19X1 Apr. 1	Balance	✓			450 00
24	Invoice 543	S1	1280 00		1730 00
May 6	Return on Invoice 543; CM1	J3		80 00	1650 00

Notice that the Sales Returns and Allowances account is debited for the amount of the return ($80). The same amount is credited to two accounts—the Accounts Receivable account in the general ledger and the customer's account in the accounts receivable ledger. It is necessary to decrease the balances of these two accounts because the customer now owes less money to the business. (Remember that the Accounts Receivable account shows the total amount owed by all credit customers.)

At the end of the accounting period, the total of the sales returns and allowances is reported on the income statement. This amount appears in the Operating Revenue section. It is deducted from the sales revenue for the period.

```
Operating Revenue
    Sales Revenue                               $12,850
    Less Sales Returns and Allowances   $190
         Sales Discount                  227      417
    Net Sales                                   $12,433
```

Notes Receivable

A credit customer will sometimes request an extension of time to pay the balance due on an account. In order to set a definite date for payment, the seller may want the customer to issue a *promissory note*. Such notes usually bear interest.

Promissory Note: A written promise to pay a stated amount of money on a specified date.

Notes Receivable: Promissory notes that a business has received.

When a business obtains a promissory note from a credit customer, the amount owed is no longer a part of the asset accounts receivable. Instead, the amount owed becomes part of the asset *notes receivable*. This change must be entered in the seller's financial records.

On May 23, the Capitol Appliance Store asked Modern Appliance Distributors for an extension of 60 days in which to pay an invoice. The store issued a promissory note for $880, the amount owed. The note is for 60 days and bears interest at 9 percent. When Modern Appliance Distributors receives the note, the transaction is entered in the general journal and posted to the general ledger and the accounts receivable ledger.

GENERAL JOURNAL   PAGE 3

DATE	DESCRIPTION OF ENTRY	POST. REF.	DEBIT	CREDIT
19X1 May 23	Notes Receivable	111	880 00	
	Accounts Receivable/Capitol Appliance Store	112/✓		880 00
	Received a 60-day, 9% note.			

182 Accounting Fundamentals

Notes Receivable — NO. 111

DATE	EXPLANATION	POST. REF.	DEBIT	DATE	EXPLANATION	POST. REF.	CREDIT
19X1 May 23	60-day, 9% note	J3	880 00				

Accounts Receivable — NO. 112

DATE	EXPLANATION	POST. REF.	DEBIT	DATE	EXPLANATION	POST. REF.	CREDIT
19X1 May 1	Brought Forward	✓	2610 00	19X1 May 6	Return, CM1	J3	80 00
				23	60-day, 9% note	J3	880 00

NAME: Capitol Appliance Store
ADDRESS: 164 Bond Street
Austin, TX 78750
TERMS: 2/10, n/30

DATE	DESCRIPTION	POST. REF.	DEBIT	CREDIT	BALANCE
19X1 Apr. 7	Invoice 541	S1	250 00		250 00
17		CR1		250 00	— 00
29	Invoice 544	S1	880 00		880 00
May 23	60-day, 9% note	J3		880 00	— 00

The Notes Receivable account is debited to record the new asset that the business gained. Two accounts are credited—the Accounts Receivable account in the general ledger and the customer's account in the accounts receivable ledger. The balances of these two accounts must be reduced by the amount of the note.

Notes receivable appear in the Current Assets section of the balance sheet.

```
              Assets

Current Assets
  Cash                         $3,967
  Petty Cash                       50
  Notes Receivable                880
```

The note issued by the Capitol Appliance Store will become due on July 22. When Modern Appliance Distributors receives the money, an entry is made in the cash receipts journal. The Cash account is debited for the total received ($893.20). The Notes Receivable account is credited for the amount of the note ($880), and the Interest Revenue account is credited for the amount of the interest ($13.20).

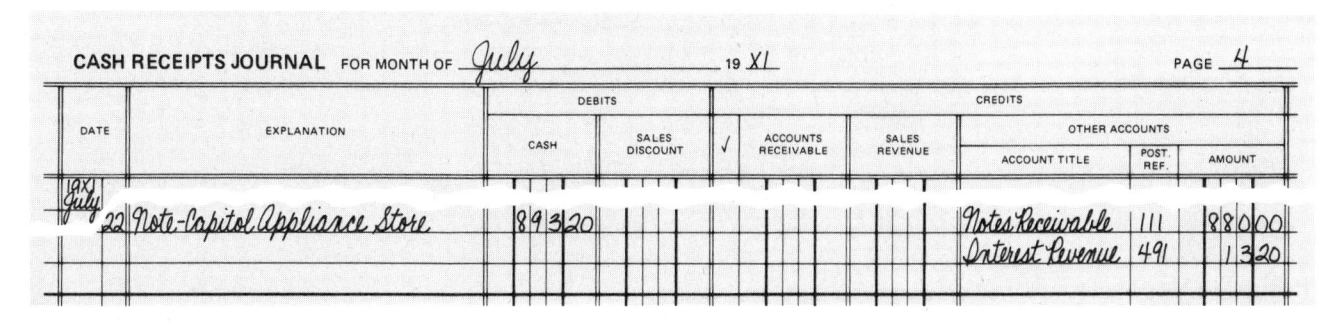

CASH RECEIPTS JOURNAL FOR MONTH OF July 19X1 — PAGE 4

DATE	EXPLANATION	CASH (DR)	SALES DISCOUNT (DR)	✓	ACCOUNTS RECEIVABLE (CR)	SALES REVENUE (CR)	ACCOUNT TITLE	POST. REF.	AMOUNT
19X1 July 22	Note-Capitol Appliance Store	893 20					Notes Receivable	111	880 00
							Interest Revenue	491	13 20

Special Procedures Related to Sales

Interest revenue appears in the Other Revenue section of the income statement.

```
Other Revenue
    Interest Revenue                                        $13.20
```

Sales Taxes

Sales Tax: A tax levied on retail sales.

Some states and cities impose a *sales tax* on many types of merchandise sold at retail. Under typical sales tax regulations, the customer must pay the tax. The business is responsible for collecting the tax and sending the total collected to the sales tax agency at regular intervals (usually monthly).

The collection of sales tax on a cash sale is recorded in the cash receipts journal. A special column called Sales Tax Payable Credit is used. The following illustration shows how an entry for a $50 sale with a 5-percent sales tax ($2.50) is made at the Kent Clothing Center, a retail store.

CASH RECEIPTS JOURNAL FOR MONTH OF *January* 19 XI   PAGE 1

DATE	EXPLANATION	CASH DEBIT	✓	ACCOUNTS RECEIVABLE	SALES TAX PAYABLE	SALES REVENUE	OTHER ACCOUNTS – ACCOUNT TITLE	POST. REF.	AMOUNT
19XI Jan. 1	Balance on hand, $4,200								
2	Cash sale, Sales Slip 101	52 50			2 50	50 00			

The entry for sales tax on a charge sale is made in the sales journal. Look at the entry for Sales Slip 102 recorded at the Kent Clothing Center. The Accounts Receivable account and the customer's account are debited for $210—the amount of the sale ($200) plus the amount of the sales tax ($10). Offsetting credits are recorded in the Sales Tax Payable account ($10) and the Sales Revenue account ($200).

SALES JOURNAL FOR MONTH OF *January* 19 XI   PAGE 1

DATE	SALES SLIP NO.	CUSTOMER'S NAME	✓	ACCTS. REC. DEBIT	SALES TAX PAYABLE CREDIT	SALES REVENUE CREDIT
19XI Jan. 2	102	Joseph D'Avanzo	✓	210 00	10 00	200 00
3	103	Robert Evans	✓	63 00	3 00	60 00

Notice that the sales journal used by the Kent Clothing Center has an Accounts Receivable Debit column and a Sales Tax Payable Credit column as well as a Sales Revenue Credit column. The totals of the Sales Tax Payable Credit columns in the cash receipts journal and the sales journal are posted to the general ledger at the end of the month in the same way as the other special columns are posted.

The amount of sales tax payable appears in the Current Liabilities section of the balance sheet.

```
                Liabilities and Owner's Equity
Current Liabilities
    Accounts Payable                              $2,160
    Sales Tax Payable                                341
```

184   Accounting Fundamentals

The following entry is made in the cash payments journal when the tax is sent to the sales tax agency. The Sales Tax Payable account is debited, and the Cash account is credited.

CASH PAYMENTS JOURNAL FOR MONTH OF February 19 X1										PAGE 2
				DEBITS					CREDITS	
DATE	CHECK NO.	EXPLANATION	✓	ACCOUNTS PAYABLE	MERCHANDISE PURCHASES	OTHER ACCOUNTS			PURCHASES DISCOUNT	CASH
						ACCOUNT TITLE	POST. REF.	AMOUNT		
19X1 Feb. 3	168	Jan. sales tax sent to state				Sales Tax Payable	203	341 00		341 00

The debit to the Sales Tax Payable account is posted individually from the cash payments journal. After the posting, the balance of the account is zero. The taxes collected from customers and held during the month have now been paid to the sales tax agency. The same procedure is followed from month to month. The liability for sales taxes is recorded each month and paid the following month.

Sales Tax Payable   NO. 203

DATE	EXPLANATION	POST. REF.	DEBIT	DATE	EXPLANATION	POST. REF.	CREDIT
19X1 Feb. 3		CP2	341 00	19X1 Jan. 31		S1	211 00
				31		CR1	130 00
							341 00

Bad Debts

From experience, business managers know that some credit customers will not be able to pay their bills when the amounts become due. Uncollectible amounts owed by credit customers are referred to as *bad debts*. They represent an expense for the business.

There is no way to tell in advance which customers will fail to pay. However, bad debts expense should be recorded in each accounting period so that it can be matched against the revenue earned during the period. This is done by estimating the bad debts loss for the period.

A number of methods can be used to estimate the amount of bad debts loss. One common method is to take a percentage of the accounts receivable at the end of the period. For example, suppose that the total of the accounts receivable is $5,000, and the rate of loss is expected to be 2 percent. The amount of the estimated bad debts loss for the period is $100 ($5,000 × 0.02). The expected rate of loss is usually determined by the business's actual losses in previous periods.

An adjustment for the estimated bad debts loss is made on the worksheet, as shown on page 186. Notice that the Bad Debts Expense account is debited, and an account called Allowance for Bad Debts is credited. This information is also recorded in the general journal along with the other adjusting entries.

Bad Debts: Uncollectible amounts owed by credit customers.

Special Procedures Related to Sales   **185**

Kent Clothing Center
Worksheet
Month Ended January 31, 19X1

ACCT. NO.	ACCOUNT NAME	TRIAL BALANCE DR.	TRIAL BALANCE CR.	ADJUSTMENTS DR.	ADJUSTMENTS CR.	ADJUSTED TRIAL BALANCE DR.	ADJUSTED TRIAL BALANCE CR.	INCOME STATEMENT DR.	INCOME STATEMENT CR.	BALANCE SHEET DR.	BALANCE SHEET CR.
112	Accts. Receivable	5000 00				5000 00				5000 00	
113	Allow. for Bad Debts				(A) 100 00		100 00				100 00
519	Bad Debts Expense			(A) 100 00		100 00		100 00			

GENERAL JOURNAL PAGE 2

DATE	DESCRIPTION OF ENTRY	POST. REF.	DEBIT	CREDIT
19X1 Jan. 31	Bad Debts Expense	519	100 00	
	Allowance for Bad Debts	113		100 00
	Estimated bad debts loss for January.			

The Bad Debts Expense account appears in the Operating Expenses section of the income statement. The Allowance for Bad Debts account is a contra asset account. It appears in the Current Assets section of the balance sheet as a deduction from the Accounts Receivable account ($5,000 − $100). The resulting figure ($4,900) is the amount that the business expects to collect from its credit customers.

```
                          Assets

Current Assets
   Cash                                    $ 2,860
   Petty Cash                                   30
   Notes Receivable                            600
   Accounts Receivable           $5,000
   Less Allowance for Bad Debts     100      4,900
   Merchandise Inventory                    11,480
      Total Current Assets                         $19,870
```

When a bill becomes overdue, various steps are taken to obtain payment from the customer. The business sends collection letters and may hire a collection agency. If such efforts are not successful, the customer's account is *written off*. This is done by making the following entry in the general journal.

Writing Off a Customer's Account: Reducing the balance of the account to zero because it is uncollectible.

GENERAL JOURNAL PAGE 6

DATE	DESCRIPTION OF ENTRY	POST. REF.	DEBIT	CREDIT
19X1 Mar. 28	Allowance for Bad Debts	113	63 00	
	Accounts Receivable/Robert Evans	112/✓		63 00
	Writeoff of uncollectible account.			

The Allowance for Bad Debts account is debited for the amount being written off. Two accounts are credited for this amount. The Accounts Receivable account in the general ledger must be credited to decrease its balance by the uncollectible amount. The customer's account in the accounts receivable ledger must be credited to reduce its balance to zero.

The Bad Debts Expense account is not involved in this transaction. It is only used when the estimated bad debts loss for a period is recorded.

Bank Credit Card Sales

Many retail businesses allow customers to use bank credit cards, such as Master Charge and Visa. This arrangement is convenient because the retailer can offer charge account services but does not have to wait for payment, keep charge account records, and send monthly statements to the customers.

When a retailer makes a sale involving a bank credit card, information about the transaction is recorded on a special multicopy sales slip form supplied by the bank. Then the customer's credit card and the sales slip are placed in an imprinting device. This device is used to print the customer's name and credit card number as well as other data on the sales slip. (Refer to the illustration on page 72.) The customer signs the sales slip and receives one copy. The retailer keeps the other copies.

Before the sale is completed, the retailer may need to obtain credit authorization for the transaction. This is usually done by calling a credit office, which determines whether the customer is within his or her credit limit. The credit office also has a list of lost, stolen, and invalid cards.

At the end of the day, the retailer adds the amounts of all the sales slips for bank credit card sales. The total is entered on a summary form, such as the one shown below. Notice that the retailer has also entered a *discount*. This is a fee that the bank charges for handling credit card sales. The discount is a percentage of the total sales. In this case, the rate is 3 percent. After the discount is computed, it is subtracted from the total sales to find the net amount that the retailer will receive ($179.80 − $5.39 = $174.41).

Discount on Credit Card Sales: A fee charged for handling credit card sales.

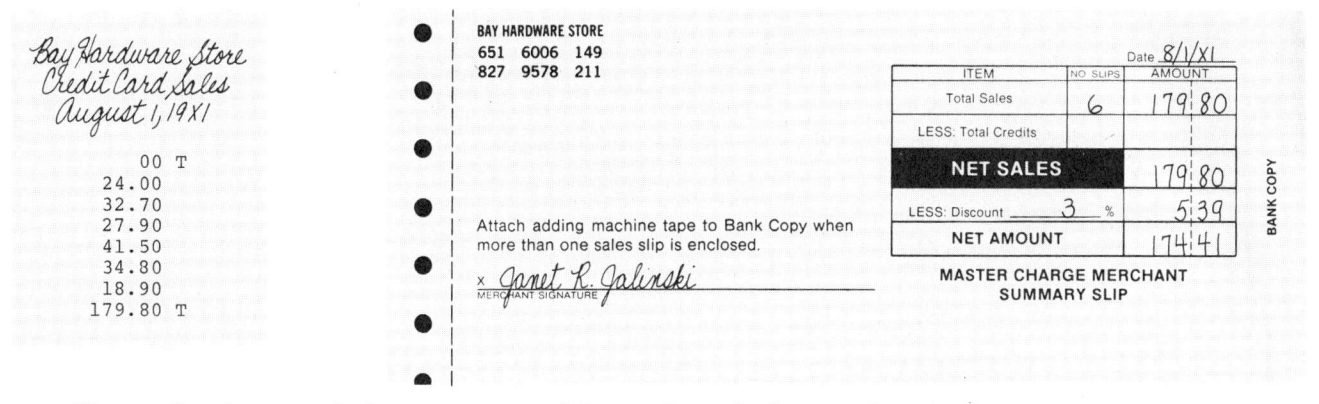

The retailer also records the net amount of the credit card sales on a deposit slip. Then the retailer takes the deposit slip, the summary form, and a copy of each credit card sales slip to the bank. When the bank processes the deposit, it adds the net amount of the credit card sales to the balance of the business's checking account.

Bank credit card sales are treated as cash sales by the retailer. After the deposit is made, these sales are entered in the cash receipts journal. The Cash account is debited for the net amount of the sales. An account called Credit Card Fee Expense is debited for the discount. The Sales Revenue account is credited for the total sales.

Special Procedures Related to Sales 187

Credit Card Fee Expense appears in the Operating Expenses section of the income statement. Some businesses set up a special account for credit card sales revenue so that they can have a separate record of these sales.

Certain banks do not deduct the discount when the credit card sales slips are deposited. Instead, they add the total amount of these sales to the retailer's account. At the end of the month, the bank computes the total discount for the period and deducts it from the account balance. When the bank statement arrives, the retailer makes an entry in the cash payments journal. The Credit Card Fee Expense account is debited, and the Cash account is credited. With this procedure, no entries are made for the discount during the month. (Each entry in the cash receipts journal consists of a debit to Cash and a credit to Sales Revenue for the total of the credit card sales.)

Chapter Summary

- The Sales Returns and Allowances account is used to record the decrease in sales revenue that results when a customer returns merchandise or receives an allowance. This account is debited for all returns and allowances. If the customer is given a cash refund, the Cash account is credited. If the amount is deducted from a balance that the customer owes, the Accounts Receivable account and the customer's account are credited.
- The Sales Returns and Allowances account appears as a deduction from the Sales Revenue account in the Operating Revenue section of the income statement.
- Promissory notes received by a business are an asset and are known as notes receivable. The interest on these notes is revenue. The Notes Receivable account is debited when a note is obtained and credited when the money is received for the note. The Interest Revenue account is credited for the amount of interest received.
- The Notes Receivable account is listed in the Current Assets section of the balance sheet. The Interest Revenue account is listed in the Other Revenue section of the income statement.
- Some states and cities impose a sales tax. The retailer collects this tax from customers. When sales are made, the amount of sales tax is credited to the Sales Tax Payable account.
- The Sales Tax Payable account appears in the Current Liabilities section of the balance sheet.
- The retailer sends the sales tax to a government agency at regular intervals, such as every month. At this time, the Sales Tax Payable account is debited, and the Cash account is credited.
- Bad debts are uncollectible amounts owed by credit customers. At the end of each accounting period, the bad debts loss is estimated. An adjusting entry is made to record this amount. The Bad Debts Expense account is debited, and the Allowance for Bad Debts account is credited.
- It is necessary to estimate the amount of bad debts because most losses from the current period's sales will probably not occur until the next period. However, the bad debts expense for the current period must be matched against the revenue earned in this period.
- The Bad Debts Expense account appears in the Operating Expenses section of the income statement. The Allowance for Bad Debts account appears as a deduction from the Accounts Receivable account in the Current Assets section of the balance sheet.
- When a customer's account is found to be uncollectible, it is written off. The Allowance for Bad Debts account is debited. Two accounts are credited—the Accounts Receivable account and the customer's account.
- Many retail businesses make bank credit card sales. The bank charges a discount (fee) for handling such sales. The discount is subtracted from the total of the sales. The bank adds the net amount of the credit card sales to the retailer's checking account after the retailer deposits the necessary forms.
- Bank credit card sales are treated as cash sales by the retailer. They are recorded in the cash receipts journal.

□ The Credit Card Fee Expense account is debited for the amount of discount that the bank deducts. This account appears in the Operating Expenses section of the income statement.

Checking Your Knowledge

BUSINESS APPLICATION

Problem 26-1. Some of the transactions that took place at the Gracious Living Furniture Store during June 19X1 are listed below.

1. Record each of these transactions in the proper journal. Use the sales journal, cash receipts journal, cash payments journal, and general journal on pages 131 and 132 of the workbook. (Before you begin, make a memorandum entry in the cash receipts journal for the cash balance of $3,100 on June 1.)
2. Pencil-foot the sales journal and the cash receipts journal. Use the cross-footing method to prove their accuracy.
3. Total and rule the sales journal and the cash receipts journal.

June 1 Received a 30-day, 9-percent promissory note from Gary Smith, a credit customer. Smith issued the note to settle an overdue bill for $800.
 2 Issued Check 663 for $372 to pay the sales tax collected in May to the state sales tax agency.
 3 Sold merchandise for $420 on credit to Lois Klein; Sales Slip 1201. The total of the merchandise is $400, and the sales tax is $20.
 7 Sold merchandise for $1,161.30 in cash during the first week of June. The total of the merchandise is $1,106, and the sales tax is $55.30.
 9 Sold merchandise for $650 on credit to David Luce; Sales Slip 1202. Since Luce is a decorator and will resell the merchandise to a client, there is no sales tax on this transaction. (Luce will collect sales tax from his client and pay it to the state.)
 13 Issued Credit Memorandum 28 for $120 to David Luce for damaged merchandise that he returned.
 14 Sold merchandise for $1,279.95 in cash during the second week of June. The total of the merchandise is $1,219, and the sales tax is $60.95.
 16 Sold merchandise for $598.50 on credit to Ellen Casey; Sales Slip 1203. The total of the merchandise is $570, and the sales tax is $28.50.
 18 Received a 60-day, 9-percent promissory note from Mark Lane, a credit customer. Lane issued the note to settle an overdue bill for $1,200.
 21 Sold merchandise for $1,554 in cash during the third week of June. The total of the merchandise is $1,480, and the sales tax is $74.
 24 Received $420 in cash from Lois Klein in payment of Sales Slip 1201.
 27 Received $806 in cash from Gary Smith in payment of his promissory note. Of this amount, $6 is interest.
 28 Sold merchandise for $1,077.30 in cash during the fourth week of June. The total of the merchandise is $1,026, and the sales tax is $51.30.

Problem 26-2. On December 31, 19X1, the Erie Supply Company had total accounts receivable of $26,000. On January 4, 19X2, the business was notified that Martin Products, a credit customer, had gone bankrupt. This customer owed $370.

1. Estimate the bad debts loss for the the year ended December 31, 19X1. The expected rate of loss is 3 percent of the total accounts receivable.
2. Make an adjusting entry as of December 31, 19X1, to record the estimated bad debts loss for the year. Use the general journal on page 133 of the workbook.
3. Make an entry as of January 4, 19X2, to write off the account of Martin Products. Use the general journal on page 133 of the workbook.

Problem 26-3. The information shown below and at the right was taken from the general ledger of the Playtime Toy Company at the end of the yearly accounting period on December 31, 19X1.

1. Prepare the Operating Revenue section of the income statement. Use the form at the top of page 134 of the workbook.

Sales Revenue	$268,473
Sales Returns and Allowances	6,186
Sales Discount	3,428

2. Prepare the Current Assets section of the balance sheet. Use the form at the bottom of page 134 of the workbook.

Cash	$14,562
Petty Cash	125
Notes Receivable	3,000
Accounts Receivable	21,240
Allowance for Bad Debts	637
Merchandise Inventory	43,100
Supplies	1,800

MANAGERIAL ANALYSIS

Case 26. Sally Fox manages the Fashion House, a retail clothing store. She is concerned because the store's sales returns and allowances have increased a great deal during the last two years. However, the sales revenue has remained about the same.

1. What problems might cause a large increase in sales returns and allowances?

2. What policies might the store adopt to reduce sales returns and allowances?

Special Procedures Related to Purchases

27

In a well-run business, all merchandise purchases are carefully inspected soon after they arrive. If any goods are unsatisfactory, they are returned to the supplier or an allowance is requested. This chapter discusses procedures for handling purchases returns and allowances as well as other special procedures related to purchases.

Purchases Returns and Allowances

When a business returns goods or receives an allowance, there is a decrease in the cost of its merchandise purchases. This decrease is usually recorded in an account called Purchases Returns and Allowances.

Returns and Allowances on Cash Purchases. Most businesses expect a cash refund if they return goods purchased for cash or request an allowance on such goods. The supplier sends a check for the necessary amount. For example, on May 1, Modern Appliance Distributors made a cash purchase for $260. When the merchandise was unpacked, an item costing $30 was found to be defective. The item was returned, and Modern Appliance Distributors received a check from the supplier on May 5. This transaction is recorded in the cash receipts journal. The Cash account is debited, and the Purchases Returns and Allowances account is credited.

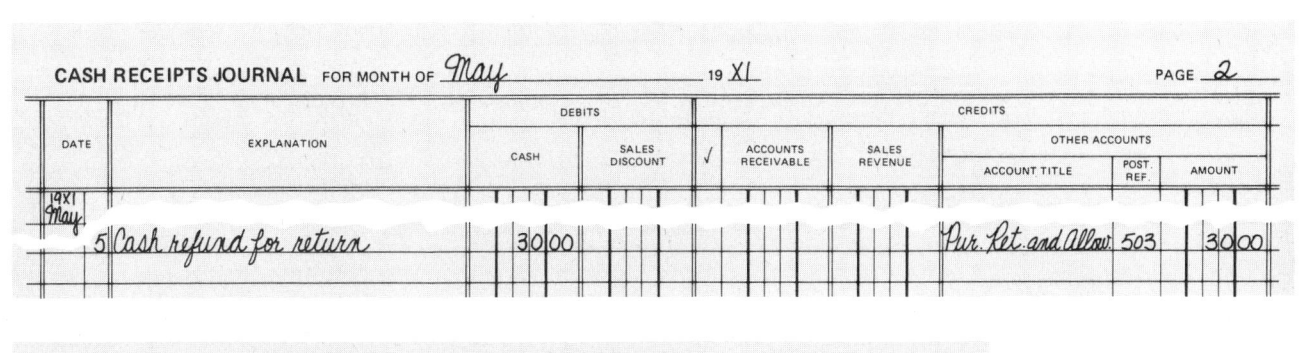

CASH RECEIPTS JOURNAL FOR MONTH OF May 19 X1								PAGE 2
		DEBITS			CREDITS			
DATE	EXPLANATION	CASH	SALES DISCOUNT	✓	ACCOUNTS RECEIVABLE	SALES REVENUE	OTHER ACCOUNTS	
							ACCOUNT TITLE / POST. REF.	AMOUNT
19X1 May 5	Cash refund for return	30 00					Pur. Ret. and Allow. 503	30 00

Purchases Returns and Allowances NO. 503

DATE	EXPLANATION	POST. REF.	DEBIT	DATE	EXPLANATION	POST. REF.	CREDIT
				19X1 May 5	Return	CR2	30 00

Special Procedures Related to Purchases 191

Returns and Allowances on Credit Purchases. If merchandise is purchased on credit, the supplier usually issues a credit memorandum for a return or allowance. The credit memorandum shows that the supplier will reduce the purchaser's account balance by the amount of the return or allowance.

Modern Appliance Distributors purchased merchandise for $1,750 on credit from Dow Industries. Items costing $50 arrived in a damaged condition. Modern Appliance Distributors returned these items and received a credit memorandum on May 7. The return is entered in the general journal and posted to the general ledger and the accounts payable ledger.

GENERAL JOURNAL PAGE 3

DATE	DESCRIPTION OF ENTRY	POST. REF.	DEBIT	CREDIT
19X1 May 7	Accounts Payable/Dow Industries	202/✓	50 00	
	Purchases Returns and Allowances	503		50 00
	Received Credit Memorandum 19 for the return of merchandise purchased on Invoice 327			

Accounts Payable NO. 202

DATE	EXPLANATION	POST. REF.	DEBIT	DATE	EXPLANATION	POST. REF.	CREDIT
19X1 May 7	Return	J3	50 00	19X1 May 1	Brought Forward	✓	5550 00

Purchases Returns and Allowances NO. 503

DATE	EXPLANATION	POST. REF.	DEBIT	DATE	EXPLANATION	POST. REF.	CREDIT
				19X1 May 5	Return	CR2	30 00
				May 7	Return	J3	50 00

NAME: Dow Industries
ADDRESS: 62 Bradshaw Avenue
San Antonio, TX 78201
TERMS: 3/10 EOM

DATE	DESCRIPTION	POST. REF.	DEBIT	CREDIT	BALANCE
19X1 Apr. 24	Invoice 327, 4/21/X1	P1		1750 00	1750 00
May 7	Return on Invoice 327; CM19	J3	50 00		1700 00

As a result of the return, Modern Appliance Distributors owes less money to the supplier. Thus, the Accounts Payable account in the general ledger and the supplier's account in the accounts payable ledger are debited for $50 to decrease their balances. (Remember that the Accounts Payable account shows the total amount that the business owes to all suppliers.) The Purchases Returns and Allowances account is credited for $50 to record the reduction in the cost of purchases.

When Modern Appliance Distributors pays the invoice, the return is deducted from the invoice total before the cash discount and the amount of the payment are computed.

Accounting Fundamentals

Invoice total	$1,750
Less return	50
Net purchase	$1,700
Rate of discount	0.03
Amount of discount	$51.00

Net purchase	$1,700
Less discount	51
Amount of payment	$1,649

At the end of the accounting period, the total of the purchases returns and allowances is reported on the income statement. This amount is shown in the Cost of Goods Sold section as a deduction from the amount of merchandise purchases. (See the partial income statement on page 194.)

Freight In

When a business purchases merchandise, it may be required to pay transportation charges from the supplier's warehouse. These charges are an added cost of the merchandise. However, they are usually recorded in a separate account called Freight In, or Transportation In.

Transportation charges may cover parcel post, motor freight, railway freight, or air freight. The invoice issued by the supplier usually shows who will pay the transportation charges. The term *FOB shipping point* on the invoice means that the purchaser must pay. The term *FOB destination* means that the supplier must pay.

Payment of transportation charges can be handled in two ways. In some cases, the purchaser is asked to pay the transportation company directly. In other cases, the supplier lists the transportation charges on the invoice. The purchaser pays the supplier for both the merchandise and the transportation charges when the invoice becomes due.

On May 12, Modern Appliance Distributors received some merchandise from a supplier. A check was issued to the Acme Motor Freight Company to pay transportation charges of $18 on the merchandise. This transaction is recorded in the cash payments journal. The Freight In account is debited, and the Cash account is credited.

FOB: Free on board.

FOB Shipping Point: The purchaser pays transportation charges.

FOB Destination: The supplier pays transportation charges.

CASH PAYMENTS JOURNAL FOR MONTH OF May 19 X1 PAGE 3

DATE	CHECK NO.	EXPLANATION	✓	ACCOUNTS PAYABLE	MERCHANDISE PURCHASES	ACCOUNT TITLE	POST. REF.	AMOUNT	PURCHASES DISCOUNT	CASH
19X1 May 12	125	Transportation charges				Freight In	502	18 00		18 00

On May 14, an invoice from a new supplier arrived at Modern Appliance Distributors. This invoice listed a credit purchase of $400 and transportation charges of $22. In order to be able to record such invoices easily, Modern Appliance Distributors has expanded its purchases journal as shown below.

PURCHASES JOURNAL FOR MONTH OF May 19 X1 PAGE 2

DATE	PURCHASED FROM	INV. NO.	INVOICE DATE	TERMS	✓	ACCTS. PAY. CREDIT	MERCHANDISE PURCHASES DEBIT	FREIGHT IN DEBIT
19 X1 May 14	United Manufacturing Co.	1223	5/11/X1	2/10, n/30	✓	422 00	400 00	22 00

Special Procedures Related to Purchases 193

Notice how the May 14 entry is made. The Merchandise Purchases account is debited for the price of the goods ($400), and the Freight In account is debited for the transportation charges ($22). The Accounts Payable account is credited for the total of the invoice ($422). (This amount is also credited to the supplier's account in the accounts payable ledger.)

At the end of the month, the column totals of the purchases journal are posted to the general ledger. The postings to the accounts payable ledger are made individually during the month.

When Modern Appliance Distributors pays the invoice owed to United Manufacturing Company, the cash discount is taken on the price of the goods, but not on the transportation charges. The discount and the amount of the payment are computed as follows.

Price of goods	$400	Price of goods	$400
Rate of discount	0.02	Plus transportation charges	22
Amount of discount	$8.00	Invoice total	$422
		Less discount	8
		Amount of payment	$414

The amount of transportation charges for the period is shown on the income statement. Notice that the balance of the Freight In account is added to the balance of the Merchandise Purchases account to find the total cost of purchases.

```
Cost of Goods Sold
  Merchandise Inventory, May 1, 19X1                           $ 7,500.00
  Merchandise Purchases                         $8,350.00
  Freight In                                        92.00
  Total Cost of Purchases                       $8,442.00
  Less Purchases Returns and Allowances $100.00
       Purchases Discount                143.50    243.50       8,198.50
  Total Merchandise Available for Sale                         $15,698.50
  Less Merchandise Inventory, May 31, 19X1                      9,500.00
     Cost of Goods Sold                                                    $6,198.50
```

Notes Payable

If a business does not have enough cash to pay the balance owed to a creditor, it will usually request some extra time. The creditor may grant the extra time, but ask for a promissory note. This arrangement gives the creditor more assurance of receiving its money. The note provides a written promise to pay and sets a definite date for the payment.

Assume that Modern Appliance Distributors issues a note for $800 to Reliable Products on May 29. The note will run for 60 days and bear interest at 9 percent. This note does not pay the debt. It merely changes the form of the liability from an account payable to a note payable. (Promissory notes given to creditors are called *notes payable.*) Because the form of the liability has changed, the following entry is made in the general journal of Modern Appliance Distributors. This entry is posted to the general ledger and the accounts payable ledger.

Notes Payable: Promissory notes that a business has issued.

DATE	DESCRIPTION OF ENTRY	POST. REF.	DEBIT	CREDIT
19X1 May 29	Accounts Payable/Reliable Products	202/✓	800.00	
	Notes Payable	201		800.00
	Issued a 60-day, 9% note.			

GENERAL JOURNAL PAGE 3

194 Accounting Fundamentals

Accounts Payable — NO. 202

DATE	EXPLANATION	POST. REF.	DEBIT	DATE	EXPLANATION	POST. REF.	CREDIT
19X1 May 7	Return	J3	50 00	19X1 May 1	Brought Forward	✓	5550 00
29	60-day, 9% note	J3	800 00				

Notes Payable — NO. 201

DATE	EXPLANATION	POST. REF.	DEBIT	DATE	EXPLANATION	POST. REF.	CREDIT
				19X1 May 29	60-day, 9% note	J3	800 00

NAME: Reliable Products
ADDRESS: 3221 Lincoln Expressway
Dallas, TX 75207
TERMS: n/60

DATE	DESCRIPTION	POST. REF.	DEBIT	CREDIT	BALANCE
19X1 Apr. 1	Balance	✓			2200 00
4		CP1	1400 00		800 00
May 29	60-day, 9% note	J3	800 00		— 00

The Accounts Payable account in the general ledger and the creditor's account in the accounts payable ledger are debited to record the decrease in their balances. The Notes Payable account is credited to record the new liability.

Notes payable appear in the Current Liabilities section of the balance sheet.

```
                Liabilities and Owner's Equity

Current Liabilities
    Notes Payable                                    $  800
    Accounts Payable                                  3,230
```

The note given to Reliable Products will become due on July 28. When Modern Appliance Distributors issues the necessary check, an entry is made in the cash payments journal. The Notes Payable account is debited for the amount of the note ($800), and the Interest Expense account is debited for the amount of the interest ($12). The Cash account is credited for the total amount paid ($812).

CASH PAYMENTS JOURNAL FOR MONTH OF July 19 X1 — PAGE 7

DATE	CHECK NO.	EXPLANATION	✓	ACCOUNTS PAYABLE (DR)	MERCHANDISE PURCHASES (DR)	ACCOUNT TITLE	POST. REF.	AMOUNT	PURCHASES DISCOUNT (CR)	CASH (CR)
19X1 July 28	164	Note — Reliable Products				Notes Payable	201	800 00		812 00
						Interest Expense	591	12 00		

Special Procedures Related to Purchases

Interest expense appears in the Other Expenses section of the income statement.

```
Other Expenses
    Interest Expense                    $12.00
```

Chapter Summary

- The Purchases Returns and Allowances account is used to record the decrease in the cost of merchandise purchases that results when a business returns goods or receives allowances. This account is credited for all returns and allowances. If the business is given a cash refund, the Cash account is debited. If the amount is deducted from a balance that the business owes, the Accounts Payable account and the supplier's account are debited.
- The Purchases Returns and Allowances account appears as a deduction from the Merchandise Purchases account in the Cost of Goods Sold section of the income statement.
- The purchaser may be required to pay transportation charges on merchandise. These charges are debited to the Freight In account.
- The balance of the Freight In account appears in the Cost of Goods Sold section of the income statement. This amount is added to the balance of the Merchandise Purchases account to find the total cost of purchases.
- The purchaser cannot take a cash discount on the amounts of returns and allowances or transportation charges.
- Promissory notes given by a business are a liability and are known as notes payable. The interest on these notes is an expense. The Notes Payable account is credited when a note is issued and debited when the note is paid. The Interest Expense account is debited for the amount of interest paid.
- The Notes Payable account is listed in the Current Liabilities section of the balance sheet. The Interest Expense account is listed in the Other Expenses section of the income statement.

Checking Your Knowledge

BUSINESS APPLICATION

Problem 27-1. Some of the transactions that took place at the Varsity Sporting Goods Store during August 19X1 are listed below.

1. Record each of these transactions in the proper journal. Use the purchases journal, cash payments journal, cash receipts journal, and general journal on pages 135 and 136 of the workbook. (Before you begin, make a memorandum entry in the cash receipts journal for the cash balance of $2,890 on August 1.)
2. Pencil-foot the purchases journal and the cash payments journal. Use the cross-footing method to prove their accuracy.
3. Total and rule the purchases journal and the cash payments journal.

Aug. 1 Issued a 30-day, 9-percent promissory note to Devon Industries, a creditor, to settle an overdue bill for $1,000.
     3 Purchased merchandise for $595 on credit from Champion Products; Invoice 1271, dated 8/1/X1, terms 2/10, n/30. The price of the goods is $570, and the transportation charge is $25.
     6 Issued Check 446 for $250 to make a cash purchase of merchandise.

196 Accounting Fundamentals

Aug. 9 Issued Check 447 to Champion Products for Invoice 1271. (Compute the amount of the discount and the amount of the payment.)

10 Returned some defective merchandise purchased on August 6. Received a cash refund of $25 from the supplier.

12 Purchased merchandise for $380 on credit from Elco Sports Equipment; Invoice 3692, dated 8/9/X1, terms 3/10, n/30.

12 Issued Check 448 for $14 to Rapid Freight Company to pay a transportation charge on merchandise.

15 Returned some damaged merchandise that arrived on August 12. Received Credit Memorandum 112 for $60 from Elco Sports Equipment.

17 Issued Check 449 to Elco Sports Equipment for Invoice 3692 less the return. (Compute the amount of the discount and the amount of the payment.)

24 Issued a 60-day, 9-percent promissory note to Gem Bicycles, a creditor, to settle an overdue bill for $680.

Aug. 27 Purchased merchandise for $826 on credit from Champion Products; Invoice 1334, dated 8/25/X1, terms 2/10, n/30. The price of the goods is $790, and the transportation charge is $36.

29 Issued Check 450 for $1,007.50 to pay the promissory note given to Devon Industries. Of this amount, $7.50 is interest.

Problem 27-2. The following information was taken from the general ledger of the Warren Wholesale Grocery Company at the end of the yearly accounting period on December 31, 19X1.

Merchandise Inventory, Jan. 1, 19X1	$12,500.00
Merchandise Purchases	55,867.00
Freight In	471.90
Purchases Returns and Allowances	618.50
Purchases Discount	832.20

A physical count was made of the merchandise inventory on December 31. The total is $12,000.

Prepare the Cost of Goods Sold section of the income statement. Use the form on page 137 of the workbook.

MANAGERIAL ANALYSIS

Case 27. John Dexter owns a business that deals in farm equipment and tools. He needs to purchase some new merchandise. Two suppliers have offered similar goods for the same price ($4,000) but with different terms.

Supplier A has terms of 3/20, n/60 and will add a transportation charge of $135. Supplier B has terms of 1/10, n/30 and will pay for transportation.

1. From which supplier would you suggest that Dexter make his purchase?

2. If Dexter were to pay within the discount period, what would be the cost of the purchase from each supplier?

The Combined Journal

Combined Journal: Multicolumn journal that combines features of the general journal and several special journals.

Special journals provide an efficient way of recording transactions. However, some small businesses prefer to use a single multicolumn journal. This journal combines the features of the general journal and several special journals in one book. It is therefore known as the *combined journal*.

Recording Transactions in the Combined Journal

The combined journal is suitable for a business that has a limited number of entries each month. The Rainbow Paint Store is an example of such a business. Its combined journal is shown on pages 200 and 201. Notice that there are special columns for the following accounts: Cash, Accounts Receivable, Accounts Payable, Merchandise Purchases, and Sales Revenue. These columns make it easier to record the types of transactions that occur most often in the business. All other transactions are recorded in the Other Accounts section of the journal.

The advantages and disadvantages of the combined journal can be seen by examining the entries made at the Rainbow Paint Store during June 19X1.

Cash Balance. At the beginning of each month, a memorandum entry is recorded in the combined journal to show the cash balance. Notice how this entry was made on June 1. A line was drawn through the Cash section, and "Cash balance, $4,187" was written in the Explanation column.

Payment of Expenses. The Rainbow Paint Store made several cash payments for expenses during June. For example, Check 413 for $500 was issued on June 2 to pay the rent. Because the business's combined journal does not have any special columns for expense accounts, the title of the account to be debited (Rent Expense) must be written in the Other Accounts section. The amount is recorded in the Other Accounts Debit column and the Cash Credit column. Additional examples of cash payments for expenses appear on lines 6, 7, and 24. The entries on lines 35 and 36 show the expenses that were recorded when the petty cash fund was replenished. The entry on line 37 is for the expense incurred when the bank deducted a service charge from the business's checking account.

Purchases of Merchandise on Credit. On June 3, the Rainbow Paint Store purchased merchandise for $1,700 on credit from the Durable Paint Company. The amount is recorded in the Merchandise Purchases Debit column and the Accounts Payable Credit column. Other entries for purchases of merchandise on credit appear on lines 12 and 20.

Purchases of Fixed Assets. On June 4, the Rainbow Paint Store purchased an electronic calculator for use in the office. Check 414 for $165 was issued to pay for this purchase. The account to be debited (Office Equipment) is written in the Other

Accounting Fundamentals

Accounts section. The amount is recorded in the Other Accounts Debit column and the Cash Credit column.

Sales of Merchandise on Credit. The Rainbow Paint Store makes most of its sales for cash to individuals. However, the business sells on credit to several firms that paint houses, apartments, and offices. The terms for all credit customers are 2/10, n/30. On June 5, the Rainbow Paint Store sold merchandise for $420 on credit to the Perez Decorating Service. The amount is recorded in the Accounts Receivable Debit column and the Sales Revenue Credit column. Other entries for sales on credit appear on lines 9 and 19.

Sales of Merchandise for Cash. During the week of June 1–6, the Rainbow Paint Store had cash sales of $1,875. These sales were entered on June 6 by recording the total amount in the Cash Debit column and the Sales Revenue Credit column. Other entries for cash sales appear on lines 14, 18, 22, and 34.

Payments to Creditors. On June 9, the Rainbow Paint Store issued Check 417 for $1,666 to the Durable Paint Company for Invoice 931 ($1,700) less discount ($34). The total of the invoice is recorded in the Accounts Payable Debit column. Because there is no special column for purchases discount, the title of this account must be written in the Other Accounts section. The amount of the discount is entered in the Other Accounts Credit column. The amount of the cash payment is recorded in the Cash Credit column. Another entry for a payment to a creditor appears on line 21.

Cash Purchases of Merchandise. On June 10, the Rainbow Paint Store purchased merchandise for $440 in cash. Check 418 was issued for this purchase. The amount is recorded in the Merchandise Purchases Debit column and the Cash Credit column.

Cash Received From Credit Customers. On June 13, the Rainbow Paint Store received $411.60 in cash from the Perez Decorating Service for Sales Slip 689 ($420) less discount ($8.40). The amount of cash received is recorded in the Cash Debit column. Because there is no special column for sales discount, the title of this account must be written in the Other Accounts section. The amount of the discount is entered in the Other Accounts Debit column. The total of the sales slip is recorded in the Accounts Receivable Credit column. Another entry for cash received from a credit customer appears on line 16.

Withdrawals by the Owner. On June 15, the owner of the Rainbow Paint Store wanted to make a cash withdrawal of $900. Check 419 was issued for this purpose. The account to be debited (Carl Miller, Drawing) must be written in the Other Accounts section. The amount is recorded in the Other Accounts Debit column and the Cash Credit column.

Returns and Allowances on Credit Purchases. The Rainbow Paint Store returned some merchandise to the Ideal Paint Corporation and received Credit Memorandum 95 for $80 on June 19. The title of the account to be credited (Purchases Returns and Allowances) is written in the Other Accounts section. The amount is recorded in the Accounts Payable Debit column and the Other Accounts Credit column.

Returns and Allowances on Credit Sales. On June 29, the Rainbow Paint Store issued Credit Memorandum 37 for $25 to the Bell Contracting Company. This credit memorandum is for a return of merchandise that was sold on credit. The title of the account to be debited (Sales Returns and Allowances) is written in the Other Accounts section. The amount is recorded in the Other Accounts Debit column and the Accounts Receivable Credit column.

Employee Earnings and Deductions. The Rainbow Paint Store pays its employees at the end of each month. The payroll register prepared on June 30 showed total earnings of $1,600, total income tax deductions of $172.30, total FICA tax deductions of $98.08, and total net pay of $1,329.62. An entry was made in the combined journal to record these amounts. Refer to lines 25–28. Because there are no special columns for the payroll accounts, the Other Accounts section must be used for this type of entry.

Employer's Payroll Taxes. The Rainbow Paint Store had the following taxes on the June payroll: employer's FICA tax, $98.08; federal unemployment tax, $11.20; and state unemployment tax, $43.20. These amounts were recorded in the combined journal on June 30. Refer to lines 29–32. Again, the Other Accounts section must be used.

COMBINED JOURNAL — FOR MONTH OF June 19X1

#	Cash Debit	Cash Credit	Date	Check No.	Explanation	✓	A/R Debit	A/R Credit
1			19X1 June 1		Cash balance, $4,187			
2		500.00	2	413	Rent for June			
3			3		Durable Paint Co.-Inv. 931; 6/1; 2/10, n/30			
4		165.00	4	414	Purchase of electronic calculator			
5			5		Perez Decorating Service-Sales Slip 689	✓	420.00	
6		107.40	6	415	Electric bill			
7		89.60	6	416	Telephone bill			
8	1,875.00		6		Cash sales for June 1-6			
9			8		Hudson Painters-Sales Slip 690	✓	380.00	
10		1,666.00	9	417	Durable Paint Co.-Inv. 931			
11		440.00	10	418	Cash purchase of merchandise			
12			11		Ideal Paint Corp.-Inv. 1233; 6/9; 2/20, n/60			
13	411.60		13		Perez Decorating Service-Sales Slip 689	✓		420.00
14	1,790.00		13		Cash sales for June 8-13			
15		900.00	15	419	Withdrawal by owner			
16	372.40		17		Hudson Painters-Sales Slip 690	✓		380.00
17			19		Ideal Paint Corp.-CM 95 on Inv. 1233			
18	1,947.00		20		Cash sales for June 15-20			
19			22		Bell Contracting Co.-Sales Slip 691	✓	445.00	
20			23		Variety Paints, Inc.-Inv. A468; 6/20; n/30			
21		1,862.00	27	420	Ideal Paint Corp.-Inv. 1233 less CM 95			
22	2,231.00		27		Cash sales for June 22-27			
23			29		Bell Contracting Co.-CM 37 on Sales Slip 691	✓		25.00
24		67.00	30	421	Delivery Service for June			
25			30		Payroll for June			
26								
27								
28								
29			30		Employer's payroll taxes for June			
30								
31								
32								
33		1,329.62	30	422	Payment of payroll			
34	463.00		30		Cash sales for June 29 and 30			
35		39.00	30	423	Replenish petty cash fund			
36								
37		5.00	30	—	Bank service charge for June			
38	9,090.00	7,170.62			Totals		1,245.00	825.00
39	(101)	(101)					(112)	(112)

200 Accounting Fundamentals

Payment of the Payroll. On June 30, Check 422 for $1,329.62 was issued to obtain the cash needed to pay the employees of the Rainbow Paint Store. The account to be debited (Wages Payable) is written in the Other Accounts section. The amount is recorded in the Other Accounts Debit column and the Cash Credit column.

Posting From the Combined Journal

During the month, the amounts in the Other Accounts section of the combined journal are posted individually to the general ledger accounts listed. As each amount is posted, the account number is written in the Posting Reference column of the

Posting From the Combined Journal:
- During the month, post individual entries in Other Accounts section to general ledger. Post individual entries in Accounts Receivable section and Accounts Payable section to subsidiary ledgers.
- At end of month, post all column totals to general ledger except totals in Other Accounts section.

PAGE 6

√	Accounts Payable Debit	Accounts Payable Credit	Mdse. Purchases Debit	Sales Revenue Credit	Account Title	Post. Ref.	Other Accounts Debit	Other Accounts Credit	
					Rent Expense	517	500 00		2
√		1700 00	1700 00						3
					Office Equipment	123	165 00		4
				420 00					5
					Utilities Expense	519	107 40		6
					Telephone Expense	518	89 60		7
				1875 00					8
				380 00					9
√	1700 00				Purchases Discount	504		34 00	10
			440 00						11
√		1980 00	1980 00						12
					Sales Discount	403	8 40		13
				1790 00					14
					Carl Miller, Drawing	302	900 00		15
					Sales Discount	403	7 60		16
√	80 00				Purchases Ret. and Allow.	503		80 00	17
				1947 00					18
				445 00					19
√		630 00	630 00						20
√	1900 00				Purchases Discount	504		38 00	21
				2231 00					22
					Sales Ret. and Allow.	402	25 00		23
					Delivery Expense	512	67 00		24
					Wages Expense	520	1600 00		25
					Employee Income Taxes Pay.	221		172 30	26
					FICA Taxes Payable	222		98 08	27
					Wages Payable	225		1329 62	28
					Payroll Taxes Expense	516	152 48		29
					FICA Taxes Payable	222		98 08	30
					Fed. Unemp. Taxes Pay.	223		11 20	31
					State Unemp. Taxes Pay.	224		43 20	32
					Wages Payable	225	1329 62		33
				463 00					34
					Miscellaneous Expense	515	18 70		35
					Office Expense	521	20 30		36
					Miscellaneous Expense	515	5 00		37
	3680 00	4310 00	4750 00	9551 00			4996 10	1904 48	38
	(202)	(202)	(501)	(401)			(X)	(X)	39

The Combined Journal 201

journal. The abbreviation *C* and the journal page number are recorded in the ledger accounts to identify the source of the entry.

The amounts in the Accounts Receivable section and the Accounts Payable section are posted individually to the subsidiary ledger accounts shown in the Explanation column. As each amount is posted, a check mark is placed in the journal.

At the end of the month, the money columns of the combined journal are pencil-footed. Then a proof is prepared to check the equality of the debits and credits recorded in the journal.

Rainbow Paint Store
Proof of Combined Journal
Month Ended June 30, 19X1

Column	Debit	Credit
Cash	9090.00	7170.62
Accounts Receivable	1245.00	825.00
Accounts Payable	368.00	4310.00
Merchandise Purchases	4750.00	
Sales Revenue		9551.00
Other Accounts	4996.10	1904.48
Totals	23761.10	23761.10

After the proof is completed, the column totals are entered in ink and the journal is ruled. The totals are posted to the general ledger accounts named in the column headings. As these postings are made, the account numbers are recorded below the totals in the journal. The letter *X* is entered below the totals of the Other Accounts section to show that they are not posted. (Remember that the amounts in the Other Accounts section are posted individually during the month.)

The combined journal is convenient for the Rainbow Paint Store. However, it would present problems for a business that had more transactions to record. The large number of columns increases the likelihood of making errors when entering amounts. Also, only one person at a time can journalize or post transactions. In contrast, when special journals are used, several employees can do accounting work at the same time.

Chapter Summary

☐ Some small businesses use a combined journal. These businesses find it more convenient to have a single multicolumn journal than a general journal and several special journals.

☐ In the combined journal, special columns are provided for recording the types of transactions that occur most often, such as those involving cash, accounts receivable, accounts payable, merchandise purchases, and sales revenue.

☐ During the month, the amounts in the Other Accounts section are posted individually to the general ledger. The amounts in the Accounts Receivable section and the Accounts Payable section are posted individually to the subsidiary ledgers.

☐ At the end of the month, the money columns of the combined journal are pencil-footed. Then the equality of the debits and credits is proved.

☐ After the combined journal is totaled and ruled, the totals of the special columns are posted to the general ledger.

Checking Your Knowledge

BUSINESS APPLICATION

Problem 28-1. The transactions that took place at the Royal Carpet Store during May 19X1 are listed below. This business makes most of its sales for cash to individuals. However, some merchandise is sold on credit to decorators and various organizations. The terms for such sales are 2/10, n/30.

1. Record each of the May transactions in the combined journal. Use the form on pages 140 and 141 of the workbook. Before you begin, make a memorandum entry for the cash balance of $4,327.85 on May 1.
2. Pencil-foot the money columns. Then prepare a proof of the combined journal as of May 31, 19X1. Use the form on page 139 of the workbook.
3. Enter the column totals, and rule the combined journal.

May 1 Issued Check 323 for $550 to pay monthly rent for the store.
2 Sold merchandise for $685 on credit to Mary Dumont; Sales Slip 220.
3 Issued Check 324 for $142.50 to pay for newspaper advertisements.
4 Purchased merchandise for $3,218 on credit from Drake Carpet Company; Invoice 2417, dated 5/1/X1, terms 2/10, n/30.
6 Sold merchandise for $1,892.75 in cash during May 1–6.
8 Issued Check 325 for $3,153.64 to Drake Carpet Company for Invoice 2417 ($3,218), less discount ($64.36).
10 Sold merchandise for $2,186 on credit to Bayside Motel; Sales Slip 221.
11 Received $671.30 in cash from Mary Dumont for Sales Slip 220 ($685), less discount ($13.70).
13 Sold merchandise for $1,327.92 in cash during May 8–13.

May 15 Purchased merchandise for $2,280 on credit from Beacon Rugs, Inc.; Invoice 961, dated 5/12/X1, terms 1/20, n/60.
17 Issued Check 326 for $276.50 to purchase an electric typewriter for use in the office.
19 Received $2,142.28 in cash from Bayside Motel for Sales Slip 221 ($2,186), less discount ($43.72).
20 Sold merchandise for $1,594.68 in cash during May 15–20.
22 Returned some damaged merchandise that was purchased from Beacon Rugs, Inc. (Invoice 961). Received Credit Memorandum 72 for $130.
24 Issued Check 327 for $129.67 to pay the electric bill. (Debit Utilities Expense.)
25 Sold merchandise for $346 on credit to Howard Voss; Sales Slip 222.
27 Sold merchandise for $1,721.40 in cash during May 22–27.
29 Issued Check 328 for $1,200 for a cash withdrawal by Susan Roth, the owner.
31 Issued Check 329 for $189.70 to pay for delivery service during May.
31 Computed the payroll for May. The amounts are as follows: total earnings, $1,710; total income tax deductions, $256.50; total FICA tax deductions, $104.82; total net pay, $1,348.68.
31 Computed the business's payroll taxes for May. The amounts are as follows: employer's FICA tax, $104.82; federal unemployment tax, $11.97; state unemployment tax, $46.17.
31 Issued Check 330 for $1,348.68 to obtain the cash needed for payment of the payroll.
31 Sold merchandise for $789.65 in cash during May 29–31.

MANAGERIAL ANALYSIS

Case 28. Frances Hoffman owns and operates a retail clothing store. The business has a large number of transactions, including many transactions with charge account customers. On some days, it is necessary for the office secretary and a cashier to help the accounting clerk to make journal entries and post to the ledgers. Ms. Hoffman is now considering a change from special journals to a combined journal.

Would you suggest that this business use a combined journal? Why or why not?

COMPREHENSIVE PROJECT

This project presents transactions that took place at the Casual Clothing Center during June 19X1. You will do all the firm's accounting work for the month. The activities you perform will provide practical application of the accounting principles discussed in the text.

The Business

The Casual Clothing Center is a retail store that sells sportswear for men and women. The store is located in a busy suburban shopping mall. It is owned and operated by Gary Larson. Mr. Larson is assisted by one full-time employee and two part-time employees.

Most sales are made for cash. However, the store provides charge accounts to a small number of steady customers. Merchandise is usually purchased on credit.

The Accounting System

The accounting system of the Casual Clothing Center includes a general journal and special journals for sales, purchases, cash receipts, and cash payments. The business also has a general ledger and subsidiary ledgers for accounts receivable and accounts payable. The chart of accounts for the general ledger is shown below.

General Instructions

The journal forms that you will need for the project are given on pages 143–150 of the workbook. The ledger accounts appear on pages 151–164. The June 1 balances have already been entered.

Record each of the transactions for June in the proper journal. Use the following procedure to post individual entries. At the end of each week, post to the general ledger from the general journal and the Other Accounts column of the cash receipts journal and the cash payments journal. Also post all journal entries affecting the subsidiary ledgers.

Before you begin work, make a memorandum entry in the cash receipts journal to show the cash on hand as of June 1.

CASUAL CLOTHING CENTER
Chart of Accounts

Assets

101 Cash
102 Petty Cash
111 Notes Receivable
112 Accounts Receivable
113 Merchandise Inventory
114 Supplies
121 Store Equipment
122 Accum. Depr.—Store Equipment
123 Office Equipment
124 Accum. Depr.—Office Equipment

Liabilities

201 Notes Payable
202 Accounts Payable
221 Employee Income Taxes Payable
222 FICA Taxes Payable
223 Federal Unemployment Taxes Payable
224 State Unemployment Taxes Payable
225 Wages Payable
231 Sales Tax Payable

Owner's Equity

301 Gary Larson, Capital
302 Gary Larson, Drawing
399 Revenue and Expense Summary

Revenue

401 Sales Revenue
402 Sales Returns and Allowances
491 Interest Revenue

Costs and Expenses

501 Merchandise Purchases
502 Freight In
503 Purchases Returns and Allowances
504 Purchases Discount
511 Advertising Expense
512 Delivery Expense
513 Depr. Expense—Store Equipment
514 Depr. Expense—Office Equipment
515 Miscellaneous Expense
516 Payroll Taxes Expense
517 Rent Expense
518 Supplies Expense
519 Utilities Expense
520 Wages Expense
591 Interest Expense

Transactions for June 1–2

June 1 Issued Check 223 for $450 to pay monthly rent for the store.
   1 Issued Check 224 for $50 to set up a petty cash fund.
   1 Issued a 30-day, 10-percent promissory note for $1,410 to Davis Sportswear, a creditor.
   2 Received $293.73 in cash from Alice Murphy for the balance she owes.

2 Issued Check 225 for $60 to pay for advertising display materials.

2 Received a 30-day, 9-percent promissory note for $480 from George Anton, a charge account customer.

2 Sold merchandise for $764.72 in cash during June 1 and 2. The total of the merchandise is $728.30, and the sales tax is $36.42. *Be sure to post the individual entries as specified in the instructions.*

Transactions for June 4–9

June 4 Sold merchandise for $80.01 on credit to Donna Chase; Sales Slip 113. The total of the merchandise is $76.20, and the sales tax is $3.81.

4 Issued Check 226 for $698.25 to Ward Apparel Company for Invoice 1924 ($712.50), less discount ($14.25).

5 Issued Check 227 for $45 to pay for a newspaper advertisement.

5 Received $75.07 in cash from Paul Steiner for the balance he owes.

6 Sold merchandise for $89.15 on credit to Anthony Lopez; Sales Slip 114. The total of the merchandise is $84.90, and the sales tax is $4.25.

8 Issued Check 228 for $345.65 to make a cash purchase of merchandise.

8 Issued Check 229 for $16 to pay transportation charges on merchandise.

9 Issued Check 230 for $33.10 to pay the telephone bill.

9 Issued Check 231 for $248.90 to Leisure Time Fashions for Invoice A762.

9 Issued a 30-day, 10-percent promissory note for $1,230 to Paragon Shirt Company, a creditor.

9 Sold merchandise for $1,550.75 in cash during the week of June 4–9. The total of the merchandise is $1,476.90, and the sales tax is $73.85. *Be sure to post the individual entries as specified in the instructions.*

Transactions for June 11–16

June 11 Issued Check 232 for $128 to purchase an electronic calculator for the office.

12 Sold merchandise for $44.89 on credit to Paul Steiner; Sales Slip 115. The total of the merchandise is $42.75, and the sales tax is $2.14.

13 Purchased merchandise for $500 on credit from Ward Apparel Company; Invoice 2432, dated 6/11/X1, terms 2/10, n/30.

14 Issued Check 233 for $25 to pay for cleaning service. (Debit Miscellaneous Expense.)

14 Purchased merchandise for $985.35 on credit from Paragon Shirt Company; Invoice 9388, dated 6/12/X1, terms 2/20, n/60.

14 Issued Check 234 for $37 to pay transportation charges on merchandise.

14 Sold merchandise for $25.57 on credit to Karen Pace; Sales Slip 116. The total of the merchandise is $24.35, and the sales tax is $1.22.

14 Issued Check 235 for $359 to pay employee income taxes and total FICA taxes for May. The amount of the income taxes is $192, and the amount of the FICA taxes is $167.

14 Issued Check 236 for $371.65 to pay the sales tax collected in May.

15 Computed the payroll for the biweekly period ended June 15. The amounts are as follows: total earnings, $600; total income tax deductions, $82.10; total FICA tax deductions, $36.78; total net pay, $481.12. (Make the necessary entry in the general journal.)

15 Computed the business's payroll taxes for the biweekly period ended June 15. The amounts are as follows: employer's FICA tax, $36.78; federal unemployment tax, $4.20; state unemployment tax, $16.20. (Make the necessary entry in the general journal.)

15 Issued Check 237 for $481.12 to pay the June 15 payroll.

15 Issued Check 238 for $74 to pay for a newspaper advertisement.

16 Received $140.47 in cash from Harold Watson for the balance he owes.

16 Sold merchandise for $1,594.01 in cash during the week of June 11–16. The total of the merchandise is $1,518.10, and the sales tax is $75.91. *Be sure to post the individual entries as specified in the instructions.*

Transactions for June 18–23

June 18 Returned some damaged merchandise that was purchased from Paragon Shirt Company (Invoice 9388). Received Credit Memorandum 316 for $125.

19 Issued Check 239 for $30 to pay for the mailing of advertising circulars.

19 Purchased merchandise for $1,291.50 on credit from Harmony Slacks and Jeans; Invoice 3033, dated 6/16/X1, terms 2/10, n/30.

Comprehensive Project

19 Issued Check 240 for $45 to pay transportation charges on merchandise.

19 Issued Check 241 for $490 to Ward Apparel Company for Invoice 2432 ($500), less discount ($10).

20 Sold merchandise for $183.75 on credit to Harold Watson; Sales Slip 117. The total of the merchandise is $175, and the sales tax is $8.75.

21 Sold used store equipment for $100 in cash.

21 Issued Check 242 for $479.85 to make a cash purchase of merchandise.

22 Accepted a return of merchandise sold to Harold Watson (Sales Slip 117). Issued Credit Memorandum 12 for $42. Of this amount, $40 is for the merchandise and $2 is for sales tax. (Debit Sales Returns and Allowances for $40. Debit Sales Tax Payable for $2. Credit Accounts Receivable and the customer's account for $42.)

22 Sold merchandise for $68.04 on credit to Alice Murphy; Sales Slip 118. The total of the merchandise is $64.80, and the sales tax is $3.24.

23 Issued Check 243 for $1,265.67 to Harmony Slacks and Jeans for Invoice 3033 ($1,291.50), less discount ($25.83).

23 Sold merchandise for $1,750.98 in cash during the week of June 18–23. The total of the merchandise is $1,667.60, and the sales tax is $83.38.

Be sure to post the individual entries as specified in the instructions.

Transactions for June 25–30

June 25 Purchased merchandise for $402.50 on credit from Leisure Time Fashions; Invoice A798, dated 6/22/X1, terms n/30.

25 Sold merchandise for $164.33 on credit to Donna Chase; Sales Slip 119. The total of the merchandise is $156.50, and the sales tax is $7.83.

25 Issued Check 244 for $30 to pay for repairs to store equipment. (Debit Miscellaneous Expense.)

26 Accepted a return of merchandise sold to Donna Chase (Sales Slip 119). Issued Credit Memorandum 13 for $73.50. Of this amount, $70 is for the merchandise and $3.50 is for sales tax. (Record this transaction in the same way as the June 22 return.)

26 Purchased merchandise for $1,056 on credit from Ward Apparel Company; Invoice 2498, dated 6/24/X1, terms 2/10, n/30.

27 Issued Check 245 for $110 to pay for supplies that will be used in the business.

28 Received $483.60 in cash from George Anton in payment of his promissory note. Of this amount, $3.60 is interest.

28 Sold merchandise for $223.13 on credit to Anthony Lopez; Sales Slip 120. The total of the merchandise is $212.50, and the sales tax is $10.63.

29 Returned some damaged merchandise that was purchased from Ward Apparel Company (Invoice 2498). Received Credit Memorandum 177 for $106.

29 Issued Check 246 for $1,421.75 to pay the promissory note given to Davis Sportswear. Of this amount, $11.75 is interest.

30 Issued Check 247 for $104.90 to pay the electric bill.

30 Received a 60-day, 10-percent promissory note for $340 from Karen Pace, a charge account customer.

30 Issued Check 248 for $63.80 to pay for delivery service during June.

30 Computed the payroll for the biweekly period ended June 30. The amounts are as follows: total earnings, $630; total income tax deductions, $89.25; total FICA tax deductions, $38.62; total net pay, $502.13.

30 Computed the business's payroll taxes for the biweekly period ended June 30. The amounts are as follows: employer's FICA tax, $38.62; federal unemployment tax, $4.41; state unemployment tax, $17.01.

30 Issued Check 249 for $502.13 to pay the June 30 payroll.

30 Issued Check 250 for $1,100 for a cash withdrawal by Gary Larson, the owner.

30 Issued Check 251 for $43.90 to replenish the petty cash fund. The expenses involved are as follows: Advertising Expense, $10.50; Delivery Expense, $21.30; Miscellaneous Expense, $12.10.

30 Sold merchandise for $1,981.09 in cash during the week of June 25–30. The total of the merchandise is $1,886.75, and the sales tax is $94.34.

Be sure to post the individual entries as specified in the instructions.

End-of-Period Procedures

Perform the following end-of-period procedures for the Casual Clothing Center.

1. Pencil-foot the sales journal, cash receipts journal, and cash payments journal. Use the cross-footing method to check the accuracy of these journals.

2. Total and rule the sales journal, purchases journal, cash receipts journal, and cash payments journal. Then post the column totals to the proper general ledger accounts. (Remember that the totals of the Other Accounts columns should not be posted.)

3. Prepare a schedule of accounts receivable. Use the form on page 164 of the workbook. Compare the total of this schedule with the balance of the Accounts Receivable account in the general ledger. The two amounts should be the same.

4. Prepare a schedule of accounts payable. Use the form on page 167 of the workbook. Compare the total of this schedule with the balance of the Accounts Payable account in the general ledger. The two amounts should be the same.

5. Prepare a worksheet. Use the forms on pages 165 and 166 of the workbook. The heading, account numbers, and account names have already been entered.

   a. Complete the Trial Balance section. Remember that the column totals should be equal.
   b. Complete the Adjustments section. Supplies costing $60 were used during June. The monthly depreciation on the store equipment is $45, and the monthly depreciation on the office equipment is $19.
   c. Complete the Adjusted Trial Balance section in order to check the equality of the debits and credits again.
   d. Record the merchandise inventory of $9,700 on June 30. Then complete the Income Statement section and the Balance Sheet section.

6. Prepare financial statements for the business. Use the forms on pages 168–170 of the workbook. Obtain the necessary amounts from the worksheet.

   a. Complete an income statement for the month ended June 30, 19X1. (Review the income statements on pages 143 and 194 of the text before you start work.)
   b. Complete a statement of owner's equity for the month ended June 30, 19X1. (Review the statement of owner's equity on page 144 of the text before you start work.)
   c. Complete a classified balance sheet as of June 30, 19X1. (Review the balance sheet on page 144 of the text before you start work.)

7. Record the adjusting entries in the general journal. Obtain the necessary information from the Adjustments section of the worksheet. Post the adjusting entries to the proper general ledger accounts.

8. Record the closing entries in the general journal. Obtain the necessary information from the Income Statement section of the worksheet. Post the closing entries to the proper general ledger accounts.

9. Rule all closed accounts in the general ledger.

10. Rule and balance each open account in the general ledger that has two or more entries.

11. Prepare a postclosing trial balance as of June 30. Use the form on page 171 of the workbook.

Index

A

Account, 13–17, 20–22, 43–47; *def.*, 13 (*see also specific accounts*)
  closing an, 55–60; *def.*, 56; *illus.*, 57–59, 153–155
  opening an, 13–15, 43–44; *illus.*, 14, 15, 45–47
  permanent, *def.*, 60
  temporary, *def.*, 60
  writing off an, *def.*, 186; *illus.*, 186
Account balance, 16–17; *def.*, 16; *illus.*, 16, 17
Account form of balance sheet, *def.*, 53; *illus.*, 3, 11, 32, 35
Accounting, 1, 63; *def.*, 1
Accounting cycle, 62; *def.*, 62
  procedures that make up, 62
Accounting equation, 2; *illus.*, 2
  balance sheet and, 2–3
Accounting period, *def.*, 29
Accounting system, beginning an, 1–2
Accounts payable, *def.*, 2
  on balance sheet, 3; *illus.*, 3, 11, 32, 53, 144
  schedule of, *def.*, 129; *illus.*, 130
Accounts payable ledger, 126–130; *def.*, 127; *illus.*, 128
  posting to, 127–129; *illus.*, 127, 128
  proving the, 129–130; *illus.*, 130
Accounts receivable, *def.*, 9
  aging of, 123
  on balance sheet, *illus.*, 11, 32, 53, 144
  schedule of, *def.*, 121; *illus.*, 121
  schedule of, by age; *def.*, 123; *illus.*, 123
Accounts receivable ledger, 117–123; *def.*, 118; *illus.*, 118–120
  posting to, 119–121; *illus.*, 119, 120
  proving the, 121–122; *illus.*, 121
  statement of account and, *def.*, 122; *illus.*, 122
Adjusting entries, 148–149, 185; *illus.*, 148, 186
Adjustments, worksheet, 134–138, 140–141, 185–186; *def.*, 134
  for bad debts, 185–186; *illus.*, 186
  for depreciation, 135–136; *illus.*, 137
  for expired insurance, 135
  for merchandise inventory, 140–141; *illus.*, 141
  for supplies used, 134–135; *illus.*, 137
Asset accounts, 13, 15–16; *illus.*, 14, 16
  debiting and crediting, 15–16; *illus.*, 15, 16
Assets, 2; *def.*, 2
  on balance sheet, 3; *illus.*, 3, 11, 32, 35, 53, 144
  current, *def.*, 145
  fixed, 135–136, 145; *def.*, 135, 145
  transactions involving, 4–5, 8–10
  useful life of, 135–136; *def.*, 135

B

Bad debts, 185–187; *def.*, 185; *illus.*, 186
Balance ledger form, 63, 118; *def.*, 63, 118
Balance sheet, 3, 30–32, 52–53, 144–145; *def.*, 3, 30; *illus.*, 3, 11, 32, 35, 53, 144
  account form of, *def.*, 53; *illus.*, 3, 11, 32, 35
  accounting equation and, 2–3
  assets on, 3; *illus.*, 3, 11, 32, 35, 53, 144
  classified, *def.*, 145; *illus.*, 144
  effect of business activities on, 3–5, 8–11
  liabilities on, 3; *illus.*, 3, 11, 32, 35, 53, 144
  opening accounts for items on, 13–15; *illus.*, 14–15
  owner's equity on, 3; *illus.*, 3, 11, 32, 35, 53, 144
  preparing, 3, 31–32, 52–53, 145
  report form of, *def.*, 53; *illus.*, 53, 144
  worksheet and, 49–53, 141–145; *illus.*, 51–53, 141, 143, 144
Balances of accounts, 17; *illus.*, 17, 18
Bank credit card sales, 187–188; *illus.*, 187
Bank statement, 160–163; *def.*, 160; *illus.*, 161
Banking procedures, 158–163
  making bank deposits, 158–159
  opening a checking account, 158
  other bank services, 163
  reconciling the bank statement, 160–163; *def.*, 161; *illus.*, 162
  writing checks, 159–160; *illus.*, 160
Beginning inventory, 140–142; *def.*, 140
Blank endorsement, 158; *illus.*, 159
Book value, 136, 145; *def.*, 136
Business data processing, *def.*, 63
Business transactions, 3–5, 8–10, 22; *def.*, 3

C

Canceled checks, 160–163; *def.*, 160
Capital, *def.*, 2
  on balance sheet, 31, 52; *illus.*, 3, 11, 32, 35, 53, 144
Capital account, 14–16, 20, 22, 31, 52, 55–57, 60, 149–150, 155
Capital statement, *def.*, 30 (*see also* Statement of owner's equity)
Cash discount, 73, 78, 80–81, 192–194; *def.*, 73
  for purchase of merchandise, 78–79; *illus.*, 78, 79
  for sale of merchandise, 80–81; *illus.*, 80, 81
Cash over, *def.*, 168
Cash payments journal, 107–114; *def.*, 111; *illus.*, 111
  posting from, 113–114, 127–129; *illus.*, 111, 113, 114, 127, 128
  recording transactions in, 112–113
  setting up, 111–112
Cash purchases, 76–77, 107–112; *illus.*, 76, 77, 107–111
Cash receipts, *def.*, 103
Cash receipts journal, 99–105; *def.*, 101; *illus.*, 101, 104, 184, 187
  posting from, 103–105, 119–121; *illus.*, 104, 105, 119, 120
  recording transactions in, 102–103
  setting up, 101–102
Cash received report, 103; *illus.*, 103
Cash sales, 69–70, 79, 99–103; *illus.*, 70, 79, 99–103
Cash short, *def.*, 168
Certified check, *def.*, 163
Change fund, *def.*, 168
Charge account sales, 70–71 (*see also* Credit sales)
Charge accounts, *def.*, 69
Chart of accounts, 36, 43, 81; *def.*, 36; *illus.*, 36, 82
Check, 159–160; *def.*, 159; *illus.*, 160
  canceled, 160, 162–163; *def.*, 160
  certified, *def.*, 163

Index 209

Check (*continued*)
  endorsement of, *def.*, 158; *illus.*, 159
  outstanding, 162; *def.*, 162
  stop payment order for, *def.*, 163
Check register, 159–160; *def.*, 159
Check stub, 113, 159–160; *def.*, 159; *illus.*, 113, 160
Chronological order, 34, 74; *def.*, 34
Classified balance sheet, *def.*, 145; *illus.*, 144
Closing an account, 55–60; *def.*, 56; *illus.*, 57–59, 153–155
Closing entries, 55–57, 149–150; *def.*, 57; *illus.*, 56, 149
Closing the ledger, 55–60; *def.*, 55; *illus.*, 56–60
Combined journal, 198–202; *def.*, 198
  posting from, 201–202; *illus.*, 200–201
  proving, 202; *illus.*, 202
  recording transactions in, 198–201; *illus.*, 200–201
    cash balance, 198
    cash purchases of merchandise, 199
    cash received from credit customers, 199
    employee earnings and deductions, 200
    employer's payroll taxes, 200
    payment of expenses, 198
    payment of payroll, 201
    payments to creditors, 199
    purchases of fixed assets, 198–199
    purchases of merchandise on credit, 198
    returns and allowances, 199
    sales of merchandise, 199
    withdrawals by the owner, 199
Commission plan, *def.*, 170
Compound entry, *def.*, 39; *illus.*, 39
Computer, 65–66; *def.*, 65; *illus.*, 65
Contra account, 136, 186; *def.*, 136
Control account, 122, 129; *def.*, 122
Cost accounts, 76, 78
  on income statement, 142, 193, 194; *illus.*, 143, 194
Credit, entering, in account, 14
Credit balance, 16, 17; *illus.*, 18
Credit card sales, 70–71
  bank, 187–188; *illus.*, 187
  discount on, 187–188; *def.*, 187
  recording, 72, 187–188; *illus.*, 72, 187
Credit cards, 70–71; *def.*, 70
Credit memorandum, 181, 192; *def.*, 181; *illus.*, 181
Credit purchases, 73–74, 76, 94–96; *illus.*, 74, 76, 94–96

Credit sales, 70–73, 79, 89–91; *illus.*, 71, 72, 79, 89–91
Credit side of ledger account, *def.*, 13; *illus.*, 13, 42
Credit slip, 181 (*see also* Credit memorandum)
Credit terms, 73
Crediting, *def.*, 14
  asset accounts, 15–16; *illus.*, 15, 16
  liability accounts, 15–16; *illus.*, 15, 16
  owner's equity accounts, 15–16; *illus.*, 15, 16
  rules for, 15
Creditors, *def.*, 2
Cross-footing, 104, 113, 174; *def.*, 104
Current assets, *def.*, 145
Current liabilities, *def.*, 145

D

Data processing
  business, *def.*, 63
  electronic, 65–66; *def.*, 65; *illus.*, 65, 66
  manual, 63–64; *def.*, 63; *illus.*, 63, 64
    adding machines and calculators, 63–64; *illus.*, 64
    journals and ledgers, 63; *illus.*, 63
    pegboard, *def.*, 64; *illus.*, 64
Debit, entering, in account, 14
Debit balance, 16, 17
Debit side of ledger account, *def.*, 13; *illus.*, 13, 42
Debiting, *def.*, 14
  asset accounts, 15–16; *illus.*, 15, 16
  liability accounts, 15–16; *illus.*, 15, 16
  owner's equity accounts, 15–16; *illus.*, 15, 16
  rules for, 15
Debts, bad, 185–187; *def.*, 185; *illus.*, 186
Deposit slip, 159; *def.*, 159; *illus.*, 159
Depreciation, 135–136; *def.*, 135
  adjustment for, 135–136; *illus.*, 137
Disposal value, *def.*, 136
Drawer of checks, *def.*, 160
Drawing account, 22, 31, 52, 55–57, 60, 150; *def.*, 22

E

Electronic data processing, 65–66; *def.*, 65; *illus.*, 65, 66
Employee deductions, 172–173
  federal income tax withholding, 172
  social security (FICA) tax, 172–173

Employee earnings records, *def.*, 174; *illus.*, 175
Ending inventory, 140–142; *def.*, 140
Endorsement, *def.*, 158; *illus.*, 159
Expense accounts, 21–22, 55–57, 60, 150 (*see also* Expenses)
  recording amounts in, 21–22; *illus.*, 22
Expenses, *def.*, 8 (*see also* Expense accounts)
  on income statement, 29, 142–143; *illus.*, 30, 52, 143

F

Federal income tax withholding, 172
Financial interest, 2
Financial statements, 3, 29–32, 51–53, 142–145
  accounting period and, *def.*, 29
  balance sheet, 3, 30–32, 52–53, 144–145; *def.*, 3, 30; *illus.*, 3, 11, 32, 35, 53, 144
  income statement, 29–30, 52, 142–143; *def.*, 29; *illus.*, 30, 52, 143
  statement of owner's equity, 30–31, 52, 143–144; *def.*, 30; *illus.*, 31, 52, 144
  worksheet and, 49–53, 141–145; *illus.*, 51, 141
Fiscal year, *def.*, 29
Fixed assets, 135–136, 145; *def.*, 135, 145
FOB, *def.*, 193
Freight in, 193–194; *illus.*, 193, 194
Full endorsement, 158; *illus.*, 159

G

General journal, 34–39, 114; *def.*, 34; *illus.*, 35, 38, 39, 84–87
  posting from, 42–43; *illus.*, 43–47
  recording a business's transactions in, 35–36, 39; *illus.*, 35, 38, 39, 84–87
  use of, 34–35; *illus.*, 35
General ledger, 42–47; *def.*, 13, 43; *illus.*, 42, 45–47
  adjusting the, 148–149, 185; *def.*, 148; *illus.*, 148, 151, 152, 154, 155
  balance ledger account for, 63; *illus.*, 63
  closing the, 55–60, 149–150; *def.*, 55, 149; *illus.*, 56–59, 149, 151–155
  postclosing trial balance for, 60, 155; *def.*, 60; *illus.*, 60, 155
  posting to, 42–43; *illus.*, 43, 45–47
  ruling and balancing accounts, 59–60, 150; *illus.*, 57–59, 150–155

210   Index

General ledger (*continued*)
    setting up and using accounts in, 43–44, 47; *illus.*, 45–47
    standard ledger account for, 42; *illus.*, 42
    trial balance for, 25–27, 47; *illus.*, 26, 47
Gross earnings, 170–171; *def.*, 170
    computing, 171–172

H

Hourly-rate plan, 170, 172; *def.*, 170

I

Income, 8 (*see also* Revenue)
Income statement, 29–30, 52, 142–143; *def.*, 29; *illus.*, 30, 52, 143
    worksheet and, 49–52, 141–143; *illus.*, 51, 52, 141, 143
Interest expense, 195, 196
Interest revenue, 183–184
Inventory
    merchandise, *def.*, 81
    updating, 140–141
Inventory sheet, *def.*, 140; *illus.*, 140
Investment, *def.*, 2
Invoice, 71, 73–74, 91, 96, 193; *def.*, 71; *illus.*, 72, 74, 91, 96
    credit terms for, 73
    purchase, 73–74, 96; *illus.*, 74, 96
    sales, 71, 73, 91; *illus.*, 72, 91

J

Journal, *def.*, 34
    cash payments journal, 107–114; *def.*, 111; *illus.*, 111
    cash receipts journal, 99–105; *def.*, 101; *illus.*, 101, 104, 184, 187
    combined journal, 198–202; *def.*, 198; *illus.*, 200–201
    data processing and, 63, 66
    general journal, 34–39, 114; *def.*, 34; *illus.*, 35, 38, 39, 84–87
    purchases journal, 94–97; *def.*, 95; *illus.*, 95, 96, 193
    sales journal, 89–92; *def.*, 90; *illus.*, 90, 92, 184
Journalizing, 34; *def.*, 34

L

Ledger, *def.*, 42
    accounts payable ledger, 126–130; *def.*, 127; *illus.*, 128
    accounts receivable ledger, 117–123; *def.*, 118; *illus.*, 118–120
    data processing and, 63, 66

Ledger (*continued*)
    general ledger, 42–47; *def.*, 13, 43; *illus.*, 42, 45–47
Liabilities, *def.*, 2
    on balance sheet, 3; *illus.*, 3, 11, 32, 35, 53, 144
    current, *def.*, 145
    long-term, *def.*, 145
    transactions involving, 4–5
Liability accounts, 14, 16–17; *illus.*, 14, 16, 17
    debiting and crediting, 15–17; *illus.*, 15, 16, 17
Long-term liabilities, *def.*, 145

M

Magnetic disk, 66; *illus.*, 66
Magnetic tape, 66; *illus.*, 66
Manual data processing, 63–64; *def.*, 63; *illus.*, 63, 64
Matching principle, *def.*, 134
Memorandum entry, 102, 198; *def.*, 102; *illus.*, 101, 200
Merchandise, *def.*, 69
    purchases of, 73–74, 76, 94–97; *illus.*, 74, 76–77, 94–97
    sales of, 69–73, 79, 89–92; *illus.*, 70–72, 79–80, 89–92
Merchandise inventory, 81, 140–141; *def.*, 81
Merchandising business, *def.*, 69
    chart of accounts for, 81; *illus.*, 82
    recording typical transactions for, 81–83; *illus.*, 84–87
    sales and purchases procedures in, 69–74
        making purchases, 73–74
        selling at retail, 69–71
        selling at wholesale, 71–73
    special accounts for, 76–81
        purchases of merchandise, 76, 78–79; *illus.*, 76–79
        sales of merchandise, 79–81; *illus.*, 79–81

N

Net income, 8, 29, 50–52, 142–143; *def.*, 8
Net loss, 8, 29, 142; *def.*, 8
Net pay, 173–174; *def.*, 173
Net profit, *def.*, 8 (*see also* Net income)
Net worth, *def.*, 2 (*see also* Owner's equity)
Night depository, *def.*, 163
Notes payable, 194–196; *def.*, 194; *illus.*, 194–196
Notes receivable, 182–184; *def.*, 182; *illus.*, 182–184

O

Opening entry, *def.*, 36; *illus.*, 38
Overtime, 171–172; *def.*, 171
    computing, 172
Owner's equity, *def.*, 2
    on balance sheet, 3; *illus.*, 3, 11, 32, 35, 53, 144
    statement of, 30–31, 52, 143–144; *def.*, 30; *illus.*, 31, 52, 144
    transactions involving, 4–5, 8–10, 22
Owner's equity accounts, 14, 16, 20–23; *illus.*, 14, 16, 20–23
    capital account, 14, 16, 20; *def.*, 22
    debiting and crediting, 15–16; *illus.*, 15, 16
    drawing account, 22; *def.*, 22
    expense accounts, 21–22; *def.*, 22
    revenue accounts, 20–21, *def.*, 22
    relationship of revenue, expenses, and withdrawals, 23; *illus.*, 23

P

Paid on account, *def.*, 10
Pay plans, 170–171; *illus.*, 170, 171
Pay statement, *def.*, 175
Payee, *def.*, 160
Payroll records, 170–177
    computing gross earnings, 171–172
    computing net pay, 173–174
    determining employee deductions, 172–173
    pay plans, 170–171; *illus.*, 170, 171
    paying the employees, 175
    preparing
        employee earnings records, *def.*, 174; *illus.*, 175
        payroll register, *def.*, 174; *illus.*, 174
        payroll tax forms, 177
    recording employer's payroll taxes, 176–177; *illus.*, 176, 177
    recording the payroll, 175–176; *illus.*, 175, 176
Payroll taxes, employer's, 176–177; *illus.*, 176, 177
Pegboard, *def.*, 64; *illus.*, 64
Pencil footing, *def.*, 17; *illus.*, 17, 18
Permanent accounts, *def.*, 60
Personal account, 22 (*see also* Drawing account)
Petty cash fund, 165–168; *def.*, 165
    proving, 166; *def.*, 166; *illus.*, 167
    replenishing, 166–168; *def.*, 166; *illus.*, 167
    setting up, 165; *illus.*, 165
    using, 166; *illus.*, 166
Petty cash voucher, *def.*, 166; *illus.*, 166

Index 211

Physical inventory, *def.*, 140
Piece-rate plan, *def.*, 170
Plant assets, 135 (*see also* Fixed assets)
Postclosing trial balance, 60, 155; *def.*, 60; *illus.*, 60, 155
Posting, 42–43; *def.*, 42
    to accounts payable ledger, 127–129; *illus.*, 127, 128
    to accounts receivable ledger, 119–121; *illus.*, 119, 120
    to general ledger, 42–43; *illus.*, 43, 45–47
    from cash payments journal, 113–114, 127–129; *illus.*, 111, 113, 114, 127, 128
    from cash receipts journal, 103–105, 119–121; *illus.*, 104, 105, 119, 120
    from combined journal, 201–202; *illus.*, 200, 201
    from general journal, 42–43; *def.*, 43; *illus.*, 43–47
    from purchases journal, 96–97, 127–129; *illus.*, 96, 97, 127, 128
    from sales journal, 91–92, 119–121; *illus.*, 92, 119, 120
Profit
    net, *def.*, 8 (*see also* Net income)
Program, computer, *def.*, 65
Promissory note, 182–184, 194–196; *def.*, 182
Proprietor, *def.*, 1
Proprietorship, *def.*, 2
Proving petty cash, *def.*, 166; *illus.*, 167
Purchase invoice, 73–74, 96; *illus.*, 74, 96
    controlling, 74
Purchases, credit (*see* Credit purchases)
Purchases discount, 78–79; *illus.*, 78, 79
Purchases journal, 94–97; *def.*, 95; *illus.*, 95, 96, 193
    posting from the, 96–97, 127–129; *illus.*, 96, 97, 127, 128
    recording transactions in, 95–96; *illus.*, 95
Purchases of merchandise, 73–74, 76, 94–97; *illus.*, 74, 76, 77, 94–97
Purchases returns and allowances, 191–193
    on cash purchases, 191; *illus.*, 191
    on credit purchases, 192–193; *illus.*, 192

R

Received on account, *def.*, 10
Record of final entry, 42
Record of original entry, 34

Replenishing petty cash, 166–168; *def.*, 166; *illus.*, 167
Report form of balance sheet, *def.*, 53; *illus.*, 53, 144
Restrictive endorsement, 158; *illus.*, 159
Retailers, 69–71; *def.*, 69
Revenue, 8, 69; *def.*, 8 (*see also* Revenue accounts)
    on income statement, 29, 142; *illus.*, 30, 52, 143
Revenue accounts, 20–21, 55–57, 60, 79–81, 150 (*see also* Revenue)
    recording amounts in, 20–21, 79–80; *illus.*, 21, 79–81

S

Salary-commission plan, *def.*, 171
Salary plan, *def.*, 170
Sales, bank credit card (*see* Bank credit card sales)
Sales, cash (*see* Cash sales)
Sales, credit (*see* Credit sales)
Sales invoice, 71, 73, 91; *illus.*, 72, 91
Sales journal, 89–92; *def.*, 90; *illus.*, 90, 92, 184
    posting from the, 91–92, 119–121; *illus.*, 92, 119, 120
    recording transactions in, 90–91; *illus.*, 90, 91
Sales of merchandise, 69–73, 79, 89–92; *illus.*, 71, 72, 79, 80, 89–92
Sales returns and allowances, 180–182
    on cash sales, 180; *illus.*, 180
    on credit sales, 181–182; *illus.*, 181, 182
Sales slip, 70, 91; *def.*, 70; *illus.*, 71
Sales taxes, 184–185; *def.*, 184; *illus.*, 184, 185
Schedule of accounts payable, *def.*, 129; *illus.*, 130
Schedule of accounts receivable, 121–122; *def.*, 121; *illus.*, 121
    by age, *def.*, 123; *illus.*, 123
Service charge, bank, *def.*, 160
Signature card, 158, 160; *def.*, 158
Social security (FICA) tax, 172–173
Solvency, *def.*, 145
Source documents, *def.*, 62
Special journal, *def.*, 90 (*see also* Cash payments journal; Cash receipts journal; Purchases journal; Sales journal)
Statement of account, 70–71, 122; *def.*, 70; *illus.*, 71, 122
Statement of owner's equity, 30–31, 52, 143–144; *def.*, 30; *illus.*, 31, 52, 144
Statements (*see* Financial statements)

Stop payment order, *def.*, 163
Straight-line method of depreciation, 136; *def.*, 136
Subsidiary ledger, *def.*, 118 (*see also* Accounts payable ledger; Accounts receivable ledger)

T

T accounts, 13–18, 20–22, 25–26; *def.*, 13; *illus.*, 13–18, 20–22, 25, 26
Take-home pay, *def.*, 173 (*see also* Net pay)
Tax base, 173
Taxes (*see specific taxes*)
Temporary accounts, *def.*, 60
Time cards, 171–172, 174; *def.*, 171; *illus.*, 171
Time clock, *def.*, 171; *illus.*, 171
Time sheets, *def.*, 171
Travel advances, *def.*, 168
Trial balance, 25–27, 47; *illus.*, 26, 47
    adjusted, on worksheet, 136–138; *illus.*, 137
    errors not revealed by, 27
    finding errors, 26–27
    on worksheet, 49; *illus.*, 50, 137
    taking the, 25–26; *def.*, 25; *illus.*, 25, 26

U

Unpaid invoices file, 74, 96; *def.*, 74
Useful life of fixed assets, 135–136; *def.*, 135

W

Wholesalers, 69, 71; *def.*, 69
Worksheet adjustments, 134–138, 140–141, 185–186; *def.*, 134
    for bad debts, 185–186; *illus.*, 186
    for depreciation, 135–136; *illus.*, 137
    for expired insurance, 135
    for merchandise inventory, 140–141; *illus.*, 141
    for supplies used, 134–135; *illus.*, 137
Worksheets, 49–51, 136–138, 141–142; *def.*, 49, 134; *illus.*, 50, 51, 137, 141, 186
    financial statements and, 49–53, 141–145
    preparing, 49–51, 136–138, 141–142; *illus.*, 50, 51, 137, 141
    result of operations and, 50–51, 142; *illus.*, 51, 141
Writing off an account, *def.*, 186

Y

Year-to-date earnings, *def.*, 174

NOTES

NOTES

NOTES

NOTES